Religion and the Schools

by Paul Blanshard

An Outline of the British Labor Movement

What's the Matter With New York? (with Norman Thomas)

Investigating City Government

Democracy and Empire in the Caribbean

American Freedom and Catholic Power

Communism, Democracy and Catholic Power

The Right to Read

The Irish and Catholic Power

God and Man in Washington

Freedom and Catholic Power in Spain and Portugal

Religion and the Schools: The Great Controversy

Paul Blanshard has had a varied career as a lawyer, author, journalist, and public official. Under Mayor La Guardia he was head of New York City's Department of Investigations and Accounts, and attracted national attention with his exposure of graft. He served for two years as an associate editor of *The Nation*. During World War II he was a State Department official in Washington and the Caribbean. He has studied both theology and law, and is a recognized authority on church-state issues. Among his most notable books are *God and Man in Washington* and *American Freedom and Catholic Power*.

From the book . . .

" The controversy is eternal because the issues are eternal. They will continue to plague and inspire men as long as they disagree about the best methods of bringing moral and spiritual ideals to their children."

Religion and the Schools

The Great Controversy

by Paul Blanshard

Beacon Press   Boston

CONTENTS

CHAPTER 1

Jefferson to Kennedy:

The Continuing Controversy

When the Supreme Court of the United States on June 25, 1962, outlawed a simple, non-denominational prayer used in the public schools of New Hyde Park, New York, many Americans treated the event as if it were a surprise attack upon religion by self-willed judges who had acted without precedent. It is true that the banned prayer was so simple and so apparently innocuous that the controversy over it seemed like much ado about nothing. The prayer read:

> "Almighty God, we acknowledge our dependence upon Thee, and we beg Thy blessing upon us, our parents, our teachers and our country."[1]

The Supreme Court's decision was not a surprise to those who were familiar with the legal history of church-state relations in this country. It was only one manifestation, one incident, in a great controversy about religion and its place in the educational process that has been going on in America for more than three hundred years. That controversy, as much political as it is religious, centers on the use and abuse of state power in connection with religion. In this country, as we shall see, religious issues often demand political solutions, solutions which must be worked out by citizens as citizens regardless of their religious faith or the lack of it.

The heart of the present controversy can be expressed in two basic questions, both of which involve public law and public educational policy for the whole country. How much religion should be taught in our public classrooms? How much public money should be poured into religious classrooms? These questions are two of the most important and controversial issues in American life today.

Controversy concerning them began in Europe even before our forefathers came to these shores. It waxed and waned throughout the whole nineteenth century and burgeoned into a nationwide struggle in the 1940's and 1950's. It seems to me to be one of the most basic conflicts in American life today. Certainly it is too important to ignore or evade, and if the discussion is to be intelligent and intelligible it must be conducted as part of a wider discussion of the whole religious-educational scene in the United States.

The controversy over religion and our schools involves deep and sincere moral conviction, and also ethnic prejudice, verbal distortion and clerical self-interest. Many devout Christian believers see the elimination of prayer, Bible-reading and religious instruction from public schools as a repudiation of Godly truth and a threat to the character of their children. Equally sincere religious liberals, Jews, and unbelievers are convinced that the whole conflict is a basic struggle between two value systems, one based on revealed Christianity and the other on modern scientific knowledge. In between these two extremes are millions of baffled and somewhat confused citizens who do not take a firm position either way. They maintain some kind of conventional religious affiliation and endorse a vague concept known as the separation of church and state without defining that concept clearly in their own minds.

The whole religion-and-schools controversy has been made more complex and more political by the fact that America's largest church, the Roman Catholic, does not accept the religious neutrality of the American public school system. Simultaneously, its leaders are demanding that its own church-related schools operate at public expense side by side with public schools. In Washington the financial demands of these leaders are holding up the whole national program for the expansion and improvement of the public school system. At the same time their ideological attacks on the public schools as "Godless" are making it more and more difficult to maintain the religious neutrality of those schools in our pluralistic society. This double intransigence of Roman Catholic policy adds immeasurably to the tensions involved in the religion-and-schools controversy. Defenders of the separation of church and state in education feel that they are living in a besieged city. Every tiny breach in the wall of separation causes special alarm when it may be used for more substantial breaches later on.

There are many special difficulties in discussing any religious issue as it applies to all of the people of the United States. We are not one people religiously. The edges of the pieces in the jigsaw puzzle of our religious pluralism are very ragged. It is impossible to speak of any religion-in-education policy as *the* American policy. When an author writes about religion in Spain, he is writing essentially about Roman Catholicism; in Sweden about Lutheranism; in Pakistan about Islam. In the United States there is no design for religion in education that can be considered wholly typical of the whole country. We are not only a people of diverse faiths and doubts—it is commonly estimated that we have at least 256 competing religious sects and perhaps 70,000,000 citizens outside all churches[2]—but we are also a people whose machinery of government for dealing with religion and education is infinitely varied. Our local authorities differ as much in their religious and educational predilections as the climate of Key West differs from that of Nome, Alaska.

Our Constitution, unlike that of many European nations, has assigned to local and state governments the primary responsibility for education and also a minimal responsibility for church-state relations at the local level. We have no national department of religious affairs and our national Office of Education has neither the power nor the will to impose upon the American public school any general educational program, much less a religious program. Our government of education is a mosaic, differing from state to state and from town to town.

Of course, this inevitable, and desirable, localism is partly cancelled out by certain great centripetal forces. We have one national Constitution whose guarantees of personal rights have been brought down to the level of the smallest community by a forthright Supreme Court. We have the enormous cohesive power of one national language. We have in the American public school an institution which, in spite of its exclusively local ownership, is morally and emotionally a national institution, as traditionally American as the Capitol and the flag. In spite of our religious differences the overwhelming majority of our people believe in public responsibility for education and they are eager to work out a plan of friendly coexistence between the public schools and religion.

Two primary areas of discussion and conflict are clearly distinguishable in the field of religion and education. Area 1 is the area of religion within the public, tax-supported schools. This includes not only full-blown religious instruction within public schools and tax-supported universities but also incidental religious ceremonies and exercises such as prayers, Bible reading and released-time religious classes. Private schools, sectarian or non-sectarian, do not enter into this area of discussion because they freely choose their own type of religious programs without reference to government policy.

Area 2, which is even more controversial, involves the support or non-support of religious schools by public treasuries. This is the area in which the traditional way of education in the United States differs from so many European and Latin American countries. It is the area in which the largest church functioning on American soil, the Roman Catholic Church, is asking for a change in American law and practice.

The problem of prayer and Bible-reading in public schools naturally belongs in Area 1. The question of tax support for sectarian schools belongs in Area 2. Area 1 is basically a problem in the relationship of Protestantism to the state, involving widespread discrimination against Jews and unbelievers, and some discrimination against Catholics. Area 2 involves primarily Catholic relations to the state.

For the sake of clariy, Area 1 will be discussed in the chapters on the New York State Regents' prayer decision, Bible-reading and the Lord's Prayer. The field of Area 2 will be discussed in the chapter headed "Tax Dollars for Church Schools?" Certain miscellaneous problems which spread into both areas—such problems as tax payments for textbooks, bus appropriations, baccalaureate services etc.—will be brought together in the chapter "Buses, Books and Teachers." At the end of the discussion of these areas there will be an attempt, in a final chapter on "Truth and Consequences," to predict the nature of coming conflicts and to suggest possible solutions for the controversial issues involved.

The desire of those Americans who want "God in education" spreads clear across both areas. Often the same people want prayer in public schools and public money for church schools, and their motives in making each demand may overlap or reveal amazing inconsistencies. When a clerical leader passionately advocates an undenominational prayer in a public school, his chief motive may be to discredit that school as a suitable place for educating *any* children, and then, having achieved that end, to secure public money for a separate, sectarian system.

We shall see later that this may have been the primary motive of Cardinal Spellman in his bitter attack on the Regents' prayer decision within twenty-four hours after its delivery. And, lest anyone should believe that Cardinal Spellman is unique among clerics in clothing his opposition to the Constitution in pious words, it should be pointed out that the most open violations of the First Amendment now taking place in American public classrooms are violations by devout Protestants, particularly in the South.

Indeed, one of the most obvious lessons to be derived from America's religious history—a lesson which can be noted here only in passing—is that the common people cannot always trust professional religious leaders to remain unselfish in observing the law when their ecclesiastical interests are involved. They have before them the richest human harvest in history, the more than 46,000,000 children in America's elementary and secondary schools. They naturally wish to make those children into faithful followers of their own particular way of life. They would be more than human if they did not participate in the controversies over religion and the schools as devoted partisans.

One is reminded of the experience of James Madison when he was opposing a Virginia bill in 1784, a bill that would have provided tax payments to teachers of the Christian religion. When he had fought successfully against such payments to the established church of his colony, the Church of England, he had gained the zealous support of Virginia's Presbyterians. But, later on, when the Anglican Church had lost its exclusive privileges in Virginia life, the Presbyterians reversed their policy and favored tax payments to churches *if* they could secure a portion for themselves. This horrified Madison. In writing to Monroe he described the situation as "shameful." "They seem as ready," he said, "to set up an establishment which is to take them in as they were to pull down that which shut them out."[3]

A Glance at the Past

In order to appreciate the meaning of the great religious controversy in American education we should take a brief preliminary look at American church-state history. Roughly four stages in the development of the religion-and-schools issue may be noted since Massachusetts passed a common school law in 1647.

In the first or colonial stage before the Revolution, most American colonies had established churches in the European manner. The churches controlled the only schools in evidence—there were very few—and they were Protestant or Protestant-oriented schools. Then came the period from the Revolution to about 1840 when churches were slowly and gradually disestablished and when American Protestantism, rather reluctantly, accepted the idea of the public school as the common training ground for the children of all faiths. Protestantism was then so strong in the United States that many Protestant features remained on the periphery of the public school system without much opposition, giving American common-school education a distinctly Protestant flavor.

Then came the period after 1840, which stretched on for a century to 1940. Great hordes of Catholic immigrants and some Jewish immigrants came to the Eastern and Midwestern cities. These people and their Americanized children soon began to challenge Protestant features in public education. Catholic leaders, claiming that they could not get fair treatment in public schools, demanded public money for their own elementary system. This may be called the period of change and challenge. During the course of this hundred-year span the whole position of American Protestantism and American Catholicism underwent a striking reversal. The Roman Catholic Church grew from the smallest to the largest church in the United States.

Finally, we have arrived at the present period of religion-and-education development, beginning roughly in 1940, which some writers have defined as a post-Protestant era. In this era there has been a tremendous increase in Catholic political power, largely due to the increase in the Catholic population, and an increasingly insistent demand for government support for Catholic schools. Simultaneously there has been a great increase in the social bulk of American institutional Protestantism, but American Protestants have not seriously attempted to develop Protestant school systems. Although Jews do not comprise more than 3 per cent of the total population they have become increasingly important in religion-and-schools controversies in recent years, and they are now demanding their minority rights more insistently than ever before.

The Supreme Court, beginning in 1940, has calmly walked into the eye of a denominational hurricane with its decisions concerning the separation of church and state in the schools. It has asserted new authority over vast areas previously ignored by Supreme Court decisions. It has firmed and buttressed the constitutional wall of separation between church and state, as championed by Thomas Jefferson, until the position of religion in education, both within the public schools and outside the public schools, has become one of the hottest legal issues in American life today, second only to that of racial segregation.

Partly because of this new legal definiteness we are now in the midst of a period of crisis in the history of religion and education in this country. All the great controversial issues are out in the open, with the Supreme Court on one side and enormously powerful religious groups on the other side. The issues in that battle are not wholly different from the issues which stirred Jefferson and Madison so deeply at the beginning of our national history.

In the first common schools of colonial days, freedom *from* religion was as difficult to come by as freedom *for* an unpopular religion. Religion was virtually defined as the dominant religion in each colony. At least nine of the thirteen colonies had either an established church or established churches, imposed on the people at public expense. A child in school was supposed to accept the god of the state or stay away from school altogether. In Massachusetts, after 1647, he did not even have that alternative. He was compelled to go to a school where all learning revolved around the virtues of a stiff-necked Puritan God who had the sexual philosophy later incarnated in Anthony Comstock.

The Massachusetts colonial legislature provided in 1701 that every master of a grammar school must be approved by the town minister, and the town minister was always a dogmatic Calvinistic Congregationalist. To make sure that the Protestant doctrine of the churches should be preserved in all aspects of Massachusetts life, a penalty of death was provided for idolatry and blasphemy, and both Quakers and Jesuits were forbidden to enter the colony. If parents did not like this kind of dogmatism for themselves or their children, they could get out of Massachusetts.

The Protestant sectarian dogmatism that characterized almost all of our first colonial schools was very specific. It did not admit of any equivocation or doubt. Belief was belief and some form of Protestant creed was necessary for salvation. The Bible was the Word of God and it belonged at the top of the list of all school textbooks. That meant no nonsense about contradictions or inconsistencies in the text. The children read the Book and accepted the Book. For them the Trinity was as real as Plymouth Rock and just as granitic.

The most famous and popular textbook used in the schools of Massachusetts before the adoption of the Constitution was the *New England Primer*. It was almost all religion, Protestant Christian religion. It taught the alphabet in terms of biblical stories and provided advanced reading in the form of the Westminster Catechism, the sermons of leading Protestant divines and lurid tales of Catholic cruelty. "Mr. John Rogers," said one story illustrated by a crude drawing of a man in a bonfire, "minister of the gospel in London, was the first martyr in Queen Mary's reign, and was burnt at Smithfield, February 14, 1554. His wife with nine small children, and one at her breast following him to the stake; with which sorrowful sight he was not in the least daunted, but with wonderful patience died courageously for the gospel of JESUS CHRIST." His wife and children in the picture look quite happy while their husband and father breathes the flames from large bundles of faggots.

The book ends with a solemn adjuration that good children should obey their parents, their Bible and their catechism, since at the Day of Judgment "all that are not fit for heaven must be sent to hell." One of the interesting facts about this famous text is that it was reprinted with these same features as late as 1843, and there were still enough schools in New England which accepted its point of view to provide a profitable market.

In 1654 the Massachusetts Bay Colony passed a law officially banishing anybody who was convicted of obstinately opposing infant baptism. Later on, in most of the colonies, no one could vote who denied the deity of Jesus Christ.[4] Colonial statutes excluded from the rights of citizenship not only all Jews but many of the open or secret Unitarians and Deists who constituted an important segment of the intellectual elite shortly before the Revolution. Ag-

nostic taxpayers were compelled to pay part of the salaries of orthodox Protestant clergymen; and in some of the colonies these same
agnostics were compelled to sit—or sleep—through those tedious
biblical sermons which came two or three times every Lord's Day,
constituting the only weekly "entertainment" for most of the
populace.

Sanford H. Cobb, in his authoritative study *The Rise of Religious Liberty in America,* says that even after the Declaration of
Independence at the time the American Union was formed, only
two of the states allowed complete religious freedom, Rhode Island
and Virginia.

Six of the states, namely, New Hampshire, Connecticut, New Jersey, the two Carolinas, and Georgia insisted on Protestantism. Two
were content with the Christian religion; Delaware and Maryland.
Four, Pennsylvania, Delaware and the Carolinas, required assent
to the divine inspiration of the Bible. Two, Pennsylvania and
South Carolina demanded a belief in heaven and hell. Three, New
York, Maryland, and South Carolina, excluded ministers from civil
office. Two, Pennsylvania and South Carolina, emphasized belief
in one eternal God. One, Delaware, required assent to the doctrine
of the Trinity. And five, New Hampshire, Massachusetts, Connecticut, Maryland and South Carolina adhered to a religious establishment.[5]

The word "Protestant" was not dropped from the North Carolina
Constitution until 1835, and then the word "Christian" was substituted for it.

Enter Jefferson and Madison

In the struggle to establish the separation of church and state
and to destroy the old establishments in the colonies, the Virginia
battle for religious freedom just after the Revolution was one of
the most important struggles in our history. In many ways it provides a singular parallel to the struggle that is going on today in the

United States, although it did not directly involve public schools because Virginia had virtually no public schools at that time.

Virginia had established the Church of England one year before the Pilgrims landed on Plymouth Rock. The believers in an established church were finally defeated not only by the opposition of deists and theological liberals but also by the rising sects of dissenters, the Methodists and the Baptists. A strange alliance—paralleled to a certain extent by the alignments of today—sprang up between the new orthodox sects of the common people and the modernists or skeptics, represented by men like Jefferson and Madison. Madison had grown up in the Church of England and had studied for the ministry, but he did not continue as an orthodox church member in his mature years. In the Virginia struggle he played an even more important role than Jefferson, particularly through his famous 1785 *Memorial and Remonstrance Against Religious Assessments*.[6] Although he was a very tolerant man, he was very strongly opposed to any importation into the United States of the European idea of religious establishments. "In the Papal System," he wrote in 1832, "Government and Religion are in a manner consolidated, and that is found to be the worst of Government."[7]

The usual story of America's religious beginnings is too often confined to the account of Christian institutions. It is true that the first common schools were saturated with Christian orthodoxy but it is also true that many of the intellectual leaders of the Revolution and a large segment of the people were deists or skeptics or unchurched. All available estimates indicate that at least seven out of eight Americans did not formally belong to any church when the nation was founded.[8] The French Encyclopedists, including Voltaire, were not unknown in America at the time of the Revolution, and some of the antagonism against clerical power which later manifested itself in the French Revolution had come to America by way of England. The spirit of the young intellectuals in the new country was, to appropriate a phrase that was used in describing the French *Encyclopédie,* "theistic and heretical." That weird combination of terms meant that they were reverently anti-orthodox. They were willing to tip their hats politely toward the Deity, as they did in the Declaration of Independence, but they showed no enthusiasm for Christian creeds, particularly those creeds that discriminated definitely against opposing varieties of Christianity. They did not mention God in the Constitution, and the omission was surely not accidental. John Locke, universally recognized as the philosopher who had the most influence on the teaching of the founding fathers, argued that religion was outside the power of government.

The most influential men who built the new nation were believers in the separation of church and state not only because they wanted to avoid the wars of religion that had played such an important part in ruining the old world but also because they were unorthodox in their views about Christian theology. Washington was the only one of the five greatest founders who clung quietly to his membership in a regular church without indication of heresy, and even he has sometimes been classed as a Deist. Jefferson, Franklin, Madison and John Adams can rightly be classified as extreme religious liberals, either Unitarians or Deists. Jefferson, although he was a passionate admirer of Jesus, was both anti-Calvinist and anti-Catholic in the institutional sense. "The care of every man's soul belongs to himself," he wrote in his "Notes on Religion" in 1776. "I cannot give up my guidance to the magistrates, because he knows no more of the way to heaven than I do. . . ." And again he declared: "In every country and in every age the priest has been hostile to liberty. He is always in alliance with the despot, abetting his abuses in return for protection of his own." Jefferson's biographer, Saul K. Padover, summed up his attitude on church and state by saying: "Religion was a menace to a free society when it was either an instrument of the State, as was the case with Lutheranism in Prussia, or when it used the State for its sanguinary purposes, as was the case in Inquisition-ridden Spain. There was sufficient historical evidence to prove that the partnership of Church and State had always led, and perforce must lead, to tyranny and oppression."[9]

The first crucial battle after the Revolution in the fight to dis-establish all churches in education culminated in Virginia in 1779 when Jefferson and Madison united to defeat a bill to pay teachers of Christianity out of the Virginia treasury. Jefferson described these Virginia debates over a general assessment for religion as "the severest struggles in which I have ever engaged." It was primarily Madison who won the final battle for dis-establishment by persuading his fellow statesmen to adopt the First Amendment: "Congress shall make no law respecting an establishment of religion, or prohibiting the free exercise thereof."

In perspective these two men, Jefferson and Madison, emerge from the pages of our early history as among the greatest of modern statesmen. They were far in advance of most of their confreres in religious tolerance and in their appreciation of the need for general education. They were convinced believers in free public schools for the masses. Jefferson had introduced in the Virginia legislature in 1779 a bill for the "More General Diffusion of Knowledge," which would have given the state a public school system without religious instruction. Failing in this enterprise at first, he devoted nearly all of the last years of his life to the building of a public system of education in his own state.

It would be agreeable to report that this greatest pioneer in the religion-and-education controversy was always free to express his honest sentiments and that he was honored for his intellectual integrity when he dissented from the American majority. In fact, Jefferson was so consistently vilified throughout his life as an "atheist" and an "infidel" that he felt obliged to refrain from full public disclosure of his dissident views until after his retirement from politics. Alexander Hamilton called him "an atheist in religion and a fanatic in politics." When he was Vice-President in 1796, a Connecticut parson prayed publicly: "O Lord, wilt Thou bestow upon the Vice-President a double portion of Thy Grace, for Thou knowest he needs it." The Reverend Timothy Dwight, president of Yale, described him as possessing "in no contemptible degree, the talent, which is styled cunning. . . . Mr. Jefferson has taught us that

Infidelity is an unprofitable guide in the management of national interests."

Even the memory of Jefferson was dishonored by conservative religious leaders. The public library of Philadelphia refused to admit his writings to its shelves in 1830, four years after his death, on the ground that these writings were morally dangerous.[10] A leading historian of American Christianity, writing fourteen years later, described him as an arch infidel who chuckled as he degraded Christianity through his advocacy of separating church and state.

Enter the Public School

The first great movement for public, secular schools in the new United States was largely the work of ordinary Protestant Christians who happened to reach the conclusion that common education was primarily and properly a responsibility of local democratic government. Some of them probably wanted Protestant schools but decided that the task of paying for them was too monumental. They were often confused as to the most practical limits between church and state in education, partly because the whole concept of the public schools was so new. But they chose public elementary education rather than church-controlled education quite specifically. Nearly all the states in the years shortly after the Revolution wrote prohibitions into their constitutions and laws against the expenditure of public money for sectarian schools; state legislators were persuaded that the safest policy for a nation with many differing creeds was to set up a system under non-church auspices and make it free to all children.

Many of the early Protestants did not object to some general Christian features in such schools provided there was no preaching or proselytizing for any particular Christian sect, or any compulsory tax levy to support any separate church schools. On this latter point they were virtually unanimous after the 1840's. New Jersey, Massachusetts and Pennsylvania did give some public money to

religious schools in the 1830's and 1840's, and there were a few isolated instances of small appropriations to church schools after that
date, but these were the exceptions that proved the rule.

The erection of a clearly defined "wall of separation between
church and state"—Jefferson's immortal phrase in his letter to the
Danbury Baptists in 1802—inside of the burgeoning new public
school system was a slow process. Partisan sectarian propaganda
was banned almost immediately; that is to say, propaganda favor-
ing one Protestant denomination against another Protestant denomination. But general Protestant propaganda for Christianity,
not possessing a denominational label, was often blandly accepted
as quite proper. The Jew and the atheist were fair targets for everybody.

Ellwood Cubberley in his history of public education in the
United States cites a pro-Christian arithmetic problem from an
early public school textbook which shows how Christian propaganda was inserted:

Fifteen Christians and 15 Turks bound at sea in one ship in
a terrible storm, and the pilot declaring a necessity of casting one
half of these persons into the sea, that the rest might be saved, they
all agreed that the persons to be cast away should be set out by lot
in this manner, viz., the 30 persons should be placed in a round
form like a ring and then, beginning to count at one of the pas-
sengers and proceeding regularly every ninth person should be cast
into the sea until of the 30 persons there remained only 15. The
question is, how these 30 persons ought to be placed that the lot
might fall infallibly upon the 15 Turks, and not upon any of the
15 Christians.[11]

Such partisan ferocity gradually declined during the first half
of the nineteenth century as public school systems became established throughout the country. In perspective American Protestantism deserves enormous credit for accepting a relatively broad-
gauged policy. Protestants might have followed the English pattern
of the church schools of Europe, supported by grants-in-aid from
local governments with systematic Christian instruction as part of

the curriculum. They chose to extend the principle of the separation of church and state into the new elementary school systems of the various states and to renounce denominational claims for ownership and control of these school systems. Of course, one reason for the adoption of this policy was that the multiplicity of sects made multiple religious establishments somewhat impractical.

The Protestant choice of secular schools was not altogether deliberate and conscious, and for a long time the schools continued enough incidental Protestant features to make both Catholics and Jews very uncomfortable. But the drift was steady toward the elimination of religion in the schools. Samuel W. Brown in his 1912 work, *The Secularization of American Education,* was able to say with full documentation: "For somewhat over a century there has been going on in the United States a gradual but widespread elimination of religious and church influences from public education."[12]

Horace Mann, Massachusetts Unitarian, is commonly considered the great hero and champion of the religiously neutral conception of the American public school, although the secular concept was actually accepted before his educational career began. Certainly Mann was the most famous and aggressive pioneer in public school expansion. He met the attack of competing church interests head-on in some very lively public debates. He was famous partly because he was not only an educator but also an active and successful politician, having been elected to two terms in Congress after serving as president of the State Senate of Massachusetts and secretary of the State Board of Education for 12 years. He was an almost ideal public representative in the battle against clerical encroachments upon the new public schools.[13]

One reason why he was almost ideal for his period was that he actually accepted the idea of *some* biblical instruction in public schools. If he had opposed all ceremonies of prayer and Bible-reading it is probable that he would not have been able to hold his power in the overwhelmingly Protestant environment. He represented a compromise position on religion in education, since he was willing to admit the King James version of the Bible and some religious instruction into public classrooms as long as the instruction did not underscore any particular doctrine of any particular sect. He fought hard against the introduction into Massachusetts schools of the book list of the American Sunday School Union, not only because he considered it "sectarian" but also because he did not want public school children frightened by fundamentalist versions of hell fire. He was accused by orthodox clergymen of promoting a plan that was "a grand instrument in the hands of free thinkers, atheists and infidels for the accomplishment of their purposes."

It was fortunate for the public schools that the concepts of public ownership and control were pretty well established before the first great waves of Irish Catholic immigration arrived in the 1830's. The new public system was suddenly confronted with a religious attack on two fronts, the demand for less Protestant favoritism inside public schools and the demand for public money for separate Catholic schools. Catholic leaders would not accept the King James version of the Bible for reading by the children of their faith who attended public schools. Many Protestant educational officials stubbornly refused to allow the use of the Douay version for Catholic children and insisted on the King James version for all children. A Protestant defense organization called the American and Foreign Christian Union said that the Bible would not be thrown out of public classrooms "so long as a piece of Plymouth Rock remains big enough to make a gun flint out of."

The Union, of course, referred to the King James version. It seemed to forget that there were any Catholic versions with claims to authenticity. In Boston a hundred Catholic children were expelled from one school for refusing to join in religious exercises which their priests considered too Protestant in character, and in one case a Boston Catholic pupil was flogged because he refused to read from a Protestant Bible.

The very separateness of the Catholic school system increased the misunderstanding and the ideological bitterness. The fact that the Catholic population tended to be underprivileged in economic matters resulted in split-level systems, with both ethnic and poverty connotations. Who were these "foreigners," asked the Protestant Americans, who try to control affairs in "our" schools when they keep their children out of the public schools in any case? The group antagonism fostered by the split-level system was an important factor in creating the bitterly anti-Catholic Know-Nothing movement before the Civil War, a movement that captured nearly all of New England in the 1850's.

The most noisy and bitter religious battles before the Civil War took place in New York, Boston and Philadelphia, and in all of these battles the question of religion and the schools played some part. In sharp contrast to the present-day policy of the Catholic Church, the Catholic leaders of that period were most concerned to keep religious instruction out of the public schools. When they succeeded in challenging the monopoly status of the Protestant Bible, the Protestants were horrified. Sometimes they even responded with physical violence. In Philadelphia in 1843, after a liberal school board had allowed Catholic children to read from their own Catholic Bibles in public schools, Protestant mass meetings were called to compel a reversal of the policy. Immediately some militant Irishmen replied with equal partisanship. There were mob riots, and before they were over two Catholic churches and several Catholic schools had been burned.[14]

The most bitter conflict over religion in the schools occurred in New York City. It came to a head in 1840 and 1841 when Bishop John Hughes formed the first Catholic political party in American history in order to secure two things, a secular program—in this case meaning non-Protestant—within public schools, and the granting of public funds for his separate Catholic system.

There is no doubt that Bishop Hughes had a real grievance against the public schools of New York City as they were conducted in those days. The actual operation of those schools had been turned over to a Protestant organization, the Public School Society, and Catholic children attending the schools under the society's auspices were subject not only to biblical teaching from the Protestant

Bible but also to a considerable dosage of anti-Papal suggestions in history books. According to the estimate of William H. Seward, governor and later senator from New York, one-fifth to one-fourth of the children of New York City were left for several years to grow up without any education because of the informal strike by Catholics against "public" schools with Protestant propaganda features.[15]

Although the first Catholic political party in American history was overwhelmingly defeated in its only election test, Bishop Hughes did make some impression in his campaign against discriminatory textbooks and exclusive Protestant control of the public schools. The Public School Society was divested of its authority in 1842 and the New York schools were made formally public. Also, by 1844, a great many public schools in predominantly Catholic areas had given up Bible-reading altogether in public classrooms. But the bitterness continued in many localities and manifested itself in school board elections, in state politics, in the daily press and, eventually, on a national scale in the Know-Nothing political party.

Even the Civil War did not completely halt the controversy over religion in the schools. After the war, the most militant opponent of sectarian schools ever to occupy the White House, Ulysses S. Grant, came into power. He even favored taxation of churches, and in his 1876 speech as President to the Convention of the Army of the Tennessee at Des Moines, he uttered those challenging words that were to be quoted by four justices of the Supreme Court in 1948 when they banned religious instruction from all American public schools:

Encourage free schools and resolve that not one dollar appropriated for their support shall be appropriated for the support of any sectarian schools. Resolve that neither the state nor the nation, nor both combined, shall support institutions of learning other than those sufficient to afford every child growing up in the land the opportunity of a good common school education, unmixed with sectarian, pagan, or atheistical dogmas. Leave the matter of religion to the family altar, the church, and the private school, supported entirely by private contributions. Keep the church and state forever separated.[16]

Both Grant and Garfield thought that this principle should be embodied in a new federal Constitutional amendment as a precautionary measure to make sure that public money could never be appropriated for any sectarian school system by any state. Their suggestions for an amendment were defeated largely because most Congressmen thought that no new law on the subject was necessary. Already nearly all the states had prohibited appropriations to sectarian schools in their constitutions or statutes.

The New Supreme Court Wall

The present stage in the controversy over religion in the schools began in 1940 when, for the first time, the Supreme Court asserted in specific terms its authority to extend to all citizens in the states the guarantees in favor of religious freedom and against establishment of religion in the First Amendment, as brought down to the local level by the Fourteenth Amendment.[17] Since the discussion of the legal implications of this new policy will be postponed until later, it will be appropriate here only to note certain incidental facts about the political and cultural meaning of this shift.

Until 1940 the Supreme Court had been somewhat vacillating and inconsistent in handling minor problems concerning the legal frontier between church and state in education. In 1930 it had permitted state funds to be used in Louisiana for lending textbooks to sectarian elementary schools without even discussing the question of whether this was an illegal establishment of religion under the First Amendment.[18] It had refused to hear important cases involving the use of the Bible in public schools on the ground that complaining taxpayers lacked standing to sue.[19] On the same grounds, it had ducked consideration of one phase of the prayer issue, as embodied in a complaint against appropriations for Congressional chaplains.[20]

One reason for the apparent dodging of issues by the Supreme Court was that the two biggest problems in the religion-and-schools controversy had not been brought directly to the Court. No state had granted public funds directly to a clearly sectarian school for its central activities. The grants that had been made were always protected by some special excuse connected with welfare, science or defense. And no plaintiff had reached the court with a direct challenge to formal religious instruction inside public schools, although there had been many *state* decisions on Bible-reading, pro and con.

It was quite natural that before 1940—before the Supreme Court had asserted its authority to protect all Americans against an unlawful establishment of religion—that a great many inconsistent practices should have developed in handling religious matters. There was no national judicial policy on the subject. Bible-reading in public schools actually increased at the very moment when some states were declaring it unconstitutional—we shall discuss the details later. Some states that welcomed Bible-reading and the Lord's Prayer in their schoolrooms had essentially the same prohibitions in their constitutions and statutes as the states that banned the phenomena. The same words held different meanings for different judges.

The lawyers for the sect known as Jehovah's Witnesses finally persuaded the Supreme Court in 1940 that it had a responsibility under the First Amendment to protect the religious freedom of all citizens even against the statutes of their own states.[21] When the Witnesses won "equal protection of the laws" for their somewhat unusual tactics, more conventional sects were able to go forward from that point and claim protection against any kind of religious establishment or discrimination even when it was completely sanctioned by local law. The litigation lid was off, and many local lawsuits were filed demanding both religious freedom and the end of religious establishment. Soon "states rights" in education and religion were compelled to yield to the fundamental rights of all Americans as citizens under the federal Constitution.

Within twelve years three of the most important issues about religion and the schools, tax support for parochial buses, classes in religion inside public schools, and released-time religious classes outside public school buildings under church auspices, won incisive, though divided, judgments from the Supreme Court. These three great cases were the Everson (New Jersey) bus case of 1947, the McCollum (Illinois) religious instruction case of 1948, and the Zorach (New York) released-time case of 1952.[22] The Court validated bus appropriations under the First Amendment by a vote of five to four; outlawed religious instruction inside public schools eight to one; and permitted released-time classes at state option if a state statute authorized it by a vote of six to three. These three famous cases were to be followed by the Torcaso (Maryland) notary public case of 1961, outlawing compulsory faith for all public officials, and the most drastic decision of them all, the Regents' prayer decision of 1962.

When the 1963 decisions on Bible-reading and reciting the Lord's Prayer were handed down, their nature had been so frequently predicted in advance that the outlawing of these practices scarcely came as a surprise. As we shall see later, all of these leading recent decisions form much more of a consistent pattern than most critics of the Court are willing to recognize.

Presidential and Congressional Politics

In the modern period, the whole controversy about religion and the schools has become more acute because it has entered the realms of Congressional and Presidential politics. Fortunately for him, no religion-and-schools controversy affected Al Smith in his drive for the democratic nomination in 1924 and for the Presidency in 1928. The Catholic hierarchy, after its nineteenth-century defeats, had decided to let its financial claims for parochial schools lie dormant. If Al Smith had championed public appropriations for sectarian schools or had allowed any religious-educational policy question to enter the campaign, he would undoubtedly have been defeated even more decisively than he was.

The whole controversy about religion and the schools moved up to the federal legislative level about 1937 when two things happened. The drive for federal aid for public schools in Congress began to show real strength; and the Roman Catholic Church, switching from its former policy of all-out opposition to federal aid, began to ask Congress, somewhat cautiously at first, for tax grants that would support Catholic as well as public schools. American Protestantism and American Judaism reacted instantly against these demands—instantly and almost unanimously.

In this new conflict of interest emotions rose to fever heat, especially in the late 1940's when the Supreme Court outlawed religious instruction in public classrooms and simultaneously Congress continued to bury all proposed aid bills for sectarian schools, even for fringe benefits. Cardinal Spellman's famous quarrel with Mrs. Eleanor Roosevelt in 1949 was officially a quarrel over a very limited demand by the Cardinal for auxiliary benefits for school buses. He professed no higher financial ambition. But the public sensed the fact that the controversy was something much larger than that. It was fundamentally a conflict over the whole nature and philosophy of American education.[23]

Happily, the issue of religious instruction *within* public classrooms has never become a great issue in *national* politics in this century. Of course it may become a very critical national political issue if the movement gets underway to amend the Constitution to permit Bible-reading, the Lord's Prayer, and financial appropriations to sectarian schools. During the 1940's and 1950's, nearly all important politicians of both major parties had perfected special techniques to avoid such theological questions and to reassure any particular audience that, somehow, they were deeply sympathetic with the doctrinal aspirations of that particular group. [I believe, ladies and gentlemen, in our great American tradition of the sepa-

- ration of church and state, and I would be willing to die to defend it. But we should remember that our nation was founded upon religious values and faith in God. Surely our schools can emphasize those mighty spiritual values that have made our nation great without violating the Constitution, those great God-given values common to Protestants, Catholics, Jews, yes, even to those people outside the churches who are loyal to the American way of life, so long as they detest our great enemy, atheistic Communism. Applause.] Congress has avoided almost all record votes on religion and school issues since 1937 through the device of a voice vote or the secondary device of sending controversies back to committee for "further consideration."

John F. Kennedy was fortunate that the issue of his Catholicism in the 1960 campaign did not involve Bible-reading or prayer in public schools. As we shall see later, these issues are closer to being Protestant issues than Catholic issues, since the most open violations of law have been fostered by Protestantism. Kennedy could correctly say that his Catholicism, meaning his personal religious faith, was a private matter and that this phase of his life should not be dragged into the arena of the campaign. It *was* dragged in, but the dragging probably did him more good than harm since relatively few Americans were ready to challenge any man's right to hold a personal creed of his own choice.

There were, however, two aspects of his church's policy that were quite relevant to his fitness for the Presidency, and they were not merely personal. Both aspects were brought into the campaign. One was the official Catholic bishops' interpretation of the Constitution and the separation of church and state which set forth the theory that across-the-board grants to sectarian schools would be perfectly legal if they were given indiscriminately to all church schools; and the other was the Catholic canonical boycott of public schools contained in Canon 1374.[24] This canon lays down the general rule that no Catholic may send his children to a public school without the special permission of his bishop.

Kennedy was shrewd enough to see that the policy of his

church's hierarchy concerning tax aid to parochial schools was a major issue and that it could not be avoided. It was a political issue partly because the bishops of his own church had announced their intention in 1948 to alter national policy on the separation of church and state as defined by the Supreme Court. These bishops had begun a national drive to secure federal money for their schools on the theory that the granting of federal funds would be constitutional.

Kennedy wisely chose to meet the issue head-on long before the Democratic nominating convention by declaring that he considered direct aid to sectarian schools unconstitutional. After his nomination, in his famous speech to the Protestant ministers of Houston, Texas, he underscored that judgment. He declared: "I believe in an America where the separation of church and state is absolute."[25] Then he added two points to that generalization, setting forth his belief in an America "where no church or church school is granted any public funds or political preference," and emphasizing the fact that, according to his record, he was against any boycott of public schools. That was a personal repudiation of Canon 1374 of his own church, even though he did not mention the canon.

During the question period at that famous Houston meeting, Mr. Kennedy claimed that "the American Bishops' statement of 1948 clearly supported" the separation of church and state. That claim was inaccurate,[26] and it is amazing that no great newspaper caught the inaccuracy. The American bishops' statement of 1948 supported partial financial union of church and state in the schools. But this did not affect the sincerity of the candidate or the validity of Kennedy's own personal stand. The important fact was that, even before Houston, Kennedy had disagreed with the hierarchy of his own church on religion and school policy. And his conduct after his inauguration showed that he was committed to his own view of the Constitution, not to the narrowly partisan view of Cardinal Spellman and his associates.

In the long struggle over federal aid to education in the

Eighty-seventh and Eighty-eighth Congresses, Kennedy found that the Catholic demand for an equal share in financial benefits for Catholic schools blocked his whole federal aid program. The conduct of the Catholic bishops in challenging both the Supreme Court and the first Catholic President proved beyond doubt that the apprehensions of many Americans about Catholic official policy on religion and education were well grounded. The Kennedy victory had cleared the air of one type of religious bigotry by ending the Protestant monopoly of the White House, but it had not settled the primary political issue behind the "religious issue," the location of the wall of separation between church and state in education.

In fact, the whole story of the religion-and-schools controversy from Jefferson to Kennedy shows that Amercia has swung in an almost complete circle since the days of Thomas Jefferson. The battle in Virginia during Jefferson's day was partly a battle for freedom from narrow dogmatism and partly a battle against religious establishment of teachers of Christianity through tax assessments. Both public dollars and a public philosophy of education were involved. Today in the battles over prayer, Bible-reading and tax payments to parochial schools the same fundamental issues are at stake. The controversy is eternal because the issues are eternal. They will continue to plague and inspire men as long as they disagree about the best methods of bringing moral and spiritual ideals to their children.

CHAPTER 2

The Supreme Court Examines
A New York Prayer

The public reception of the decision of the Supreme Court on the New York Regents' prayer on June 25, 1962 was the greatest publicity explosion that ever greeted an American decision about religion. It even exceeded the public storm that had greeted the McCollum (Illinois) decision against religious instruction in public schools in 1948. The flood of letters descending upon the Court was even greater than the flood produced by the anti-segregation decision in 1954.

The New York Times devoted almost eighteen columns to the prayer story on the day after the decision. The next day there was an editorial and at least three more columns of news and review. Lesser newspapers, with fewer columns available, gave the decision commensurate coverage. For many weeks the public discussion of the decision produced headlines, editorials and a flood of letters to the editor.

The Local Background

At the heart of this publicity storm, remaining as calm as was possible under the circumstances, were five parents of the little city of New Hyde Park, Long Island, a rapidly growing suburban town in Nassau County, just outside the limits of Greater New York.[1] This town is occupied largely by New York City commuters whose point of view cannot be described as rural. The five parents involved had eleven children in the local public schools and were thus directly interested in the status of prayer in those schools. Two of the parents were Jewish; one was a Unitarian; another belonged to the Ethical Culture Society; one called himself an unbeliever.

It was the unbeliever, a New York businessman named Lawrence Roth, who took the initiative in the case. He placed an advertisement in local papers asking for taxpayer-parents who were willing to join him in a court challenge of the Regents' prayer. About fifty responded. At first the group included several orthodox Protestants but they dropped out. In the end no orthodox Catholics or Protestants appeared as plaintiffs, although the plaintiffs received some Protestant support during the course of the battle.

It was recognized that the prayer itself seemed a rather innocuous target: "Almighty God, we acknowledge our dependence upon Thee, and we beg Thy blessings upon us, our parents, our teachers and our country." The plaintiff parents objected to the use of the prayer because they believed that its imposition involved some coercion of their children. They believed that this coercion plus the very use of the prayer itself, even on a voluntary basis, constituted a violation of the Establishment Clause of the First Amendment of the Constitution. Some of them also objected on ideological grounds. They disagreed with the doctrinal assumptions of the prayer and did not want those assumptions taught to their children.

These doctrinal differences, however, did not enter the case in any official way. As far as the legal protest was concerned, the plaintiffs might just as well have been Adventists, Mohammedans or Roman Catholics. Their chief lawyer, in fact, had come up through religious schools and called himself a "Commonweal Catholic." Sectarian theology was omitted from the arguments.

The five parents were not only represented by their chief counsel, William J. Butler, but they were helped very materially by the New York branch of the American Civil Liberties Union whose executive director is George E. Rundquist. Mr. Rundquist played a considerable role in stimulating and guiding the whole course of the plaintiff's battle. Mr. Butler contributed his services free as a lawyer for the ACLU.

On the other side of the case, by the time it reached the Supreme Court, there were, in addition to the local school authorities who were backed by the Board of Regents, sixteen intervening parents of Catholic, Protestant and Jewish faiths who were represented by lawyers for the local school board and, eventually, in the Supreme Court, by the well-known Catholic advocate of tax support for parochial schools, Porter R. Chandler of New York.

It was not easy for the five plaintiffs to challenge the educational folkways of Nassau County. The challenged prayer had been produced and approved by a unanimous Board of Regents in the belief that it was a satisfactory compromise which would please nearly all elements in the community. Such a small gesture of moral and religious aspiration in an age of juvenile delinquency seemed to the Regents wholly appropriate.

The Board of Regents of New York State is a respected bipartisan body of unpaid leading citizens, members of various religious denominations, chosen by the state legislature and given very considerable powers over the state's educational system. In this case the governor at the time of the prayer decisions was Nelson Rockefeller, but the prayer had originally been approved by Regents chosen before Rockefeller took office. The support for the prayer was quite general in both Democratic and Republican quarters. However, it had not been very widely accepted in school districts throughout the state. New York City had carefully shelved it in order to avoid religious controversy, and probably not more than 10 per cent of the state's school districts were using the prayer at the time it was challenged in the courts.

The experience of the parents in this case was not unlike the experience of that other famous litigant in church-state matters, Mrs. Vashti McCollum of Illinois. Mrs. McCollum had been subjected to abuse and ridicule in her long battle against religious instruction in the public classrooms of Champaign, Illinois.[2] Her battle ended in an eight to one triumph in the United States Su-

preme Court, but victory came only after she had been bombarded
with hostile publicity for years and after she had lost the vote of
every single judge of every local and appellate court on her way to
the highest tribunal in Washington.

In the New York prayer case the five parents and the eleven
children were subjected to badgering, threats and ridicule. They
accumulated a whole package of obscene vilifications sent by mail,
and their telephone wires were hot with abuse. But they were not
as isolated as Mrs. McCollum had been. They represented a substantial part of the community. Nassau County has many religious
liberals who have become accustomed to an atmosphere of religious
controversy.

Before the prayer battle began there had been a great influx
of Jewish families into Nassau County and also, in recent years, an
influx of Roman Catholics. The county's population had doubled
in the 1950's. The power of the old Protestant majority had sharply
declined. In the new clash of ethnic groups the public schools had
been caught in a special type of cultural squeeze. The devout portion of the Catholic community tended to adopt a lukewarm or
hostile attitude toward the rapidly expanding public schools, and
their hostility was particularly strong against things described as
"luxuries" in the schools. Three successive proposed bond issues
for public schools in the New Hyde Park area had been defeated,
largely by Catholic opposition. Well-organized local propaganda
for public aid to parochial schools was tied in with bitter criticism
of "luxury" schools for non-Catholic children. In a sense, the religious-political struggle in the county had become largely a Catholic
versus Jewish struggle, with Protestants playing a mixed and indecisive role.

The ridicule heaped upon the plaintiffs was both local and
national. The Long Island press was hostile from the beginning,
and throughout the nation conservative columnists questioned the
sincerity and intelligence of the challenge to the school prayer. The
late reactionary columnist George Sokolsky had seized upon the

appeal of the parents as an excuse for his special type of journalistic ridicule. He asked:

How crazy can you get? The time has come for all good Americans who believe in the love and guidance of God and who wish their children to be brought up in the spirit of moral law to assert themselves valiantly. These little groups who seek to impose their will upon the great majority of our people and to shriek against conformity while they demand conformity for their notions are divisive and sometimes even subversive. . . . Atheism and agnosticism have always existed but now these two are cults and they are fighting for supremacy.[3]

Through the long battle that was to lie ahead for these Long Island parents, this constant coupling of atheism and subversion was to confront the litigants from many sources.

One factor which contributed to local tensions had been the wide circulation of the Brooklyn *Tablet,* the official organ of the Brooklyn diocese of the Catholic Church, claiming a circulation of almost 150,000. This weekly newspaper had once served as a kind of mouthpiece for the notoriously anti-Semitic Father Coughlin of Detroit. Later it was the foremost religious champion of Senator Joseph McCarthy of Wisconsin. It still frequently eulogizes the late Senator McCarthy as one of the greatest moral leaders of American history.

The *Tablet* had waged a constant battle against the "Godlessness" of public schools and had often managed by insinuation in its columns to associate religious liberalism and skepticism with Communism. It repeatedly attempted to identify Americanism with its own particular brand of sectarian piety and economic reaction. It had ardently supported a group called The Long Island Conservatives whose ideas were not unlike those of the John Birch Society.

Some elements of anti-Semitism were also apparent in the local Long Island battle. The great Jewish influx into Nassau County, consisting largely of well-to-do families, had produced economic jealousy. Local rightists played upon this feeling in their campaign against larger expenditures for public schools. The propaganda produced what Dr. Nathaniel Lehrman has described as "anti-Semitism, anti-newcomerism, and anti-wealth" in his perceptive study, "The Psychological Campaign Against Long Island's Public Schools."[4] "Gold Coast Jews" were coupled in the propaganda with reckless and extravagant school expansionists who, of course, were unwilling to give poverty-stricken Catholic schools any deserved appropriations.

Here are some samples of the comments received in the mails by Mr. and Mrs. Lawrence Roth during the course of the prayer litigation.[5]

This looks like Jews trying to grab America as Jews grab everything they want in any nation. America is a Christian nation. ... Beware Jews of trying to take over America!

So you thought you put it over on our Christian America. Wipe the smiles from your atheistic faces!

If you don't like our God, then go behind the Iron Curtain where you belong, Kike, Hebe, Filth! You are scum!

Haven't they run you out of town yet, Commie, Jew, Rat?

In the years before the Supreme Court's prayer decision, school board elections in many places in Nassau County had become essentially political struggles between conservatives and liberals, with Catholic candidates usually on one side, Jewish groups on the other, and Protestants in the middle. Catholic leaders who would not send their own children to a public school under any circumstances were sometimes elected to school boards supervising the "development and expansion" of public schools. In fact, the chairman of the school board involved in the Regents' prayer case, William J. Vitale, Jr., was himself a Catholic parent who sent his children to a parochial school.

The religious struggle had burst into flame in New Hyde Park in 1956 when the local school board voted six to one to post copies of the Ten Commandments in all public classrooms. Some local Catholic and Protestant leaders supported the board in this policy while others were strongly opposed. The local vice-president of B'nai Brith expressed the Jewish opposition to this "invidious attempt to inject religion into the schools." Then State Education Commissioner James E. Allen banned the Ten Commandments from local schools in June, 1957, not on constitutional or legal grounds but solely because the posting, he believed, would lead to unnecessary controversy. He considered his ban desirable as a means of preserving community peace. The Brooklyn *Tablet* promptly called for his resignation.[6]

The Long Island struggle over religion and the schools was not wholly uncharacteristic of recent state-wide struggles in New York. Politics and religion are inextricably mixed in that state. For a long time New York has been approaching a condition which can only be described as religious Balkanization. (I had become aware of this unpleasant reality even in the 1930's while serving in the cabinet of Mayor LaGuardia.) The late Stanley M. Isaacs, who was for many years the most conscientious reform leader in New York politics, declared in 1962: "I don't like the carefully balanced ticket that we face on Election Day . . . one-third Protestants, one-third Roman Catholics, one-third Jews. All this is not integration, but just the opposite. It emphasizes race and creed and national origin."[7]

The Die Is Cast

This was the political-religious situation in that segment of America directly involved in the Regents' prayer case. The prayer itself went back to 1951 when the Board of Regents, after a long wrangle over the extent and character of "moral education" in the New York public schools, composed what it undoubtedly considered a handsome compromise solution in regard to prayer. The simple prayer evolved was clearly undenominational, and the state authorities of New York made it doubly optional, at the option of the local school board and at the option of parents.

The Regents' prayer was part of a formal Regents' document

called "Statement on Moral and Spiritual Training in the Schools," designed for guidance for all state educational officials. The Regents, rather artlessly, proclaimed in issuing their program: "We believe that this Statement will be subscribed to by all men and women of good will, and we call upon all of them to aid in giving life to our program."

The Regents had just gone through a long and bitter struggle over the introduction in New York schools of a course described as containing "moral and spiritual values." It was a struggle in which Catholic leaders and Jewish leaders had taken opposing points of view, with Protestant leaders divided. The outcome of the struggle had not been very satisfactory for any faction but it had left a desire in some quarters to "do something definite and constructive" to promote faith and brotherhood in the schools even if no particular program could command complete denominational cooperation. The Regents' final decision in favor of the prayer was considered by Catholic journals a victory for Catholic forces and for Christian moral values. Protestants were not so sure, and the Jewish organizations were openly hostile.

When, shortly after the prayer was issued in November, 1951, the Regents accompanied the prayer with an eloquent statement to the effect that "belief in and dependence upon Almighty God was the very cornerstone upon which our founding fathers builded," the Jesuit magazine *America* declared that the Board through its statement and through the accompanying prayer had committed itself to "a pro-religious type of public schooling."[8] This comment by *America* is particularly important because it indicates the larger significance of the prayer episode. The prayer itself was considered on the Catholic side a symbol of a philosophy of education. It was not, in Catholic eyes, a satisfactory prayer in itself since it did not include any of those implications of loyalty to the one true church which Catholicism teaches. But Catholic leaders welcomed this simple theistic declaration as one tiny step toward their own conception of education.

Nominally the Regents made the use of the prayer voluntary

on all levels, but the machinery for excusing children was often completely absent from a local school system. Nominally a child could step out of the room while the prayer was being recited or stand with the other children and remain silent. There is some doubt as to whether he could receive permission to remain seated— apparently a child was expected to leave the room if he could not stand up with the others in a reverent attitude. This, at least, was the theory of the use of the prayer. It was officially voluntary, but the mechanics of administration in New Hyde Park and the very nature of discipline of teachers over young children in classrooms had made it effectively compulsory. The local New Hyde Park school board did not direct teachers to make any provision for excusing any child from the prayer until nine months after the plaintiffs in the suit had gone to court. And the local school board never stopped to ask the question: What child would want to step out of his classroom for a ceremony lasting less than one minute? He could scarcely reach the door before he would have to return for other opening ceremonies.

The long legal journey to the United States Supreme Court began in 1958 when the plaintiffs asked the New York State Supreme Court—in this instance a trial court—to stop the use of the Regents' prayer as an illegal establishment of religion under the First Amendment. As expected, the first judge in the process, Justice Bernard S. Meyer, conceded the distinctively religious nature of the prayer, but in his thoughtful, forty-six–page opinion he refused the plea of the plaintiffs to ban it. He outlined a number of safeguards against "embarrassments and pressures" on the dissident parents and children, safeguards which he considered necessary and sufficient to protect the rights of both parents and children. All parents in the school were to receive a copy of the prayer so that they could make a considered and careful judgment as to acceptance or rejection. There was to be no comment on the prayer by the teachers nor any requirement of any particular posture by the children. Dissenting children were permitted to arrive in the classroom a moment later if they asked for this alternative.

The next higher court, a branch of New York's Appellate Division, sustained Justice Meyer unanimously on the central issue, with one dissent on a minor point. Then New York's highest court, the Court of Appeals, sustained the prayer by a vote of five to two, but the two dissenting opinions, by Justice Dye and Justice Fuld, were both powerful and prophetic. The prevailing opinion in favor of the prayer was written by Chief Judge Desmond, a Catholic jurist who had long been an advocate of a loose interpretation of the Establishment Clause of the First Amendment. Said Justice Desmond, speaking for the court: "It is an indisputable and historically provable fact that belief and trust in a Creator has always been regarded as an integral and inseparable part of the fabric of our fundamental institutions." About the prayer Justice Desmond said:

> But it is not religious education nor is it the practice of or establishment of religion in any reasonable meaning of those phrases. Saying this simple prayer may be, according to the broadest possible dictionary, an act of religion, but when the Founding Fathers prohibited an establishment of religion they were referring to official adoption of, or favor to, one or more sects. They could not have meant to prohibit mere professions of belief in God for, if that were so, they themselves in many ways were violating their rule when and after they adopted it.[9]

It did not disturb Justice Desmond that this interpretation of the Constitution had been specifically rejected by the Supreme Court on several occasions. Outside the court room he continued to defy the Supreme Court quite openly and specifically. Even two months after the United States Supreme Court had again overruled this interpretation of the Constitution in its prayer decision, by a vote of six to one, he appeared at a dinner of the National Federation of Catholic College Students where he received the Archbishop Noll Award. In his address at this dinner he flatly denied that the Constitution either bars religion from public schools or prohibits public aid to church-related schools. "You and I," he said, "owe it to our country to meet and dispel and disprove the current extremist arguments of American secularists. . . . I deny that our Constitution or our tradition forbids them [religious practices in public schools]."[10]

The failure of the New York courts to sustain their point of view did not surprise the plaintiffs. They could hardly expect local victory in the New York situation. New York's elected judges are nominated in bi-partisan deals at political conventions under circumstances which handicap any judge who might "offend" any powerful religious group. The hurdle that worried the plaintiffs and their attorneys most was the admission of the case to the United States Supreme Court for a review on the merits. The precedents here were not clear. The right to sue in such a case is clouded with ambiguities and contradictory traditions. In any case, no Supreme Court is bound to accept such a case for review or to explain its grounds for refusal.

In this case there were many persuasive points to be urged against review by our highest court. The prayer was relatively insignificant. It did not mention Jesus Christ or any particular God. Obviously the dispute involved over its use was not half so extensive or important as the dispute over the reading of the Bible and the recitation of the Lord's Prayer in many public schools throughout the country. Why jump over Bible-reading and the Lord's Prayer and take up such a simple problem first?

That was the question which many sincere advocates of church-state separation asked. They did not want the Supreme Court to review the adoption of this particular prayer at this particular moment, and they believed that the Court could be more easily persuaded to hand down a complete and meaningful review of the whole problem of religion and the schools by challenging Bible-reading and the recitation of the Lord's Prayer first. Some of the critics—and I must confess that I was among them—regarded the Regents' prayer case as resembling an impatient lady at the end of a long theatre queue who insists on rushing to the head of the line and purchasing her ticket before other waiting customers. If I could have chosen in 1962 an order of precedence for the testing of the important issues in the field of religion and the law, I would have put several other issues ahead of the Regents' prayer issue, notably tax payments to sectarian schools, laws against birth control, Bible-reading and the Lord's Prayer in public schools, and compulsory chapel attendance at service academies. But, since the timing of judicial history is not always opportune and since the Supreme Court itself cannot always determine the order of judicial events, these considerations about priority constitute little more than wishful supposition.

The litigants and lawyers in the Regents' prayer case were also worried by another striking phenomenon. There was massive legal support for the prayer by attorneys general from many states. Some seventeen state attorneys general—later increased to nineteen—filed a brief with the Supreme Court, in defense of the prayer, saying:

> Our founding fathers, together with the great and God-fearing leaders of the last century and a half, would be profoundly shocked were they to have been told in their day that in this year of our Lord, One Thousand Nine Hundred and Sixty-Two, a voluntary, undenominational acknowledgment of a Supreme Being, and a petition for His blessings, recited by American children in their classrooms, is being seriously attacked as a violation of the Constitution of the United States!
> As attorneys general of our sovereign states, we recognize and defend the right of every man to believe in God or not believe as he chooses, and should he profess such a faith, as nearly all Americans do, to worship God as he desires. Nevertheless, we firmly believe that as a Nation, America must remain true to her religious heritage and tradition. Our children must continue to have every opportunity to gain an appreciation of this heritage and tradition, not only at home and in the church but also in public activities, including public schools and other governmental functions.

Powerful *amicus* briefs were filed against the prayer by the Synagogue Council (representing many Jewish religious groups), the National Community Relations Advisory Council, which includes the American Jewish Congress, and the American Ethical

Union, the national agency of Ethical Societies. This American Ethical Union argued that the use of the prayer in a public school "constitutes governmental preference for theism in violation of the First and Fourteenth Amendments." The Synagogue Council, represented by Leo Pfeffer, declared ". . . the critical test is not compulsion . . . but state aid to religion. Hence, even if pupil participation in the prayer were entirely voluntary—which we deny—the First Amendment ban on establishment would still be violated by the aid accorded religion by the State through the public school system and by State participation in religious affairs."[11]

Many church-state specialists were surprised when the Supreme Court with reasonable promptness accepted this case for review on December 4, 1961. They continued to be apprehensive about the results because the prayer seemed so inoffensive. They feared the wrong kind of precedent.

When the case was argued before the Supreme Court on April 3, 1962, the great chamber was crowded. The lawyers for both sides were eloquent and convincing—to their own partisans. The prayer, said William J. Butler, for the plaintiffs, constituted the "teaching of religion in a public institution" and as such was clearly unconstitutional. The prayer, said Bertram B. Daiker, attorney for the New Hyde Park school board, is "fully in accord with the tradition and heritage that has been handed down to us." He suggested that the First Amendment does not bar a religious state but only a state religion, and he contended that this relatively innocuous prayer did not establish a state religion in defiance of the Constitution.

One important clarification of language occurred during the colloquy between lawyers and justices. Toward the end of his presentation of the plaintiff's case, Butler was asked by Justice Frankfurter whether it was a fair representation of his point of view to say that American public schools were "frankly secular institutions."

"Absolutely yes," Butler replied.

That marked a commendable frankness in the use of the

word "secular," since the public schools are in fact secular in the true sense of that word; they are not under church control. The admission of that fact in that exalted chamber, where words must be used with exactness and integrity, was all to the good. But it gave the mouthers of loose phrases a new opportunity to proclaim that these plaintiffs were really trying to establish "the religion of secularism" in place of "the heritage of our fathers." Of such twisted strands of verbal ambiguity are the Great Falsehoods of propaganda manufactured.

At best the plaintiffs hoped for a decision against the prayer by a sharply divided court. They were delighted—and almost stunned with surprise—by a six to one victory in one of the most sweeping and significant decisions in favor of strict separation between church and state ever handed down by an American court.

The Bomb-Shell

June 25, 1962 was not just an ordinary day in the history of American justice. It was the final day of the term of the Supreme Court. It was a day for decisions only, not for arguments by lawyers. The fact that it was the final day of the session meant that the most controversial issue in the legal history of American religion either would be decided that day or would be put off until autumn.

The spectators who came to the great vaulted chamber of the Supreme Court on this warm and lazy morning in June welcomed the air conditioning and the height of the three-storey chamber with its towering Corinthian columns. Rumors had been going around Washington for weeks that the prayer decision, when it came, might shake the religious foundations of the country. But no one could tell whether the rumors had any foundation. The Supreme Court is the most hermetically sealed institution in Washington, far more leak-proof than the CIA. When the justices meet together in chambers to take a vote on a forthcoming decision, they will not even permit a stenographer to sit in the same room with them. The most rigid protocol is observed, as well as the most rigid secrecy. If someone must leave the conference room to secure something necessary for the discussion, a junior justice must serve as errand boy. When the Chief Justice calls for a vote, the junior members are asked to express their opinions first so that no one can say that they are being subjected to pressure from above. Recently a clerks' room near the sacred inner chamber where decisions are discussed has been vacated to avoid the chance that anybody might hear the voices of the justices raised in argument.

The issuance of a decision by the Court is so carefully guarded in advance that even the Supreme Court clerk is not allowed to tell reporters on the morning of a decision whether the Court will act on that particular case that day. Copies of decisions are never given to the press in advance. The first glimpse given to any reporter comes when the justice who reads the decision itself starts to read that decision. Then a publications clerk quietly passes in front of the bench, distributing copies to journalists inside the front rail.

This time the proceedings began with a special surprise ceremony in honor of Justice Hugo Black. The Alabama judge, oldest in point of service on the bench, had completed twenty-five terms on the Court. At seventy-six he was still a vigorous tennis player and an even more vigorous all-around liberal. Appointed to the Court by President Roosevelt in 1937, he had come up quite miraculously from a Ku Klux background and a Southern political past to become one of the most respected and scholarly leaders on the Court.

Black, sitting at the right hand of Chief Justice Warren on the long bench which runs across the front of the chamber, leaned back in embarrassment and surprise as Chief Justice Warren joined Solicitor General Archibald Cox in a warm tribute to his twenty-five terms of service. Then, after a few other cases had been cleared, Justice Black leaned forward a little, shuffled a thick sheaf of papers, and in his clear dry Alabama accent pronounced the words that went further toward the complete disestablishment of religion than any previous pronouncement in American history. (The com-

plete text of the decision and the dissent will be found in Appendix I.)

Reminding his hearers of the wording of that clause in the
First Amendment—"Congress shall make no law respecting an es-
tablishment of religion"—and repeating the fact that the First
Amendment had been "made applicable to the State of New York
by the Fourteenth Amendment of the said Constitution," Justice
Black said:

We think that by using its public school system to encourage
recitation of the Regents' prayer, the State of New York has
adopted a practice wholly inconsistent with the Establishment
Clause. There can, of course, be no doubt that New York's program
of daily classroom invocation of God's blessing as prescribed by the
Regents' prayer is a religious activity. It is a solemn avowal of divine faith and supplication for the blessings of the Almighty. The
nature of such a prayer has always been religious, none of the respondents has denied this and the trial court expressly so found. . . .

The petitioners contend among other things that the state
laws requiring or permitting use of the Regents' prayer must be
struck down as a violation of the Establishment Clause because
that prayer was composed by governmental officials as a part of a
governmental program to further religious beliefs. For this reason,
petitioners argue, the State's use of the Regents' prayer in its public
school system breaches the constitutional wall of separation between Church and State. We agree with that contention since we
think that the constitutional prohibition against laws respecting
an establishment of religion must at least mean that in this country
it is no part of the business of government to compose official
prayers for any group of the American people to recite as a part of
a religious program carried on by government.

By this time both reporters and spectators knew that a revo-
tionary decision was being handed down. The Hyde Park plaintiffs
had won a smashing victory. Justice Black went on to recite the
precedents in early American history for the view he was enunci-
ating, leaning heavily upon Jefferson and Madison. "By the time
of the adoption of the Constitution," he said, "history shows that
there was a widespread awareness among many Americans of the

dangers of a union of church and state. These people knew, some
of them from bitter personal experience, that one of the greatest
dangers to the freedom of the individual to worship in his own way
lay in the goverment's placing its official stamp of approval upon
one particular kind of prayer or one particular form of religious
services." Then he reasoned:

> The First Amendment was added to the Constitution to stand
> as a guarantee that neither the power nor the prestige of the Fed-
> eral Government would be used to control, support or influence
> the kinds of prayer the American people can say—that the people's
> religions must not be subjected to the pressures of government for
> change each time a new political administration is elected to office.
> Under that Amendment's prohibition against governmental estab-
> lishment of religion, as reinforced by the provisions of the Four-
> teenth Amendment, government in this country, be it state or fed-
> eral, is without power to prescribe by law any particular form of
> prayer which is to be used as an official prayer in carrying out any
> program of governmentally sponsored religious activity.

But the prayer was *voluntary*—or at least it was described as
voluntary by its defenders and by the Board of Regents. Did the
prohibitions of the First and Fourteenth Amendments require the
elimination of a *voluntary* prayer which pupils were not compelled
to recite if they asked to be excused? Justice Black and the majority
of the Court had this to say on the all-important matter of compulsion. In effect, they said that all the arguments about compulsion and voluntariness were irrelevant. The thing that counted was
establishment.

> Neither the fact that the prayer may be denominationally
> neutral, nor the fact that its observance on the part of the students
> is voluntary can serve to free it from the limitations of the Estab-
> lishment Clause, as it might from the Free Exercise Clause. . . . The
> Establishment Clause, unlike the Free Exercise Clause, does not
> depend upon any showing of direct governmental compulsion and
> is violated by the enactment of laws which establish an official reli-
> gion whether those laws operate directly to coerce nonobserving
> individuals or not. . . . When the power, prestige and financial sup-
> port of government is placed behind a particular religious belief,

the indirect coercive pressure upon religious minorities to conform to the prevailing officially approved religion is plain.

Justice Black and the Court majority must have known, of course, that such language would immediately be interpreted—or wilfully misinterpreted—as signifying hostility to religion itself. So the Court added:

It has been argued that to apply the Constitution in such a way as to prohibit state laws respecting an establishment of religious services in public schools is to indicate a hostility toward religion or toward prayer. Nothing, of course, could be more wrong. . . . It is neither sacrilegious nor antireligious to say that each separate government in this country should stay out of the business of writing or sanctioning official prayers and leave that purely religious function to the people themselves and to those the people choose to look to for religious guidance.

The Douglas Hand-Grenade

The result of the decision, the reversal of New York's highest court and the directive to outlaw the Regents' prayer, was concurred in by Chief Justice Warren and Associate Justices Black, Douglas, Clark, Harlan, and Brennan. Only Justice Potter Stewart dissented. Justice Frankfurter, who was soon to retire because of illness, had taken part in the study of the case but not in the judgment itself, so he cast no vote. Justice Byron White had just been appointed to the Court. So the vote stood six to one against the prayer with two abstentions.

Justice William O. Douglas, fiery liberal, nature lover, and defender of lost causes, startled the audience that morning by reading a *concurring* opinion that went even farther than the majority decision. He implied that if he had been able to write an opinion covering all aspects of religion and government, he might have outlawed not only this particular prayer but also such financial phenomena as tax grants for buses to parochial schools and even paid chaplains in the halls of Congress. His implications were somewhat more revolutionary than his actual conclusions. Some newspapers, and especially the opponents of the Court, seized upon the most extreme inferences in the Douglas assenting opinion and built up more headlines out of those inferences than they constructed out of the opinion of the Court itself.

The most notable thing about the rather startling opinion of Justice Douglas was that it marked a change in view by that justice. He had often been quoted with a famous "soft" line in the decision he wrote for the majority of the Court in the released time, Zorach case in 1952: "We are a religious people whose institutions presuppose a Supreme Being." That famous sentence had been seized upon by every advocate of financial support for church schools, and inflated into an epoch-making and universal "principle." Now it was the author of that sentence himself who reversed some of his own reasoning and took the other extreme. He began as if he were manufacturing excuses for approving the school prayer because of the precedents of similar concessions to religion in other branches of government. He suggested, in a point that no other justice on the Court had brought out, that the prayer might be unconstitutional as a financial phenomenon. "The point for decision is whether the Government can constitutionally finance a religious exercise. Our system at the federal and state levels is presently honeycombed with such financing. Nevertheless, I think it is an unconstitutional undertaking whatever form it takes."

Then Justice Douglas listed a whole series of borderline religious practices around the periphery of government which are now permitted under the Constitution. If he had not committed himself so explicitly to the view that these concessions were illegal, it would have seemed that he was leading up to a general approval of such grants. Quoting from Professor Fellman's *The Limits of Freedom,* he listed in his footnote the service of chaplains in both Houses of Congress; compulsory chapel services at Armed Forces academies; religious services held in federal hospitals and prisons; Presidential religious proclamations; the receipt of federal tuition money by individuals under the G.I. bill of 1944 even when the

recipients are attending theological schools; the distribution of
food to sectarian as well as to public schools under the National
School Lunch Act; the grant of public funds to sectarian hospitals
under the Hospital Survey and Construction Act of 1946; the use
of the slogan "In God We Trust" on coins; the addition of the
name of God to the pledge of allegiance to the flag; the tax exemption of churches; the granting of postal privileges to religious organizations; and the exemption from personal income taxes of
some contributions to religious organizations. He even mentioned
in the text of his decision the famous stentorian cry of the Supreme
Court Marshall, delivered each morning as the justices of the Court
assemble: "God save the United States and this honorable court."

Then, instead of using these fringe concessions to religion as
an excuse to approve the Regents' prayer, Justice Douglas implied
that all these things might be illegal, and he specifically reversed
his own position on the use of public money for parochial school
buses. (His vote in favor of the constitutionality of such bus appropriations in 1947 had swung the balance of the court to a five to
four sanction of such appropriations.) Instead of quoting himself
from that case, the Everson bus case, he quoted as "durable First
Amendment philosophy" the opinion of a justice who had differed
with him, Justice Rutledge:

There cannot be freedom of religion, safeguarded by the
state, and intervention by the church or its agencies in the state's
domain or dependency on its largesse. . . . The great condition of
religious liberty is that it be maintained free from sustenance, as
also from other interferences, by the state. . . . Public money devoted to payment of religious costs, educational or other, brings the
quest for more. It brings too the struggle of sect against sect for
the larger share or for any. Here one by numbers alone will benefit
most, there another. . . . It is the very thing Jefferson and Madison
experienced and sought to guard against, whether in its blunt or
in its more screened forms.

Justice Douglas also went further than the other justices in
regarding the use of the prayer as a *financial* concession to religion.
"In New York," he said,

... the teacher who leads in prayer is on the public payroll; and the time she takes seems miniscule.... Yet for me the principle is the same, no matter how briefly the prayer is said ... once government finances a religious enterprise it inserts a divisive influence into our communities.... The First Amendment teaches that a government neutral in the field of religion better serves all religious interests.

In the rush of ill-digested publicity which accompanied the prayer decision many legislators and some editors made more use of the alleged inferences from the language of Justice Douglas than from the Court's decision. They assumed that because Douglas had tangentially raised the question of the legality of Congressional chaplaincies, "In God We Trust," etc., the Court itself was calling the legality of these things into question.

This was not strictly true, although it was true that the Court's total reasoning in this case could be used in an attack on such phenomena as tax-supported chaplaincies and even religious-political mottoes. Justice Black, however, in an important footnote —so important that it should never have been relegated to the bottom of the page—announced clear limits to the scope of this decision. He said:

There is of course nothing in the decision reached here that is inconsistent with the fact that school children and others are officially encouraged to express love for our country by reciting historical documents such as the Declaration of Independence which contain references to the Deity or by singing officially espoused anthems which include the composer's professions of faith in a Supreme Being, or with the fact that there are many manifestations in our public life of belief in God. Such patriotic or ceremonial occasions bear no true resemblance to the unquestioned religious exercise that the State of New York has sponsored in this instance.

Stewart Dissents

Justice Potter Stewart, the lone dissenter, an Episcopalian, did not take the same attitude toward the myriad religious phenomena in government life espoused by Douglas and brushed over by Black. He took those same phenomena and underscored the alleged inconsistency of banning a simple prayer such as the Regents' prayer while permitting a score of more serious breaches in the wall of separation between church and state. It was absurd, he implied, to draw the line against the prayer while these other examples of cooperation with religion were continuing with almost universal approval.

His main point was that the majority of the justices had overstated the meaning of the First Amendment as it applied to the establishment of religion. In that respect he seemed to be in practical agreement with Justice Stanley Reed who was the lone dissenter from the Court's eight to one verdict against religious instruction in public schools in the 1948 McCollum case. In a way it was a singular circumstance that in each case, the religious instruction case of 1948 and the prayer case of 1962, there was only one out-and-out dissent on the strict interpretation of the First Amendment enunciated by the majority of the justices.

In this case Stewart's dissent was not as powerful or as well documented as Reed's dissent in the McCollum case, but it followed the same persuasive line. And it won a great deal of respectful agreement in the press and on the floor of Congress. Justice Stewart said in part—I omit the details of the religious phenomena already cited since they were virtually the same phenomena as those cited by Douglas.

... the Court says that in permitting school children to say this simple prayer, the New York authorities have established "an official religion."

With all respect, I think the Court has misapplied a great constitutional principle. I cannot see how an "official religion" is established by letting those who want to say a prayer say it. On the contrary, I think that to deny the wish of these school children to join in reciting this prayer is to deny them the opportunity of sharing in the spiritual heritage of our Nation. . . .

For we deal here not with the establishment of a state church, which would, of course, be constitutionally impermissible, but with whether school children who want to begin their day by joining in prayer must be prohibited from doing so. Moreover, I think that the Court's task, in this as in all areas of constitutional adjudication, is not responsibly aided by the uncritical invocation of metaphors like the "wall of separation," a phrase nowhere to be found in the Constitution. What is relevant to the issue here is not the history of an established church in sixteenth century England or in eighteenth century America, but the history of the religious tradition of our people, reflected in countless practices of the institutions and officials of our government.

Justice Stewart then launched into an extensive and very effective summary of practices by American government which seemed to be equally as religious as the New York prayer. He cited the fact, with voluminous quotations, that each of our Presidents from Washington to Kennedy had, upon assuming office, invoked the protection and help of God; that the third stanza of the Star Spangled Banner definitely praises God; that Congressional, military and prison chaplains are paid with public money; and that in 1952 Congress had called upon the President each year to proclaim a National Day of Prayer. Then Justice Stewart concluded:

I do not believe that this Court, or the Congress, or the President has by the actions and practices I have mentioned established an "official religion" in violation of the Constitution. And I do not believe the State of New York has done so in this case. What each has done has been to recognize and to follow the deeply entrenched and highly cherished spiritual traditions of our Nation—traditions which come down to us from those who almost two hundred years ago avowed their "firm reliance on the protection of Divine Providence" when they proclaimed the freedom and independence of this brave new world.

These carefully chosen words were not mirrored in the public reaction. Let us turn now to the violent and eloquent outbursts of condemnation and approval which swept the nation after the Court's decision.

CHAPTER 3

The National Reaction

When a great controversy arises in American life, reporters turn to both the man on the street and his heroes for quotable judgments. The assumption is that their opinions, both hasty and well-considered, will somehow disclose the national mind. Not surprisingly, in the case of the Regents' prayer decision the reporters turned first, in the absence of a direct statement from the White House, to former Presidents and those of Presidential timber. As politicians they were happy to oblige.

Said Dwight D. Eisenhower:

I always thought that this nation was essentially a religious one. I realize, of course, that the Declaration of Independence antedates the Constitution, but the fact remains that the Declaration was our certificate of national birth. It specifically asserts that we as individuals possess certain rights as an endowment from our Creator— a religious concept.

Former President Herbert Hoover was slightly more definite. Charging that the Supreme Court's decision represented "a disintegration of a sacred American heritage," Mr. Hoover said: "The Congress should at once submit an amendment to the Constitution which establishes the right to religious devotion in all governmental agencies—national, state or local."

Former President Harry S. Truman was more cautious. He simply pointed out that "the Supreme Court of course is the interpreter of the Constitution." Richard M. Nixon took time to consider the matter and then came out four months later in his unsuccessful campaign for governor of California for an amendment to the Constitution legalizing the use of non-sectarian prayers in public schools in order "to remind our children of our religious heritage."

Governor Nelson Rockefeller, the politician most directly involved in the whole controversy, was cautiously regretful. He said that he hoped "adjustments" could be made in the Regents' prayer so that it could continue to be used. He did not say what the adjustments should be. He expressed himself in favor of inculcating in the minds of children a belief in the "brotherhood of man and the fatherhood of God."

President Kennedy was more forthright and direct, although he too made use of some precautionary phrases to protect himself against the possible charge of being opposed to religion. He did not indicate any positive liking for the Court's decision but he advocated obedience. As the first Catholic President, he occupied an unusually vulnerable position on that June 27, two days after the Court's decision, when he scheduled a press conference. On the previous day the most prominent leader of his church in America, Francis Cardinal Spellman, had made a blistering attack on the prayer decision. The Cardinal was obviously attempting to rally all Catholic Americans against the Court's view.

When the press conference began, it was obvious that the President was prepared for some sharp questioning about the prayer decision. He weighed every word carefully, and his response was politically masterful even if it was factually thin. He said—and these answers came in response to several questions:

> The Supreme Court has made its judgment, and a good many people obviously will disagree with it. Others will agree with it. But I think that it is important for us if we are going to maintain our constitutional principle that we support the Supreme Court decisions even when we may not agree with them.
>
> In addition we have in this case a very easy remedy, and that is to pray ourselves; and I would think that it would be a welcome reminder to every American family that we can pray a good deal more at home and attend our churches with a good deal more fidelity, and we can make the true meaning of prayer much more important to the lives of all our children. That power is very much

open to us. I would hope that as a result of this decision that all American parents will intensify their efforts at home, and the rest of us will support the Constitution and the responsibility of the Supreme Court in interpreting it.[1]

Congress Explodes

The members of Congress responded to the prayer decision more promptly and more violently than did any other segment of American society. Within the first twenty-four hours after the decision ten Congressmen introduced strong attacks on the Supreme Court into the *Congressional Record,* and not a single voice was raised in the Court's defense on the floor of Congress during that period. Ultimately five vocal Congressmen supported the Court but forty-seven did not.

In general, the severity of the attacks tended to increase according to the square of the distance of the critic's residence below the Mason and Dixon line. This generalization, however, had a number of exceptions. Any Northern Congressman who had a large number of Catholic constituents and not many Jewish constituents tended to see an ominous threat to religious freedom in the decision.

Perhaps a number of Congressional critics regretted the first-day attack on the Court. President Kennedy's bland statement on the decision, about 48 hours after it had been handed down, tended to sober up the dissidents in Congress and to suggest that they might not be furthering their political fortunes a great deal if they disagreed too violently with the head of the government.

The attack by Southern Dixiecrats—past and present—was naturally the most vicious because these Southern leaders were grasping an opportunity not merely to attack a decision but to destroy an institution which they hated. They were striking at the Supreme Court itself, the Warren Court that had handed down the decision against racial segregation in May, 1954. They were representing a very vocal Southern bloc whose propaganda activities were extensive. Shortly after the decision an old sign appearing on the highways in northern North Carolina which read:

> Impeach Earl Warren
> Save America

was changed by the addition of a new panel at the bottom:

> Impeach Earl Warren
> Save America
> Save Prayer

On a South Carolina highway, the added panel at the bottom produced:

> Impeach Earl Warren
> Save Our Republic
> Join the John Birch Society

Since Southern Protestantism had been violating the Supreme Court's ruling against religious instruction in public schools more consistently than any other religious segment in the population, the Southern critics of the Court felt that they were on pretty safe grounds politically when they spoke out. But the attack and the defense in Congress did not run along denominational lines. More Protestants than Catholics criticized the Court, but this was to be expected since Protestants outnumber Catholics in Congress more than four to one. The disparity in oratorical decibels had a statistical explanation. Perhaps some Democratic Catholic Congressmen—and nearly all Catholic Congressmen are Democrats—were a little abashed to take the side of Cardinal Spellman against the head of their party after he had taken a much milder and more approving line.

In the whole debate about the decision in Congress, only two speakers attempted a reasonably detailed legal analysis of the issues, Senator Wayne Morse of Oregon and Senator A. Willis Robertson of Virginia. Senator Morse included a good discussion of church-state constitutional law in his filibuster against the private ownership of Telstar. Senator Robertson made an extended analysis of the law from the point of view of Southern conservatives.

Most of the speeches and insertions in the *Congressional Record* during the prayer debate were violent and jejune. The best thing about them was that, for the most part, they were not actually spoken. If they had been spoken on the floor, a quorum would rapidly have faded away. Nearly all of the alleged speeches were simply extensions in the *Record,* inserted during a short break in some debate when the presiding officer in response to a request would mumble "withoutobjectionitissoorderedbang." These insertions cost the taxpayers about $90 a page. They are permitted on the theory that their insertion supplements the right of petition granted to every citizen in the Constitution.

Quite naturally, the most vocal critic of the Court in Congress, at least on paper, was Senator Strom Thurmond of South Carolina, former Dixiecrat candidate for President. Thurmond was the most logical person to harry the Court with inserted sermons by conservative Protestant divines, editorials from small Southern dailies, and occasionally a reasoned attack on the Court by Southern lawyers. Thurmond introduced eight hostile editorials and sermons in one day's issue of the *Congressional Record,* spacing them out in seven installments. His attack went on for more than two months.

Senator Herman Eugene Talmadge, Georgia Baptist, charged that "the Supreme Court has set up atheism as a new religion" and "put God and the devil on an equal plane." Later, in January, 1963, Senator Robertson, Virginia Baptist, in the course of a well-documented criticism of the Court, admitted in response to the prodding of Senator Paul Douglas of Illinois that he thought the Fourteenth Amendment to the Constitution had never been legally adopted and that even the Thirteenth Amendment fell in that class, although he did add: "I do endorse the abolition of slavery."[2]

The extreme position taken by Robertson in reply to questions from Douglas is worth recording here since it represents the opinion of a great many of the Southern political critics of the Warren Court.

MR. DOUGLAS. Does the Senator deny that the 14th and 15th amendments to the Constitution exist and that they are legally in effect?

MR. ROBERTSON. No; I do not deny that they exist. I assert that they have been badly abused and misconstrued. The 14th amendment had nothing to do with segregation, but the great Chief Justice from California read a book by a Swedish socialist who said that our Constitution is outmoded and ought to be thrown in an ashcan. . . . So he turned the clock forward and used the 14th amendment to amend the Constitution. . . .

Of course, when the 14th amendment was adopted, the State that first gave us representative government, going back to Jamestown in 1619, was Military District No. 1, and was found by Congress to be incapable of self-government; and, at the point of the bayonet, all Southern whites were disqualified and Negroes were given office. So the amendment was illegally adopted and ratified. . . .

The decision of the Supreme Court in Brown against Board of Education in 1954, in my opinion, is not the law of the land, but it is the fact of the land. . . . With bayonets sticking in one's back, all argument ends. . . .

The 14th amendment had nothing to do with schools; it had nothing to do with the New York prayer case.

Said Senator Talmadge: "The able Senator from Virginia is not only one of the greatest lawyers and one of the greatest biblical scholars in the Senate; he is also one of the greatest historians in the Senate."

The gravamen of the Congressional attack on the Court was that it had read something into the First Amendment that was not there. It had usurped power over the states just as it had done in the segregation cases. It was taking government away from the people. Robertson was able to muster a considerable number of legal authorities who supported his argument—and that of the Catholic hierarchy and the Protestant concessionists: "Clearly, the words 'establishment of religion' in the First Amendment, were intended to mean establishment of a particular denomination—Methodist, Baptist, or Catholic—as the national religion. And clearly the 14th amendment was not intended to apply the establishment clause of the First Amendment to the states."[3]

Like most of the Congressional critics of the decision, Robertson brought into the discussion all the many features of religious recognition now taken for granted in government activity—the mention of God in the pledge of allegiance to the flag, the motto "In God We Trust," etc. For the most part, the critics ignored the cautionary limiting paragraph in Justice Black's footnote, narrowing down the possible scope of the decision and specifically exempting many of these practices from its range.

Of all the Southern leaders in the House, John Bell Williams, Mississippi Baptist, was most resourceful. He introduced into the *Record* the "consternation" of the Paul Revere Ladies of Mississippi over "the ungodly decisions of the apparently godless Supreme Court of these United States," particularly "this blasphemous one [which] offers an insult to Almighty God and invites His wrath upon the people of this Nation."[4] At one point he introduced into the *Record* a poem of 188 lines which he described as "A U.S. Supreme Court Soliloquy as Envisioned by the Scribbler, Clarence O. Amonette." An abbreviated quotation will not remind the reader of Ogden Nash.

Of the United States we are the Supreme Court.
Remaking the Constitution is our forte.
Our present Constitution is but a relic of a former day,
And we have dedicated ourselves to putting it safely away.
We have assumed the power of constitutional amendment,
Though this indeed is not within the Constitution's intendment....

We blasted the doctrine of "separate but equal,"
And are enforcing integration as the sequel....

The light of our once great Constitution now grows dim,
As we snuff it according to our judicial whim.
For our once boasted constitutional democracy,
We are substituting a judicial autocracy.
However long our aim may be deferred,
From our purpose we cannot be deterred.
For ensconced for life in our judicial tower,

We wield as we see fit our judicial power.
Our purpose and methods are indeed quite extreme,
But under the Constitution we are supreme.[5]

The Court's critics in Congress were strengthened in their assault by two events which took place in the summer of 1962: an almost unanimous demand by the Conference of American Governors, meeting in Hershey, Pennsylvania early in July, that the right to have non-denominational prayers in public schools should be restored by constitutional amendment; and the holding of abbreviated hearings on constitutional change by the Senate Judiciary Committee under the chairmanship of Senator James O. Eastland of Mississippi. Eastland gave the critics of the Court a much publicized hearing for two days, and then adjourned his committee by stalling from day to day. Many defenders of the Court were denied the opportunity to present their vocal refutation at the moment when public attention was fixed on the problem.

Bishop James A. Pike, in a powerful attack on the Court, received virtually all the publicity from the hearings. Altogether forty-nine proposed amendments to the Constitution were filed with appropriate remarks. (*See* Chapter 8.)

Almost unnoticed, a New York lawyer representing Cardinal Spellman filed a proposed amendment that would have gone far beyond the prayer issue and permitted complete federal support of Catholic schools. "The amendment," said Lawrence X. Cusack in submitting it for Cardinal Spellman, "should rather make clear what our Founding Fathers thought they had made clear, that our Constitution favors Government cooperation with religion so long as such cooperation is devoid of favored treatment to any one religion or denomination." His suggested wording for a new version was: "Congress shall make no law respecting the establishment of a state religion or, in encouraging religion, the preferment of any religion or denomination, or prohibiting the free exercise of religion. . . ."[6] Although the proposed Spellman amendment did not specifically mention tax support, the long statement by Lawyer Cusack made it clear by implication that the Catholic hierarchy wanted something much bigger than the restoration of the Regents' prayer.

The Eastland maneuver was part of a deliberate attack on the Court by Southern extremists. The resolution passed by the governors at Hershey, Pennsylvania was a quick and pious reaction by politicians in the first flush of angry resentment over the prayer decision. There is a great deal of states-rights sentiment among governors in every section of America, not merely in the South. The Hershey Conference resolution, calling for a constitutional amendment to permit prayer in public schools, gave the governors a chance to express burning resentment against the growth in federal power and the consequent downgrading of their status in American political society.[7] Also, who could criticize any politician for coming out on the side of God? Governor Rockefeller was the only governor to beg off from the vote, on the ground that he needed more time to study the matter.

The Religious Response

The first response to the Court's decision from the world of religion came as swiftly as the response of the ex-Presidents, and it was equally hostile. Probably in that month of June 1962 the four best known Catholic and Protestant leaders in America were Cardinal Spellman, Billy Graham, Reinhold Niebuhr and Bishop James A. Pike.

All four of these noted religious leaders attacked the prayer decision as morally or legally wrong or impractical. The attack by Cardinal Spellman was most bitter; the attack by Bishop Pike was most plausible and analytical. Billy Graham contented himself with a gesture against "secularism." Niebuhr emphasized the social discord and misunderstanding that would result from such a decision and said that "to exclude the Regents' prayer is to insist that the schools be absolutely secular in every respect, which is not what the First Amendment intended."[8] He criticized the decision as "an

instance of using a meat ax for solving a delicate problem that requires a scalpel."[9] It was apparent that when the chips were down
every one of these distinguished clerics tended to look at the Constitution from an ecclesiastical point of view.

Their attitude was not entirely new. They had all been in
some partial disagreement with the Supreme Court over its past
interpretations of the separation of church and state, and for them
the prayer decision was only the final error in a series of errors.
Both the Niebuhr opposition and the Spellman opposition went
back to their powerful attacks on the Supreme Court's McCollum
decision in 1948.[10]

Cardinal Spellman did not even wait to consider the decision
for a single day. In an obvious attempt to sound the keynote for
mass religious resistance, he spoke out within a few hours after the
Court's words had raced over the news tickers to all parts of the
country. In his subsequent speeches on the subject he coupled his
resistance with his well-known argument for public funds for Catholic schools. In his first caustic comment he said: "I am shocked
and frightened that the Supreme Court has declared unconstitutional a simple and voluntary declaration of belief in God by public school children. The decision strikes at the very heart of the
Godly tradition in which America's children have for so long been
raised."[11]

Spellman was much more vehement in several public ad-
dresses during the ensuing week, often coupling his attack on the
Supreme Court with a direct or indirect plea for tax funds. His
plea was so obviously motivated by self-interest that the *New York
Post* commented in an editorial entitled "Prayer and Politics":
"The indignation of the Catholic hierarchy [over the prayer deci-
sion] is understandable. It is prompted, we suspect, not by the prohibition of a prayer which many churchmen would agree has little
religious value, but by the potential impact of the decision on the
aid-to-education battle."[12]

Speaking only two days after the decision, Spellman returned
to the attack by saying to a Catholic audience: "If that simple

prayer can be interpreted as violating the separation of church and state, then I, too, can only pray 'God save the United States.' "In an address to the Fraternal Order of Eagles, the Cardinal frankly linked the movement against the school prayer with the movement against federal aid to parochial schools as "a two-pronged attack on the American way of life," characterizing the total movement as one "to take God out of the public schools and to force the child out of the private school."[13]

Most American Catholic journals followed Spellman's lead. "Democracy is 'Caricature' When Offended by Prayer" was the headline over a report of one address by Cardinal Spellman in the leading diocesan Catholic paper of the country, *The Register*.[14] The Jesuit weekly, *America*, blistering the decision in an editorial, carried the entire text of the offending prayer in a box on its cover and—without quoting a single sentence from the majority decision itself—said:

> In this case and in this decision, the secularizing tendencies at work in American society have come full circle. It is not only an unpopular decision with the vast majority of the American people. It is quite literally a stupid decision, a doctrinaire decision, an unrealistic decision, a decision that spits in the face of our history, our tradition and our heritage as a religious people. Some day, it can be hoped, the Black Monday Decision will be reversed.[15]

America did not mention in this editorial the position of the President of the United States as a defender of the Court and its decisions. The Jesuits had evidently concluded that an attack on a Catholic president would do their church more harm than good.

There was also discernible in the Catholic press a slight note of gloating over the decision. It was as if many Catholic editors said: This is what you can expect if you consign your children to Godless public schools! The decision, said *America* in the editorial just quoted, "demonstrates beyond all shadow of doubt the reasons why millions of parents insist, and will go on insisting, on their parental right to establish and maintain independent schools that are free from the enslaving limitations of secularistic dogma." Even before the adverse decision had come from the Supreme Court, the Catholic *Register,* in an editorial on "Prayer in Public Schools," had prepared its people to use a Supreme Court defeat as a weapon in the campaign for parochial school aid. "An adverse decision," it said, "may not be altogether bad. It should shock many Protestants out of their old complacency and the dogged opposition of their leadership to any aid to the religious school child."[16]

The organized wave of Catholic protest that hit Congress immediately after the prayer decision coupled Communism and the Supreme Court with an accuracy worthy of the McCarthy era. Representative Thomas J. Lane of Massachusetts, released from a federal prison for income-tax violation and triumphantly reelected by his constituents, introduced into Congress a communication from the Faithful Navigator of the Lawrence, Massachusetts chapter of the Knights of Columbus, declaring: "Our Founding Fathers would not be proud to read of this action. It seems that the highest tribunal of American justice has fallen prey to the theories of Communist-ruled countries where prayer is a sin against the state."[17]

Such extreme inferences in regard to the Supreme Court, resembling attacks by members of the John Birch Society, did not please the more sober elements in the American Catholic community. Temperate comments began to appear in some Catholic-oriented publications. The analysis of the decision by the legal department of the National Catholic Welfare Conference (the organized Catholic bishops of the United States) was hostile but quite rational.[18] It stressed the limitations of the decision and underscored the fact that the whole Court did not adopt all the inferences expressed by Justice Douglas. The *Commonweal,* an influential weekly edited without imprimatur by Catholic laymen, attacked the prayer decision as "crude, legalistic and naive," but admitted: "In the very narrow terms of the decision itself, the majority holding of the Court was neither radical nor strained."[19]

The *Commonweal* carried a debate on the prayer decision between a Catholic spokesman and Leo Pfeffer of the American Jewish Congress, who presented a powerful and frank defense of the Court. The Catholic spokesman, William B. Ball, deplored the fact that "the Supreme Court has apparently written all interested pressure groups a stack of blank checks. But when the checks are all cashed and the victories all won, as little may be left of inter-religious goodwill in the U.S.A. as Sherman left in Georgia."[20]

A few—very few—Catholic voices were raised in outright de-fense of the principles asserted by the Supreme Court. In Maine the vice-chancellor of the Portland diocese, while declaring that the Regents' prayer contained "nothing offensive to our faith," reminded Catholics that "one can easily imagine the confusion, the violence of conscience which would result from the attempt of gov-ernmental agencies to compose official prayers."[21] Robert Hoyt, editor of *The Catholic Reporter* of Kansas City, reminded his read-ers that one of the chief rights of the Bill of Rights is "the right to be free from any sort of official coercion in matters of religious be-lief and practice." "I think," he said, "this is exactly what we used to tell the Protestants when they thought we quibbled overmuch about the use of the King James Bible as a public school text."[22]

Protestant Reactions

One of the disadvantages—or is it an advantage?—of Ameri-can Protestantism is that there is no such thing as an American Protestant attitude on any subject under the sun. There is not even any loose federation which includes more than 60 per cent of all American Protestants, and the largest single denominational group, the Southern Baptist Convention, is outside of any federa-tion. The overwhelming majority of American Protestants do not believe in papal infallibility and do not want an ambassador to the Vatican; deplore drunkenness and the louder forms of gam-bling; respect the Bible and like a good sermon; profess faith in some kind of God without agreeing about what that concept means; accept what they describe as the divinity of Jesus Christ without defining that divinity in terms exact enough to make it possible for any Buddhist or Mohammedan to understand the shades of denominational difference in the definition.

The "Protestant reaction" to the prayer decision ranged all the way from horror to delight. The most unequivocal approval was expressed by Unitarians, who are denied membership in most Protestant ministerial councils in the United States because they "do not accept the Lordship of Jesus Christ." Said Dr. Dana McLean Greeley, President of the Unitarian Universalist Association: "In citing the unconstitutionality of prayer reading in the public schools, the Supreme Court has acted clearly in support of the principle of the separation of church and state as guaranteed by the First Amendment to the Constitution."[23]

On the other wing of American Protestantism, a vigorous national organization devoted solely to maintaining the separation of church and state, Protestants and Other Americans United for Separation of Church and State, hesitated a few days, and then came forth with a strong endorsement of the Court's decision. The importance of the POAU announcement was that the organization had not previously taken any official position against prayer and Bible-reading in the schools. Now its statement was signed by many conservative Protestant leaders, headed by a former president of America's largest Protestant grouping, the Southern Baptist Convention. Said POAU: "All persons who believe in prayer as the authentic thrust of the human spirit toward its Maker should welcome this decision. It is a rebuke to official religion in whatever form it may be imposed upon the American people. The Court did not outlaw prayer; it merely made prayer free of political limitation and control."[24]

Then POAU criticized the adequacy of the prayer from the Christian point of view, a criticism that had been echoed at the time of its adoption by many religious leaders. "What is the Regents' prayer, basically? It is an empty salute to religion, a gesture which falsely parades as something real. The Regents' prayer achieves acceptability by being vapid. A truly religious person ought not to lament its passing."

American Methodism was badly split on the issues raised by the prayer decision. Several of its most prominent leaders rushed into print in the days after it was made with flatly differing pronouncements as to its significance. Bishop Fred Pierce Corson, president of the World Methodist Council and later Methodist observer at the Vatican Council in Rome, said that the Court's decision was an "obvious blow to religious freedom" and "in effect [it] makes secularism the national religion." He urged Americans to use "every legitimate measure" to counter the decision. A few days later another Methodist bishop, Richard Raines of Indiana, took an exactly opposite view. Later Methodist reactions seemed to favor the Raines position.

In general, with a few marked exceptions, the Baptist pronouncements on the prayer decision tended to be favorable to the Supreme Court. American Baptists, except in a few sections of the South, have defended church-state separation in the past almost as consistently as Unitarians and Jews. Dr. C. Emanuel Carlson, executive director in Washington of the Baptist Joint Committee on Public Affairs, summed up a Baptist position rather neatly when he said:

When one thinks of prayer as sincere outreach of a human soul to the Creator, "required prayer" becomes an absurdity. The "recitation of prayer" has been called "morally uplifting" without recognizing that hypocrisy is the worst of moral corrosion. Some have felt that our "national heritage" is in danger, without realizing that the distinctive of our heritage is not legislated prayer but a people praying in freedom under the guidance of their church and of the Spirit of God.[25]

Dr. Herschel Hobbs, President of the Southern Baptist Convention, sent a warning to the Senate hearing that "any amendment as proposed to the Constitution [to permit state-written school prayer] invites disaster in the area of the separation of church and state." Billy Graham, America's most noted evangelist, a Baptist, went beyond the official words of the Court in his gloomy criticism:

This is another step toward the secularization of the United

States. Followed to its logical conclusion, we will have to take the chaplains out of the armed forces, prayers cannot be said in Congress, and the President cannot put his hand on the Bible when he takes the oath of office. The framers of our Constitution meant we were to have freedom of religion, not freedom from religion.[26]

The one agency which had the greatest right to speak for American Protestantism, the National Council of Churches, was at first slow and equivocal in its response to the prayer decision. Its first statement on the decision straddled the issues, but one of its staff officers, Dean M. Kelley, director of the Department of Religious Liberty, spoke up quickly and decisively: "Many Christians will welcome this decision. It protects the religious rights of minorities and guards against the development of 'public school religion' which is neither Christitanity or Judaism but something less than either."[27] When the Council finally came forth with an official statement on "The Churches and the Public Schools" in June 1963, the viewpoint expressed was close to that of Mr. Kelley. "We recognize the wisdom as well as the authority of this ruling," the Council said. . . . "We express the conviction that the First Amendment to our Constitution in its present wording has provided the framework within which responsible citizens and our courts have been able to afford maximum protection for the religious liberty of all our citizens."

President Henry P. Van Dusen of Union Theological Seminary in New York, in attacking the prayer decision, supported the legality of non-sectarian religious instruction in public schools. "By no legitimate stretch of language or imagination," he said, "can it be rightly held that the First Amendment intended to preclude nonsectarian religious instruction or observance in the nation's schools."[28] Van Dusen's contention was more than balanced by support for the Court from America's two most important Protestant journals, *The Christian Century* of Chicago and *Christianity Today* of Washington. These two journals, liberal and conservative respectively in theological matters, agreed that state-composed prayer did not belong in public schools. "A second look."

said *Christianity Today* in an editorial, "should lead all critics to second thoughts about the Supreme Court decision. It can be defended, and commended, as compatible both with a proper Christian attitude toward government stipulation of religious exercises, and with a sound philosophical view of freedom."[29] *The Christian Century* rounded up thirty-one leaders of American Protestantism who issued a manifesto about the prayer decision, saying: "We believe the court's ruling against officially written and officially prescribed prayers protects the integrity of the religious conscience and the proper function of religious and governmental institutions."[30] The signers of *The Christian Century* statement included a former president of the National Council of Churches, three Methodist bishops, the President of the Southern Baptist Convention, and a leading Presbyterian editor.

The strongest Protestant statement of all in support of the Supreme Court came in the spring of 1963 from the General Assembly of the United Presbyterian Church, meeting in Des Moines. It opposed Bible-reading and prayer in public classrooms, and declared: "We Presbyterians wish to live, teach and evangelize within a political order in which no church will dominate the civil authorities or be dominated by them."[31]

The most publicized opposition to the prayer decision in Protestant circles came from James A. Pike, Episcopal Bishop of California. "The Supreme Court," he said, "has deconsecrated the nation." He issued a closely reasoned legal attack on the prayer decision which will be considered in a later chapter.

Secularists and Jews

In all this denominational uproar the opinions of the approximately 70,000,000 Americans who are not identified with any Christian church or Jewish synagogue were not given much official attention. What did they think about the whole question?

One answer was provided by some of the plaintiffs in the

prayer case itself. The members of the Ethical Culture Society—
there were two of them among the plaintiffs in the prayer suit—
can be considered humanists in their religious outlook, honoring
moral values but not accepting any particular supernatural explanation of life or professing any allegiance to a theistic church. The
humanist, rationalist and ethical culture movements in this country are influential but small in numbers. Our 70,000,000 unchurched are usually voiceless in legislative halls, and no one
knows how many of them are genuine unbelievers.

Gerald Wendt, editor of *The Humanist,* a scholarly liberal
journal, said about the prayer decision:

> The decision of the U.S. Supreme Court on the New York
> Regents' prayer is a godsend to Humanists—"a desirable thing
> which comes unexpectedly as if sent by God." . . . No man needs to
> be forced to believe, or even to pretend to believe, in men and
> things and time. Those who wish to go further, to believe in eter-
> nity or to pray to an unseen deity are entirely free to do so at home
> or in their house of worship as President Kennedy serenely pointed
> out . . . no one can force them to pray, or even pretend to pray.
> Such is our enduring democracy . . . we must fight for those vast
> numbers of inarticulate Americans who never give a thought to
> religion and take their freedom for granted.[32]

In a sense the American Civil Liberties Union, which is
strictly neutral in religious matters, has represented these unchurched citizens of the United States as effectively as any other
agency. For many years it has been one of the most important forces
in the country in preserving the separation of church and state. It
has opposed all religious activities in public schools and all tax
payments to church schools. Its support of the litigants in this
prayer case was a demonstration of its attitude.

From the very beginning of the prayer controversy the Jewish
response was more articulate than that of any other religious group
supporting the Court. In fact, the whole drive against Christian
promotion within public schools in the United States in recent
years has been sparked by Jewish opinion and, to a certain extent,

financed by Jewish contributions. The most literate and detailed analyses of church-state issues in education have come from several great Jewish organizations centered in New York. When the prayer decision was handed down, these organizations burst into jubilation. For them it was the most important legal breakthrough in their long campaign against discriminatory religious practices in American public schools.

The American Jewish Congress, the American Jewish Committee and the Anti-Defamation League of B'nai B'rith are perhaps the three most important Jewish bodies in America which represent the struggle of the Jewish people for non-discriminatory civil rights. They have always been wholly committed to the separation of church and state under the First Amendment. They were among the many organizations filing friend-of-the-court briefs in the prayer case.

The strictly religious Jewish organizations of Reformed, Conservative and Orthodox Judaism have also been almost unanimous in supporting the Supreme Court's interpretation of the separation of church and state. The Synagogue Council of America, representing all three segments of religious Judaism, filed a brief in favor of the plaintiffs in the prayer case. The only Jewish dissidents in this solid Jewish bloc were a few Orthodox rabbis committed to Jewish religious day schools and eager to receive public money for those schools. It is doubtful whether they represent more than ten per cent of the American Jewish community.

The American Jewish Congress, through its counsel, Leo Pfeffer, rounded up 132 law-school deans and professors of law and political science, of every religious faith, from 42 colleges and universities throughout the country who issued a defense of the Court's decision and sent it to the Senate Judiciary Committee in November 1962. The opinion was not distinctively Jewish but it summed up very well the judgment of the American Jewish community. Said these leading scholars:

The intrusion of religion upon the public school system both threatens the separation of church and state and challenges the tra-

ditional integrity of the public schools. That intrusion, if permitted, will greatly endanger the institutions which have preserved
religious and political freedom in the United States and which prevented religious warfare in this nation. The decision of the Supreme Court in the Regents' prayer case has warded off that threat.
It would be tragic if the beneficial effects of that decision were nul-
lified by any tampering with the Bill of Rights.[33]

Up to this point in the controversy there had been no overt
anti-Semitism on a national scale, although, as we have seen, there
had been sporadic manifestations of anti-Semitism in some communities on Long Island. Then one of those unfortunate slips occurred in some Jesuit's pen in the editorial offices of *America*—or
perhaps there was in that urbane Catholic order a single writer
with a little actual anti-Semitic malice in his system. At any rate,
an editorial appeared in *America* on September 1, 1962 entitled
"To our Jewish Friends," which should in all honesty have been
called "To Our Jewish Enemies—Beware!" It piously deplored the
"disturbing hints of heightened anti-Semitic feeling" since the
prayer decision, but it obviously relished its own warning of "a
harvest of fear and distrust" against American Jews. And it said
that while "we should recognize that full responsibility for the decision . . . is not to be pinned on the Jewish community," still: "It
would be most unfortunate if the entire Jewish community were
to be blamed for the unrelenting pressure tactics of a small but
overly vocal segment within it." Then the editorial added:

We wonder, therefore, whether it is not time for provident
leaders of American Judaism to ask their more militant colleagues
whether what is gained through the courts by such victories is
worth the breakdown of community relations which will inevitably follow them. What will have been accomplished if our Jewish
friends win all the legal immunities they seek, but thereby paint
themselves into a corner of social and cultural isolation?

The Jesuit editorial had been tactless enough to couple its
criticism of the prayer decision and such organizations as the American Jewish Congress with an indirect plea for tax support for pa-

rochial schools. It warned the Jewish people against an "all-out campaign to secularize the public schools." *The New York Times, Time* and the great wire services picked up the Jesuit *faux pas* immediately and featured it in every corner of the nation.

A stream of passionate replies came not only from Jewish organizations but also from Protestant leaders. The liberal Catholic *Commonweal* rebuked its Jesuit brethren, and on September 28, 1962 published a special issue on "The Jew in American Society." The American Jewish Committee probably best represented the Jewish reaction when it reminded the Jesuits that it was the Catholics who, "throughout many decades of the 19th century and the first quarter of the 20th century" fought desperately against the reading of the King James version of the Bible in American public schools. It asked: "Have Catholics been deterred from pressing their views in the legislatures and in the courts by the worry that victory might produce 'a harvest of fear and distrust?' "

Then the Committee argued:

You naturally have every right to disagree with the Supreme Court, but your identification of the struggle to maintain the protections of the First Amendment with an "all-out campaign to secularize the public schools and public life from top to bottom" contains disturbing implications.

We do not agree that the Supreme Court decision was antireligious; nor do we believe that it will result in the increased "secularization" of American life . . . by accusing Jews of participating in a campaign to "secularize" the country on no evidence other than their commitment to the First Amendment, and by asserting that the general population is overwhelmingly opposed to this campaign, you have made it appear that the heightened anti-Semitic feelings over which you express such friendly concern are the product of righteous outrage against Jewish vigilance on the principle of the separation of Church and State. You therefore counsel the Jewish community to forestall the threat of anti-Semitism by abandoning or compromising its commitment to the First Amendment. . . .

This seems to us a very strange piece of advice indeed to offer in the name of pluralism. We believe . . . that pluralism involves the right of every American group to express its viewpoint and press its position through the impartial judicial process which our democratic state has established for such purposes.[34]

The Jesuits handled the prayer storm with dignity. They were fair enough to print the long reply from the American Jewish Committee together with many other critical letters. But the editors announced in closing the discussion: "We now withdraw from the fray—bloodied a bit, in a worthy cause, but unbowed." The Catholic press had supported *America's* position consistently. The Jesuits, while insisting that they were not inspired by anti-Semitism —and they were probably correct in this claim—continued to paint the militant defenders of church-state separation among the Jewish people as extremists who "have no mandate from the Jewish religious community."

Two conclusions became evident from this caustic public interchange. First, the American Jewish community was far more united in support of church-state separation in education than the Jesuits had imagined—the few Jewish leaders who rallied to defend *America* were quite unimpressive and unrepresentative. Second, although the Jewish people comprise, as the American Jewish Committee pointed out, "less than 3 per cent of the total population, of whom $37\frac{1}{2}$ per cent are *unchurched* gentiles," the militant stand of American Jews probably represented the viewpoint of a very large proportion of the unchurched $37\frac{1}{2}$ per cent. The Jesuits had sought to disparage Jewish opposition to the prayer decision by associating it with "militant secularists" and the general conglomeration of people of doubtful respectability described by their phrase, "an assortment of humanist groups, ethical culturists, Unitarians, secularists and atheists." Perhaps they forgot that the largest single segment in American society with a "religious" label is the one that has no religious label, the 70,000,000 outside the churches. When the Jews were associated with the secularists in an abusive editorial, it probably did the secularists more good than the Jews harm.

The Swing Toward the Court

The governors had spoken against the Court in July when feeling about the prayer decision ran very high and when nearly all the publicity in the newspapers was hostile to the Court. By the end of that summer, however, a gradual shift of sentiment had taken place. Congressmen who had earlier considered the prayer controversy a good campaign issue began to change their minds. Many sober commentators had pointed out that the Court's actual decision did not go nearly as far as some of the much publicized inferences in the assenting opinion of Justice Douglas.

Many Southern Congressmen were caught by surprise when the leaders of their chief church, the Southern Baptist Convention, endorsed the primary principle of the decision. These Southern Congressmen had counted on solid support from that quarter. Southern politicians were also disturbed by the absence of support for constitutional amendments from the chief northern leaders in Congress. While the vocal chorus in both Houses was nearly all critical, the most important Senators and Representatives chose to remain silent. One of the surprises at the Senate Committee hearing—an unpleasant surprise for Senator Eastland and his friends—was that the only Catholic member of the examining committee, Senator Philip Hart of Michigan, asked a number of embarrassing questions which indicated that at least one independent Catholic was very far from agreement with Cardinal Spellman. Hart evidently foresaw many difficulties in state-imposed prayer. What, he asked, would happen if the imposed prayer was the Catholic "Hail Mary"? What would the law be on that?

Senator Robertson, caught off guard, averred that "if it is voluntary, there might be no more objection to the 'Hail Mary' than to the Lord's Prayer." The Southern Senators squirmed a little. Unitarian Hruska from Nebraska raised further questions. When Episcopal Bishop James Pike was confronted at the same hearing with the same "Hail Mary" question, he said that such a denominational prayer "should not be selected, of course, as the official prayer for everybody."[35]

At one point in the colloquy between Bishop Pike and Senator Hart, the Bishop remarked that "perhaps this honorable body needs real prayer." Senator Dirksen of Illinois leaned forward and said in his deepest Shakespearian voice: "It sure does."

By autumn—the autumn of 1962—the general public sentiment as expressed in mail addressed to the Supreme Court had changed markedly. In the beginning a hostile mountain of mail had piled up against the decision. Before Christmas, postal sentiments had cooled down, and most of the letters arriving were favorable to the Court's decision or simply reflective and analytical.

One factor in this swing toward the Court had been the calm way in which the state authorities of New York had accepted and carried out the decision in spirit as well as in letter. State Commissioner of Education James E. Allen, Jr. and the Board of Regents announced that the Supreme Court decision was now "the law of the land and it will be so recognized." When a local school board in Hicksville, Long Island, tried to substitute for the banned prayer a religious verse of The Star Spangled Banner, Commissioner Allen ruled that this violated the decision of the Supreme Court if it was used as a prayer. The verse reads in part:

> Blest with victory and peace, may the heav'n rescued land
> Praise the Pow'r that hath made and preserved us a nation!
> Then conquer we must, when our cause it is just,
> And this be our motto " 'In God is our Trust.' "

Apparently there was no ban on singing as singing. Religious words could be used in a traditional song; the religious verse of America was not banned. Professor Arthur Sutherland of Harvard, a critic of the Court's philosophy, suggested mildly that "in the morning children like the sound of music." He disagreed with the Court's legal reasoning but, as a former local school board official himself, he wondered "whether the New Hyde Park Union Free School District Board was really wise in adopting the optional Regents' Prayer, regardless of the constitutional issue. Was the hoped-for educational gain worth its predictable cost?"[36]

Probably the major factor in swinging public sentiment gradually toward the view enunciated by the Supreme Court was the sober reaction of many of America's leading newspapers and magazines. While many small Southern dailies were spreading anti-Court sulphur on local pages, and while the Hearst newspapers were following their usual line in favor of the partial financial union of church and state, the four most influential dailies in the United States, *The New York Times, The Washington Post, The New York Herald Tribune,* and *The Christian Science Monitor,* were standing up sturdily for the Court's decision.[37] *The St. Louis Post Dispatch* and *The New York Post* took the same position. Even *Time* magazine came along on the Court's side in the weight of its news analysis.

From the first, the vast editorial influence of *The New York Times* was thrown into the battle on the side of the Court. In its first editorial on the subject, "Prayer is Personal," it said:

There is a danger of the Supreme Court's becoming too doctrinaire in enforcing the separation of church and state. It is easy to imagine religious or quasi-religious events in public activities that would not rise to the level of a constitutional violation. But nothing could be more divisive in this country than to mingle religion and government in the sensitive setting of the public schools, and under circumstances regarded by minorities as coercive. Our history counsels against that course, and the Supreme Court has wisely turned us from it.[38]

The Washington Post, which is probably read by more Congressmen than any other paper in the country, was just as forthright in supporting the Court.

The decision is an act of liberation. It frees school children from what was in effect a forced participation in an act of worship. It frees the public schools from an observance much more likely to be divisive than unifying. It frees religion from an essentially mischievous and incalculably perilous sort of secular support. A prescribed prayer however nondenominational it may be, is a form of enforced orthodoxy and is therefore an inescapable enemy to religious liberty.[39]

CHAPTER 4

Is the Supreme Court Right?

Did the Supreme Court's decision in the Regents' prayer case depart drastically from the other Court decisions of recent years in the field of church and state?

Before attempting to answer such a question it should be pointed out that there are very few certainties in the field of constitutional law, particularly when broad general principles are involved. A constitution is a charter of general aims and purposes designed to serve as moral and legal guideposts in a changing world. It may contain many narrowly specific provisions but its statements of principle, particularly when the principle involves individual rights, must be flexible enough to allow for a wide variety of circumstances. It must be like the steel frame of a great skyscraper, firm as the rock on which it is based, but designed to sway a little in the gale in order to avoid collapse under pressure.

The Bill of Rights—a purely optional title for the first ten amendments—is full of moral generalizations which can mean one thing for one generation and another thing for the next. These moral generalizations can also mean one thing to a judge sitting at one end of a long bench in the Supreme Court and quite another thing to another judge sitting at the other end of that same bench.

The Bill of Rights assures American citizens that they cannot lawfully be "deprived of life, liberty, or property, without due process of law"; that they may not be subjected to "cruel and unusual punishments"; that they shall have the right "peaceably to assemble"; that they shall have "freedom of speech" and the "free exercise" of religion; and that Congress may not make a law for them "respecting an establishment of religion."

All of these high professions of principle have blurred edges.

They do not fit neatly into any constricted pattern of interpretation. Whole libraries have been devoted to arguments about their divergent meanings. However, this conflict of testimony about meanings is not as serious as it may seem to the uninitiated. No system of government has been devised by man which produces any more stability in constitutional matters than the American system. We have left it to one agency, the Supreme Court of the United States, to tell us what constitutional principles mean. It would be a rash critic indeed who failed to appreciate how essential the role of the Supreme Court has been. The very stability of our relatively stable democracy, now one of the oldest governments among the nations, is built largely upon the recognition that we have a reasonably competent and disinterested Court to tell us what our fundamental constitutional principles mean when they are applied to a dynamic world.

In the field of religious rights the interpretative power of the Supreme Court is especially important because the words of the Constitution on religion are so few and so oblique. In the Constitution proper there is only one mention of religion, the prohibition against religious tests embodied in Article VI. And there is only one clause on religion in the Bill of Rights: "Congress shall make no law respecting an establishment of religion, or prohibiting the free exercise thereof. . . ."

As we have seen, the Fourteenth Amendment, which brought First Amendment rights to the local level, has no direct mention of religion or education in its text. There was almost no serious attempt to apply it to religion during the first sixty years after it was adopted. Its words simply guarantee to American citizens certain rights as citizens, such rights as due process of law and equal protection of the laws.

Out of these disconnected fragments—the First Amendment as applied to the states by the Fourteenth Amendment—the Supreme Court has felt obliged to construct a judicial code of religious freedom and no-establishment in a world where public education has become the most important single factor in the building of our society. Under the circumstances, the Court's task has been one of constructive legal imagination as well as exact interpretation.

If we once recognize that the Supreme Court is correct in claiming the right to review both federal and state laws—and it is now too late in our judicial history to deny this claim—then one important corollary follows. The Court is not absolutely obliged to interpret the same phrases in the Constitution in the same way from generation to generation. The meaning of a principle may change somewhat as it is applied to new circumstances. The minds of judges must have the privilege of growing—some would say of shrinking. While the Court cannot rewrite the Constitution, it can, and often it has, extended the limits of a principle in such a way as to contradict its former rulings on that very principle. As Professor Milton R. Konvitz of Cornell has put it:

> Fortunately for American life and institutions, American constitutional doctrine and law are not founded on an arid, dead historicism. Men are not chosen as justices of the Supreme Court for the records they have as antiquarians. They are chosen for their urbanity, experience, statesmanship, wisdom—for their understanding of live facts, live issues. The Constitution is a way of life for the American people, not a chart of a cemetery.[1]

The Right of Reversal

In several striking instances in recent years the Supreme Court has reversed its own interpretations of fundamental rights involved in the First and Fourteenth Amendments. One recent reversal of old positions, the 1954 segregation case, has become world famous.[2] A similar shift, not yet complete, is taking place in the Supreme Court in the matter of the separation of church and state. In 1899 the Court approved the payment of public funds to a Catholic hospital in Washington for reasons which would be considered quite evasive and superficial today.[3] In 1930 the Court allowed public money to be used for non-religious textbooks in Louisiana parochial schools in a decision which did not contain even a nod in the direction of the First Amendment.[4]

Since then the whole climate of America has changed in respect to religious minorities, particularly non-Christian minorities. Simultaneously a new sensitiveness has developed concerning the establishment of *any* religion. The United States has become a pluralistic society not merely within the Christian orbit but within an orbit recognizing all the world's great religious traditions. It is partly because of this new shift toward ethnic and religious pluralism that the Supreme Court has moved to bring both the non-religious and the religious rights guaranteed to all citizens in the First Amendment down to the level of every local community via the Fourteenth Amendment. The Court, in doing this, has demonstrated the same kind of realism that appeared in the segregation decision.

It is quite startling to go back a hundred years or more and see how American judicial opinion ignored religious rights before the United States Supreme Court had adopted modern attitudes. In 1845 the Court ruled in the case of *Permoli* v. *Municipality* (44 U.S. 589) that the City of New Orleans could prevent Catholic priests by ordinance from holding funerals in any Catholic church in the city. Although the ordinance was based on supposed health considerations, it actually singled out the Catholic church by name for discrimination. Under the ordinance, a priest named Bernard Permoli was fined $50 merely for officiating at a regular Catholic funeral held under the rules of his church. When he appealed to the Supreme Court on the ground that the ordinance restricted his free exercise of religion, the Court refused to interfere, saying: "The Constitution makes no provisions for protecting the citizens of the respective states in their religious liberties; this is left to the state constitutions and laws. . . ."

The present Supreme Court, by using the Fourteenth Amendment as a bridge, takes precisely the opposite view. It has constructed a whole scheme of religious rights and religious freedom by judicious re-interpretation of constitutional principles.

Was It Predictable?

An examination of recent Supreme Court decisions on religion bears out the claim of Edmond Cahn, professor of law at New York University, that, when seen against the whole backdrop of American judicial thought, the Supreme Court's decision on the Regents' prayer "was about as close to predictable as the judicial process ever comes."[5] The Court, having once embarked on its present interpretation of constitutional history in 1947, and having declared *any* aid to religion in the public school system unconstitutional, could not have reached any other conclusion in the prayer case without contradicting its whole recent philosophy.

Although Justice Black did not directly refer to it in his prayer decision, most of his reasoning came straight out of a famous paragraph which he wrote in 1947 when, speaking for the Court, he sanctioned as constitutional the use of state tax funds in New Jersey for the costs of parochial school buses but, at the same time, set strict legal limits beyond which the state should not go in aiding religion in public schools. His immortal paragraph, often later described as mere dictum but since labelled by the Court itself as more than dictum, said:

The "establishment of religion" clause of the First Amendment means at least this: Neither a state nor the Federal Government can set up a church. Neither can pass laws which aid one religion, aid all religions, or prefer one religion over another. Neither can force nor influence a person to go to or remain away from church against his will or force him to profess a belief or disbelief in any religion." No person can be punished for entertaining or professing religious beliefs or disbeliefs, for church attendance or non-attendance. No tax in any amount, large or small, can be levied to support any religious activities or institutions, whatever they may be called, or whatever form they may adopt to teach or practice religion. Neither a state nor the Federal Government can, openly or secretly, participate in the affairs of any religious organizations or groups and *vice versa*. In the words of Jefferson, the clause against establishment of religion by law was intended to erect "a wall of separation between church and state."[6]

These words, the most sweeping words ever written by an American court about the separation of church and state, concerned a case which was primarily financial, not ideological. The ideological problem was presented one year later in the McCollum religious-instruction case from Illinois.[7] The justices swooped upon illegal religious instruction inside American public schools with much more vehemence than they had swooped upon the problems of bus transportation. This time they voted eight to one that classes in religion taught by outside religious teachers of Protestant, Catholic and Jewish faiths *inside* the public schools, were in violation of the Establishment Clause of the First Amendment. And just to make sure that the Court's general philosophy about the wall of separation between church and state had not been changed since the bus decision, the Court repeated with approval the entire paragraph quoted above from the Everson decision.

When, three years later, the Court by a six to three vote permitted released-time religious classes *away from* public classrooms, taught by church teachers not on the public payroll, the advocates of religion within the public schools hailed the Court because it had "abandoned the McCollum philosophy of absolute separation of Church and State and reaffirmed the basic American tradition of cooperation of Church and State."[8] The quoted words are those of the Legal Department of the National Catholic Welfare Conference. Those words from the NCWC represent a too-eager overbelief based on wishful thinking. Although the Zorach released-time decision of 1952 was confused and sentimental enough to permit some wishful deductions, it did not abandon the Court's fundamental philosophy of religious neutrality in public classrooms. The justices went out of their way to say specifically: "We follow the McCollum case." They also said: "Government may not finance religious groups nor undertake religious instruction nor blend secular and sectarian education nor use secular institutions to force one or some religion on any person."[9]

It is true that in this famous Zorach decision, Justice Douglas, speaking for the Court, inserted some sentimental phrases as dicta which he must later have regretted, since his present view seems to be in sharp conflict with the inferences that have been drawn from those phrases. In order to justify the minimum amount of cooperation between state and church involved in released-time classes away from public classrooms, Douglas pointed out that: "The First Amendment, however, does not say that in every and all respects there shall be a separation of Church and State." Then he added the sentence which has become the most famous sentence in the whole church-state controversy: "We are a religious people whose institutions presuppose a Supreme Being."

How much did this sentence mean? After the Zorach case there was a rather widespread suspicion that the Supreme Court, in adopting placatory words concerning church-state cooperation, intended to move toward the church-state philosophy of the Catholic bishops and abandon the strict philosophy of church-state separation. So the Court went out of its way, nine years later in the Sunday-law cases, to deny this interpretation. Citing its own strong language in previous decisions, the Court, speaking through Chief Justice Warren in the case of *McGowan* v. *Maryland* said: "But, the First Amendment, in its final form, did not simply bar a congressional enactment *establishing a church*; it forbade all laws *respecting an establishment of religion.* . . . It has found that the First and Fourteenth Amendments afford protection against religious establishment far more extensive than merely to forbid a national or state church."[10] (Italics in orginal.)

Enter the Unbeliever

One legal factor which made the Supreme Court's majority decision in the prayer case seem quite natural was that, shortly before the decision, the Court had recognized religions without God as having a legal status. If a man could be religious without believing in God, then a Court which banned a state-composed prayer in public schools was not necessarily opposing all religion as such.

It might be opposing only certain manifestations of certain kinds of religion.

This concept was rather startling for most Americans. Most people in this country had never thought of non-theists as being in any sense religious. They thought that there must be some kind of belief in God at the core of every religion in order to be called religion. They considered the man who disbelieved in God as the very symbol of no-religion. Theodore Roosevelt had set the political fashion during his administration by calling Thomas Paine a "filthy little atheist," without apparently suffering any political penalty for his careless abuse.

It has taken the public a long time to recognize the fact that, in strictly legal terms, the United States is not a Christian country. It is a pluralistic nation guaranteeing all believers and unbelievers equal rights. In the nineteenth century the United States moved from being a Protestant country to being a Protestant and Catholic country; then it moved to the status of being a tri-partite Protestant-Catholic-Jewish country. Finally in the inaugural ceremonies for President Eisenhower and Kennedy, the United States became a quadruplicate religious society, granting ceremonial recognition to Protestant, Catholic, Jewish and Greek Orthodox faiths. The shivering spectators at the Kennedy inaugural in January 1961 were appalled when the four invited clergymen of the four dominant faiths spent more time in informing the Deity about facts which the Deity might be presumed to know already than the young President used for his entire inaugural address.

Perhaps the Supreme Court justices who had to sit through those four long petitions in freezing temperature were subconsciously conditioned for their next church-state case! At any rate, they handed down a ruling six months later, in the case of Roy R. Torcaso, a Maryland citizen who wanted to become a notary public, that went farther in recognizing the rights of atheism than any former decision in American legal history.[11] In order to become a notary public, Torcaso was required by an old Maryland statute to sign a statement professing belief in God. He refused to sign, carried his case after local defeat to the United States Supreme Court, and won a quick and unanimous victory.

Officially this Torcaso decision had nothing to do with public schools, but it was bound to have an effect on school policy because it carried the moral frontier farther into unbelievers' territory than it had ever been carried before. Justice Black tied up his decision with the previous school decisions by adding a sentence to his famous paragraph in the Everson bus case. He said: "Neither [a state nor the Federal Government] can constitutionally pass laws nor impose requirements which aid all religions as against non-believers, and neither can *aid those religions based on a belief in the existence of God as against those religions founded on different beliefs*." (Italics added.) In a footnote Justice Black added: "Among religions in this country which do not teach what would generally be considered a belief in the existence of God are Buddhism, Taoism, Ethical Culture, Secular Humanism and others."

Then Justice Black referred to an important Washington case of 1957 which involved tax exemption for the Washington Ethical Society as a religious institution. In that case the United States Court of Appeals for the District of Columbia had, by a unanimous decision, ruled that the Washington Ethical Society could qualify as a tax-exempt "religious corporation or society" in spite of the fact that the organization did not require its members to believe in any God. Religion, the Court of Appeals held, need not be narrowly interpreted. One of its definitions, cited in the court's opinion, was merely "devotion to some principle; strict fidelity or faithfulness; conscientious, pious affection or attachment."[12]

Professor Edmond Cahn, in the article already cited in the *New York University Law Review*,[5] rather playfully but with perfectly sound scholarship, lists a whole group of genuinely religious people who might reasonably be "offended" by the imposition upon their children of the text and the accompanying postures of the Regents' prayer. They include Spinoza and Einstein as believers in pantheistic religion; Buddhists, Confucianists and Ethical

Culturists; believers in polytheistic religions a la William James; all those individuals like Judge Jerome Frank who professed belief in a God who was not "almighty"; and all those who scorn to beg anything of God because they think He already knows what is best for men. Although Professor Cahn's classifications have not yet been adopted by the Supreme Court, it is probable that his assumptions quite fairly represent the views of the present justices concerning the wisdom of recognizing a wide variety of religious experience as valid religion.

It is evident from this review that the whole ideological skeleton for the Regents' prayer decision can be constructed out of the elements of the Court's decisions as they began in the Everson bus case of 1947 and progressed through the McCollum religious instruction case in 1948, then through the Zorach released-time case in 1952, then through the McGowan and other Sunday-law cases of 1961, then through the Torcaso notary public case in that same year, finally culminating in the prayer decision itself. In that whole progression—some would say devolution—the Court with only a slight backward tracing of steps in the Zorach released-time case, moved toward an ever more strict interpretation of Jefferson's wall of separation between church and state.

Legal Scholars and Common Sense

Many persons considered the legal justification of the Supreme Court in the prayer case especially indecisive for two reasons. The majority of the New York lawyers among local school board officials supported the legality of the prayer, as did most of the New York judges who passed upon the case. Also, several academic constitutional experts, speaking immediately after the decision, rebuked the justices for a "mistaken" interpretation of the First Amendment. The opposition of the *American Bar Association Journal*[13] was to be expected because of its previous bitter opposition to the McCollum decision—it reprinted in October 1962 its own caustic editorial of 1948 on that subject. The opposition to the Court's decision by Dean Erwin Griswold of Harvard was taken more seriously because Griswold in 1949 had declared that "the only sure protection for those who believe deeply in religious freedom is to maintain rigidly the line of separation between church and state." Griswold, speaking at the University of Utah in February, 1963, criticized the Court for a "species of absolutism in its reasoning, which is more likely to lead us into darkness than to light."[14] He cited the absolutism of Justice Black in opposing libel laws in a private address; actually Justice Black had not carried that absolutism into the prayer decision since he had specifically exempted many religious phenomena on the fringe of government from condemnation. And it was Justice Black who had written the decision in the Everson case conceding the constitutionality of tax grants for parochial school buses, while four dissenting justices, Jackson, Rutledge, Frankfurter and Burton, took a more absolutist position than he did.

Dean Eugene V. Rostow of the Yale Law School took a position on the prayer decision exactly contrary to that of Dean Griswold; and at the University of Chicago a noted specialist in church-state law, Professor Philip B. Kurland, who had previously committed himself to the constitutionality—not desirability—of government grants to parochial schools, endorsed the basic reasoning of the prayer decision by saying: "Indeed, when time gives the opportunity for thoughtful evaluation rather than emotional reaction, *Vitale* may come to be recognized as one of the bulwarks of America's freedom from the ills that continue to plague those countries where 'toleration' rather than 'freedom' and 'separation' are the guides to government action."[15]

When distinguished legal scholars find the precedents so contradictory, the man on the street is likely to turn to something he calls "common sense" in attempting to judge the judges. Apart from precedent, what were the chief commonsense arguments in the legal controversy over the Regents' prayer decision? Six are worth mentioning, some of them militating against the Court's decision and some supporting it.

1. *The case was trivial.* The Regents' prayer was so short, so innocuous and so noncommittal in the realms of theology that the whole case should have been refused review by the Supreme Court under the *de minimis* doctrine—which means, in effect, that it was too trifling for the Court to bother about. From the public's point of view this was the strongest single argument against the prayer decision. Even some of those lawyers who doubted the wisdom of incorporating the prayer into the curriculum in the first place thought that the justices should have refused to take it seriously enough to hear the constitutional arguments on its merits.

2. *No public money was involved.* This is not quite completely true, but it is so near to the truth that it may be accepted. Justice Douglas, in his separate assenting opinion, mentioning the fact that "the teacher who leads in prayer is on the public payroll," implied clearly that the financial principle was involved. Technically it was, but the involvement was miniscule in character. Since there was a violation involving the establishment of religion entirely apart from the tiny fraction of a teacher's salary assignable to the recitation of the prayer, the financial argument may as well be waived.

3. *The prayer represents the majority attitudes of the American people.* There is no way of proving this contention since the majority of the American people do not have prayers in public classrooms and have not been asked directly to vote on the issue. But most opinion polls indicate that believers in God are in an overwhelming majority in the American population, and the general public response to the prayer decision seemed to confirm a commitment to God rather than to the Supreme Court. It seems proper to conclude, therefore, that the Regents' prayer accorded with the religious attitudes of the majority.[16] It is not proper to conclude that this fact gave the majority any legal or moral right to impose the prayer on an American public school. The whole point of the Establishment Clause of the Constitution is that mere majority po-

litical power does not give the majority any right to impose its faith on the minority by state authority.

4. *The prayer was voluntary.*   This extremely popular argument for the prayer was weak on three counts.

First, subtle coercion is always involved in a group policy requiring a child to separate himself from his fellows in order to avoid compliance with the prevailing customs of that group. The strongest compulsions are often indirect.

Second, children in a public school are young, impressionable children, trapped in a captive audience by our compulsory education laws. They sit under the authority of teachers whom they are taught to revere as guides for social living. It is especially questionable under such circumstances to describe the prayer as voluntary when a compulsory assemblage has been gathered together for one purpose and is used for another.

Third, the Court itself met this "voluntary" argument head-on and dismissed it as entirely irrelevant, saying in effect that it is not necessary to prove overt coercion in order to prove illegal establishment of religion in a public school. The incorporation of the religious practice itself, whether it is called voluntary or coercive, is enough compulsion to satisfy the claim of illegal establishment. Establishment "does not depend on any showing of direct governmental compulsion."

This last point came as something of a shock to some school officials throughout the country. Many of them, without stopping to do any legal research on the issue, had assumed that the release of a child from a religious exercise on request made the exercise "voluntary." That they were wrong in this assumption could have been foretold. The Court had already, in the McCollum case of 1948, found it "unnecessary to consider" the coercive argument in connection with religious instruction in public classrooms. Justice Frankfurter had added this perceptive comment in his concurring opinion in that case: "That a child is offered an alternative may reduce the constraint; it does not eliminate the operation of influence by the school in matters sacred to conscience and outside the school's domain. The law of imitation operates, and non-conformity is not an outstanding characteristic of children."

5. *The prayer was permissible because it was not sectarian.* This argument was almost as popular as the "voluntary" argument. It goes back to a traditional America when nearly everybody was nominally a member of a Protestant Christian bloc in our society, even if he was not a member of a Protestant church. The word "sectarian" in those days stood for some theory or principle advocated by one sect of Protestantism and opposed by another sect of Protestantism. This kind of sectarian clash was looked upon as undesirable and therefore to be avoided. For many years American jurisprudence has been plagued with the legal corollary of this old assumption, namely that a *religious* exercise in a public classroom is different in principle from a *sectarian* exercise, and that the first is permissible while the second is not.

This distinction between religious and sectarian is, in most cases, quite artificial. It begs the question by assuming that sectarian things are in a different class legally from other religious things. The Constitution does not forbid an establishment of sectarian religion; it forbids an establishment of religion. It is the religious and not merely the sectarian feature of a phenomenon which brings it within the prohibtion of the First Amendment.

It is true that a distinctly sectarian feature in a public classroom is open to a double challenge because it may specifically offend certain religious groups as well as all non-religious groups. Some practical distinction between sectarian religion and nonsectarian religion is therefore recognized in practice. No one, for example, would defend the use of the *Book of Mormon* or Mrs. Eddy's *Science and Health With Key to the Scriptures,* or Martin Luther's 95 theses from Wittenberg, or even a prayer for the success of the Second Vatican Council, since all these phenomena represent a point of view that is definitely challenged by a considerable religious segment in American society. In some areas, also, a prayer mentioning Jesus Christ would fall into the offensive sectarian class because of the large number of Jewish pupils. However, thousands of school officials who recognize this point still believe that a general religious formula, not identified with any sect, is quite unobjectionable.

A moment's reflection will show that in a society which is as pluralistic as ours there is virtually no religious or ceremonial phenomenon that is not sectarian to somebody. Does a permissible Christian ceremonial become illegal when a Jewish child walks into a classroom where the majority of the students are Christians? Does a permissible Buddhist reading become illegal when a Christian child walks into a classroom in Hawaii, which is predominantly Buddhist?

Such questions reveal the absurdity of the all-too-prevalent attempts to make a legal distinction between sectarian and religious. As used in current controversy the distinction is plainly specious. A practice which is legal does not become illegal simply because an objection to it comes from a minority. The acceptance of such a theory would mean that we have a government by men, a government by pressure groups instead of a government by laws.

Even the Regents' prayer, the most undenominational feature in public school life to be challenged in the Supreme Court in recent years, was based on many assumptions considered sectarian to some parents even although it seemed so innocuously pious to most. It was anthropomorphically religious; that is to say, it was based squarely on an assumption not acceptable to those who reject a personal divinity, and the possibility of personal communication with that personal divinity. No one who understood the nature of prayer could pass it off as simply and solely a general bit of moral guidance.

Prayer is the core of worship and worship is the core of religion. The New York trial court properly recognized this fact from the beginning and pointed out that the Board of Regents itself recognized the religious nature of prayer. Prayer, says *Corpus Juris Secundum*, is "a reverent petition to some divinity or object of worship." It presupposes (1) a God who is personal enough to be addressed personally; (2) a God who will respond to a personal request to the extent that He will change the fortunes of teachers, parents and politicians as a result of a child's petition; (3) a child who believes that the universe and the laws of nature may be modified by this type of petition.

Such assumptions are contrary to the conviction of many parents, including the plaintiffs in the prayer case. They disbelieve in a universe which is subject to modification by simple appeal. They even consider it injurious to the morals of their children, in the larger sense, to be taught that their personal wishes can alter the operation of natural law.

6. *The prohibition of public school religion establishes secularism as the national religion.* This is an extremely effective and emotional debating point which has been resorted to even by some reputable scholars and clergymen.[17] It has a double fallacy familiar to all students of even the first lesson in logic. The absence of a thing does not prove the existence of its opposite. When I say that A is not white, that does not mean that A is necessarily black. To assert that the absence of religion in classrooms establishes another opposing religion, the religion of secularism, is reminiscent of the tricky fallacies of the McCarthy era when many good men were branded as pro-Communists simply because they did not accept the particular type of overstatement produced by the junior senator from Wisconsin.

Actually, the charge that a religion of secularism is being established in the American public schools is refuted by mountains of solid evidence familiar to all citizens. It is a well-known fact that no public school textbooks are permitted to advocate secularism. On the contrary, all school officials in the United States know that the textbooks must be consistently respectful toward religion. If any passage offensive to any religious sect creeps into a textbook, there is immediate local uproar. No teachers are allowed to promote either secularism or atheism in American classrooms. Countless illustrations could be cited of teachers in various parts of the country who have lost their positions or their promotions for even suggesting that they champion unbelief.

The Argument from History and Tradition

These commonsense arguments for and against the prayer decision do not bear as much weight with the lawyers as the historical arguments. If they choose to oppose the decision, the law experts and dissenting judges usually say that it flies in the face of many historic traditions and religious practices on the periphery of government, and that it is based on a misreading of the intention of the Founding Fathers in using the language of the First Amendment. Justice Potter Stewart based his lone dissent primarily on the first of these two points. He also endorsed the second without going into details. He did not stop to point out that one reason why so many peripheral religious ceremonials have been permitted in connection with government is that taxpayers have been prevented from stopping them by litigation. Taxpayers, for example, have been denied standing to sue to challenge the appointment of Congressional chaplains. The litigants in the Regents' prayer case were themselves quite uncertain whether the Supreme Court would hear their challenge on the merits, and at least one constitutional expert argued that the Court had made new law by accepting the case for review.[18]

How much weight should be given to the contention that the authors of the First Amendment intended only to prevent the establishment of *one* favored church, not the establishment of *all* churches and religious schools? Of course, their *primary* purpose was to prevent the establishment of a national church because, in the first place, the single established church was the obnoxious and familiar feature of colonial society that they were most anxious to eliminate, and, in the second place, they had no power at that time to eliminate the establishment of *state* churches because the power over state churches was not given to the national government until 1868 by the Fourteenth Amendment.

The debates over the Constitution in the Philadelphia Constitutional Convention in 1787 and in the first Congress in 1789 are in themselves somewhat inconclusive. Those debates were not reported verbatim as in the present-day style. The comments were paraphrased in the British parliamentary fashion, which leaves much to be desired when original meanings are in dispute. Madison, the chief pilot of the forces demanding separation of church and state, emphasized various aspects of his separation doctrine in various statements. He was occasionally forced into the position of a compromising politician, accepting some amended wordings which he may not have preferred. The paraphrased statements from Madison in the early constitutional proceedings can be given varying interpretations. At one point "he apprehended the meaning of the words [of a proposed amendment] to be that Congress should not establish a religion, and enforce the legal observation of it by law, nor compel men to worship God in any manner contrary to their conscience." Later Madison said that he thought the Establishment Clause was necessary because "the people feared one sect might obtain a pre-eminence, or two might combine together and establish a religion to which they would compel others to conform."

In June 1789, Madison offered a draft amendment which read: "The civil rights of none shall be abridged on account of religious belief or worship, nor shall any national religion be established, nor shall the full and equal rights of conscience be in any manner, or on any pretext, infringed."[19] That word "national" should not be treated as necessarily supporting the one-church doctrine since, at that time, Congress could deal only with a national religion. All power over local religions had been left with the states. The word "national" may have been inserted to reassure the states that Congress was not claiming power over state churches. Madison himself wanted the Constitution to prohibit establishments of religion by the states, but this was not to come until this century.

About a month after this form of the First Amendment was

suggested, a select committee suggested the wording: "No religion shall be established by law, nor shall the equal rights of conscience be infringed." About a month after that, the House suggested: "Congress shall make no law establishing religion or prohibiting the free exercise thereof, nor shall the rights of conscience be infringed." The Senate, still a month later, suggested: "Congress shall make no law establishing articles of faith or a mode of worship, or prohibiting the free exercise of religion . . ." Then, after conference, the compromise was adopted which now constitutes the First Amendment: "Congress shall make no law respecting an establishment of religion, or prohibiting the free exercise thereof . . ."

It is obvious that the wording finally adopted for the First Amendment was more sweeping in its prohibitions than the Senate's limited proposed ban on articles of faith and modes of worship. It is obvious also that a ban on any laws respecting an establishment of religion is broader than a ban simply on a single church. The burden of proof in the inconclusive controversy would seem to be on those who wish to confine the intention of the Founding Fathers to the disestablishment of a single church. Schools were not mentioned in these debates because America had virtually no public school system at that time, either federal or local.

Professor Leonard Levy, Dean of the Graduate School of Brandeis University, has pointed out a supplementary reason why the narrow constructionists of the First Amendment must remain on the defensive.[20] When the new states were adopting the First Amendment in 1789, six of them already had, potentially or in active operation, a system of multiple establishments of religion. They were Massachusetts, New Hampshire, Connecticut, Maryland, South Carolina, and Georgia. These new states had already gone beyond the European idea of a single established church. "The framers of the First Amendment," says Professor Levy, "understood 'an establishment of religion' to mean what their experience showed them it meant." The experience of "establishment" included nonpreferential tax support for *various* churches. In the light of that experience it is inconceivable that, when they struck down "establishment of religion," they intended merely to abolish a *single* federal establishment. Professor R. Freeman Butts of Columbia has advanced and ably defended a similar thesis.[21]

Justice Rutledge in his classic history of the First Amendment in his dissenting opinion in the Everson case reached a similar conclusion, and his judgment has been virtually accepted as official gospel by later Supreme Court decisions:

> The Amendment's purpose was not to strike merely at the official establishment of a single sect, creed or religion, outlawing only a formal relation such as had prevailed in England and some of the colonies. Necessarily it was to uproot all such relationships. But the object was broader than separating church and state in this narrow sense. It was to create a complete and permanent separation of the sphere of religious activity and civil authority by comprehensively forbidding every form of public aid or support for religion. In proof the Amendment's wording and history unite with this Court's consistent utterances whenever attention has been fixed directly upon the question.

Perhaps more important than any of these technical points about constitutional history is the fact that the Court is not altogether bound by the intentions of the authors of constitutional words when those words are very broad and when new circumstances may demand new principles of application. In many non-church cases the Supreme Court has asserted its right to adapt original intentions and give them extended significance. That right was asserted by Chief Justice Hughes in a striking case in the darkest days of the depression in 1934, when farm mortgages were being foreclosed in many parts of the country under strict interpretations of the obligations of contract law. Rather clumsily but with tremendous force, he said: "If by the statement that what the Constitution meant at the time of its adoption it means today, it is intended to say that the great clauses of the Constitution must be confined to the interpretation which the farmers, with the conditions and outlook of their time, would have placed upon them, the statement carries its own refutation."[22] Then he quoted the Court itself from a 1922 decision: "The case before us must be considered in the light of our whole experience not merely in that of what was said a hundred years ago."

The Court followed up this thought in 1954 in the segregation decision when it said: "In approaching this problem we cannot turn the clock back to 1868 when the Amendment was adopted, or even to 1896. . . . We must consider public education in the light of its full development and its present place in American life throughout the Nation."

Chief Justice Warren reiterated this doctrine, without mentioning segregation, under dramatic circumstances in February 1963 when he spoke to the Georgia Institute of Technology while his rightist enemies were posting signs around the city "Impeach Earl Warren". "Fortunately for us," he said, "the Founding Fathers painted with a broad brush. . . . They wrote what they intended to be a living document, not one committed merely to the conditions of that day but one that could function under constantly changing conditions—even those we have today and those we will have in generations to come."[23]

This vision of the Constitution as a dynamic document reflects the realities of a complex nation in the modern age, a nation in which the public school has become the most important cultural institution in our pluralistic society. To "establish" any religion in that far-flung system—that is, to build it into the curriculum of a government institution operating under compulsory attendance laws—is to give religion a preferment far more substantial even than monetary grants to churches. It means state-supported religious promotion in the presence of the largest and most vulnerable captive audience in the history of man. It is scarcely conceivable that if Madison and Jefferson could face the realities of this issue today they would concede that their First Amendment failed to cover the situation. Although they could not have visualized the twentieth-century American public school system, their fundamental adherence to the principle of no-establishment of religion was a realistic philosophy designed for a living institution.

CHAPTER 5

Bible-Reading and the Lord's Prayer In the Public Schools

For those who had read the text of the Regents' prayer decision the 1963 ruling of the Court outlawing Bible-reading and the Lord's Prayer from devotional exercises in public schools was a foregone conclusion. Yet so many millions of ordinary Americans had failed to do their legal homework in this field that the Bible-Lord's Prayer decision of June 17, 1963 came like an extra, very loud clap of thunder.[1]

Of course this new decision was far more important and revolutionary in its immediate and practical results than the Regents' prayer decision because of the extent of Bible-reading in American schools. Possibly 40 per cent of the school children of America, when this decision was handed down, were directly affected by it as against a few thousand in the affected schools of New York. (Statistics on this point must be conjectural because no complete study has been made by federal authorities.)

The Bible has always been the core of religious instruction as well as the star of all religious ceremonials in American schools. It lies at the heart of the Protestant tradition. It is, quite simply, The Book, The Word of God. Our country was founded by European Protestants at a time when the Bible was still in a position of supreme pre-eminence, unchallenged by the cross fires of that continental and English criticism which assailed its authority in the latter part of the nineteenth century.

Of course there had been many, many challenges to Bible-reading in public schools in *state* courts long before 1963. The early state legal records are full of voluminous discussions of the issue of the Bible in public schools. Some of these early decisions can be classed as scholarly and thorough, particularly the decisions in the Ring case in Illinois in 1910 and in the Tudor case in New Jersey in 1953.[2] In fact, the reasoning in these two cases is so sound that the Supreme Court could have taken it over bodily and incorporated it into its 1963 opinion.

However, the older state decisions were in many particulars in flat contradiction with each other. Six states had pronounced Bible-reading in public schools unconstitutional under their state constitutions before the Supreme Court's 1963 decision: Illinois, Louisiana, Nebraska, South Dakota, Washington and Wisconsin. In six other states, Arizona, California, New Mexico, Nevada, Oregon and Vermont, the language of the law and the wording of attorney generals' opinions had suggested that Bible-reading in public schools *might* be considered unconstitutional.[3] This uncertainty had made statistics in this field somewhat questionable.

At the other end of the Bible spectrum came thirteen states which not only considered Bible-reading in public schools legal but required it by statute or constitutional provisions. These states were Alabama, Arkansas, Delaware, Florida, Georgia, Idaho, Kentucky, Maine, Massachusetts, Mississippi, New Jersey, Pennsylvania and Tennessee. In the middle, between these extremes in practice, came twelve states where Bible-reading might be described as permissive; it had either been upheld by courts without benefit of a statute or affirmatively permitted by law. These middle-ground twelve were Colorado, Indiana, Iowa, Kansas, Maryland, Michigan, Minnesota, New York, North Dakota, Ohio, Oklahoma and Texas.

This official state legal pattern represented only part of the Bible-reading story. Many states had left the matter of Bible-reading in classrooms so completely in the hands of local school officials that the state officers scarcely knew what the practice was in their own state. Statistics were largely guesswork. Professor Richard B. Dierenfield of Macalester College, Minnesota tried to

clear up the confusing facts about religious practices in publi
schools in a 1959 questionnaire addressed to some 4,000 schoo
systems throughout the country. About 55 per cent of them
answered. The answers indicated not only that Bible-reading and
the Lord's Prayer were very common in public schools but that, in
spite of the Supreme Court's ban on religious instruction inside o
public school buildings in the 1948 McCollum case, many, many
schools were continuing such instruction, accompanied in some
cases by outright evangelism. And in all cases the Bible, particu
larly in the South, was the core of the "devotional" sessions.[4]

Dierenfield's perceptive study indicated that in the United
States as a whole Bible-reading was conducted in about 42 per cen
of the public school systems, while a great many schools, particu
larly in the South, went far beyond simple Bible-reading and in
corporated the Bible as the central feature in a program described
as "homeroom devotional exercises." Hymns, prayer and devo
tional talks often started off the school day with something very
much like a church service. Dierenfield found that in 1959 about
one-third of the public schools of the nation had what could fairly
be described as such homeroom devotional exercises. These exer
cises tended to be Protestant in flavor, not only because a Protes
tant Bible was almost always used as the core of the exercises but
also because the style and type of hymns and moral exhortations
approximated the Protestant rather than the Catholic norm. The
Jewish norm was usually ignored.

In the South about 9 per cent of the public schools went
beyond mere Bible-reading and scheduled Bible classes, some of
them taught for school credit. The recurrence of this phenomenon
was nearly as high in the far West as in the South; it was lowest in
New England where Catholic influence was strongest.

Enter the Schempps

Oddly enough, the practice of Bible-reading in public schools
had never been initially challenged in *federal* courts until 1958.

Then the practice was challenged before a special three-man federal court in Pennsylvania by two very dignified and cultured Unitarians, with the backing of the American Civil Liberties Union, and later on of the American Jewish Congress. The Unitarians were Mr. and Mrs. Edward L. Schempp of Abington Township, a suburb of Philadelphia. Mr. Schempp is an electronics engineer. The Schempp parents made their legal challenge in defense of their own constitutional rights and the rights of their three children, Ellory, Roger and Donna Schempp, who were students in local public high schools. All three of the children attended a Unitarian Sunday school, so it could not be said that they or their parents were indifferent to religion or to religious values. Their case was a case against state-established religion and also, incidentally, against a literalist interpretation of the Bible which as modernists they were not disposed to accept.

Pennsylvania had had since 1949 a law on its statute books requiring the reading of ten verses from the "Holy Bible" each morning without comment. This ceremony—it could be called religious instruction and in fact it was so described by a federal court—was followed by a call from the teacher for all the students to rise, stand reverently, and recite the Lord's Prayer in unison. Sometimes a student led the exercises, sometimes the teacher. In Abington at the time of the Schempp challenge a special type of procedure was followed. The Bible was read over a public address system to all the students while they were seated in their own rooms. The reading was done by members of a special high school class in broadcasting. Then the students rose, bowed their heads and repeated the Lord's Prayer.

The Pennsylvania statute did not say which version of the Bible should be read, but in Abington township a Protestant version was always favored. Perhaps that is one reason why the Catholic Church did not officially enter the Schempp case. Catholic leaders could scarcely defend the Bible-reading practices without also condemning the discrimination. The Schempp lawyer, Henry W. Sawyer III, could not even persuade a Catholic authority to testify as an expert witness in the case. The local school officials bought copies of the King James version of the Bible exclusively and distributed one copy free to each teacher. Nominally pupils who read the Bible on request of the teachers could, if they wished, choose the Catholic Douay version for their reading, or even the Jewish version of the Old Testament entitled *The Holy Scriptures According to the Masoretic Text*. Nominally the addition of the Lord's Prayer to the opening ceremony was optional, but its use was taken for granted throughout Pennsylvania school systems.

At the time the Schempp case began, all Pennsylvania schools were required to start the day with Bible-reading, and no provision was made for excusing dissident minority pupils. Any teacher who refused to read the Bible could be discharged.

Ellory Schempp, the older Schempp boy, stating that he did not believe in the Trinity, the Immaculate Conception and certain other concepts included in the readings, demonstrated his objection by reading the Koran while the Bible was being read. He refused to stand for the recitation of the Lord's Prayer and asked to be excused from attendance at the exercises. After a long period when he was required to sit in an administrative office in school, he was finally directed to stay in his home room during the religious exercises in spite of his request. He obeyed the direction while continuing his protest. Actually, under the arrangements in force in his high school, Ellory could not escape the sound of Bible-reading even by remaining in his guidance counsellor's office, since the public address system reached all rooms in the school. He could only make his protest and then wait for his day in court.

When that day came, he performed effectively both in court and on a national television program of the Columbia Broadcasting System. He is a tall, handsome young man, now a student at Brown University. When he was put on the witness stand he bluntly explained the reasons for his protest.[5]

"Do you believe in God?"
"Yes."
"Do you believe in an anthropomorphic God?"

"No."

"Ellory, do you believe in your own conscience in the concept of petitional prayer?"

"No."

When his father, Edward L. Schempp, was put on the witness stand he indicated which portions of the Bible he objected to as a moral guide for his children—"Leviticus, where they mention all sorts of blood sacrifices, uncleanness and leprosy. . . . I do not want my children believing that God is a lesser person than a human father." (The Schempps never objected to the use of the Bible as literature or as auxiliary history, but only as part of a scheme of religious promotion.)

"What do you believe about Christ?" was a question addressed by the lawyers to Roger Schempp, aged fifteen.

"I believe he was a great man," said Roger, "but I do not think he was some of the other things they claim he has done and is supposed to have happened."

Although Donna Schempp, aged twelve, sometimes volunteered to read the Bible herself, usually selecting a Psalm, she testified concerning the beliefs she had acquired in Unitarian Sunday school that "where it says that the devil came down to Jesus and tempted Him, we have been taught that that was just a dream . . . also I don't think any man would have the powers to do the miracles that the Bible says He does."

The Schempp case became especially important when the Pennsylvania federal court permitted religious experts to testify as to what they thought about the sectarian or religious character of the Bible and the Lord's Prayer. They sharply disagreed. Dr. Luther A. Weigle of Yale Divinity School, a Protestant expert who had long been a champion of school Bible-reading, stated in his testimony that the Bible was a non-sectarian book. He also said: "I see nothing in the Lord's Prayer that is sectarian." But when he was pinned down, he was forced to admit that his description of the Bible as non-sectarian meant non-sectarian within the Christian tradition. He admitted that Bible-reading confined to the Old

Testament would be sectarian because the "Holy Bible," described by the law, would not be complete without the New Testament.

Rabbi Solomon Grayzel, the Jewish expert, was equally emphatic in declaring that the New Testament was utterly unsuitable for reading to Jewish children unless it could be interpreted for these children in a correct way. And, of course, the Pennsylvania law prohibited any interpretative comment by any teacher. Rabbi Grayzel pointed out that the story of the crucifixion in Matthew, picturing a Jewish mob overcoming the doubts of Pilate and refusing to exchange Barabbas as a prisoner for Jesus, had caused more anti-Jewish riots throughout the ages than anything else in history. He also testified that the concept of Jesus Christ as the Son of God in the New Testament was, for Jews, "practically blasphemous." He declared that Jesus' scathing attack on Jewish teachers —"Scribes and Pharisees, hypocrites"—would be offensive to a Jewish child.

Pennsylvania's three-man federal court found the Schempps substantially correct in all their major contentions. It declared the state Bible-reading statute unconstitutional under the First Amendment as applied to the states by the Fourteenth Amendment. It found that the practice in Abington schools constituted "religious instruction and the promotion of religiousness," and was therefore, in violation of the Constitution because it was "an establishment of religion and an interference with the free exercise of religion."

Local and state officials in Pennsylvania immediately did two things to defeat the ruling; they appealed to the United States Supreme Court against the decision, and they rushed through the legislature a revised statute making the practice of Bible-reading voluntary. Children could be excused from the exercises on their parents' written requests. It was because of this latter move that the Supreme Court, when the case reached it on appeal, decided in October 1960 to send it back to the lower federal court for further review, putting upon that lower court the burden of deciding whether the new "voluntary" character of the religious ceremonials changed its nature under the Constitution.

It did not. The Pennsylvania three-man federal court promptly came back with a new decision saying, in effect, that the practices involved were still involuntary. A teacher could be discharged for non-conforming. Again the three judges were unanimous. This time their decision was even stronger for the Schempps because they based it entirely on the Establishment Clause of the First Amendment. Back came the case to the United States Supreme Court for final adjudication in the summer of 1963.

Through this whole struggle the Schempps stood firm against a great deal of adverse opinion. The American Civil Liberties Union and the American Jewish Congress supported them, but most of the people of Abington did not. When the Abington school board held a special hearing in 1962 to decide whether to appeal again to the Supreme Court, thirty-two citizens appeared against the Schempps and only one for them. Many Protestant leaders in the area, including Methodist Bishop Fred Pierce Corson, deplored the decision as "a serious blow to the public schools." The Greater Philadelphia Council of Churches (Protestant) also deplored the ruling and warned that it opened the door to more serious restraints on religious programs in public schools.

But the Philadelphia Synod of the United Church of Christ said that "in the nature of our American pluralistic, democratic society, the court could not fairly decide otherwise"; and the Abington community was very much more gracious to the Schempps than the New Hyde Park community had been to the Roths and their fellow plaintiffs in the Regents' prayer case. There was little abuse and no overt persecution. At least one Protestant minister supported the Schempps, and the Jewish community was almost unanimously sympathetic. Abington Township is a mixed community with a rather high income rating, three Jewish synagogues, and a predominantly Protestant background. Considering the emotional nature of the issues raised by the Schempps, the local public reaction was exemplary.

Enter Bill and Madalyn Murray

The story was different in Baltimore. There a very determined lady who was an avowed and militant atheist was raising many of the same issues raised by the Schempps. The Schempp and Murray challenges were destined to cross finally in the United States Supreme Court in February, 1963 when they were argued on successive days before a packed courtroom as one consolidated case.

Bill—William J. Murray III, son of Madalyn—was only fourteen years of age when he began his fight as an atheist. He was just as convinced of the truths of atheism as his mother was—and as Percy Bysshe Shelley had been in his youth. (Shelley wrote *The Necessity of Atheism* at the age of nineteen.)

Mrs. Murray has told her own story[6] in a rather disarmingly frank narrative in which, although she is a lawyer, she admits encouraging Bill in "civil disobedience in a challenge of the constitutionality of religious ceremonies in public schools." Bill, she says, during the summer of his fourteenth year "grew four inches during the summer; turned fourteen; and even acquired two blond hairs on his chin," along with the responsibility that comes with maturity and "I encouraged him in this." Bill was to need all the encouragement his mother could give him. Before he was through he was severely beaten up by groups of teen-agers, completely ostracized by his schoolmates, and his home was pelted with stones and rotten eggs. The Murray automobile was damaged on several occasions.

However, Mrs. Murray received much encouragement and praise, together with some funds, not only from civil liberties champions but also from the militant rationalist journals. "The more I see of atheists," she explained to a rationalist audience, "all I can say of you is where have you been all my life? You are wonderful." She joined her defense of her Bill with outright praise for materialism: "We should look past trinities and angels and other theological blind alleys. We must look to materialistic philosophy which alone enables men to understand reality and to know how to deal with it." She even opposed a moment of silent meditation in public classrooms.

After her final victory in the Supreme Court in June 1963, she announced that she was establishing a colony of atheists in Kansas with a university, a radio station and a printing press.

Bill went to Woodbourne Junior High School in Baltimore which, like all the Baltimore high schools, came under an old School Board rule originally adopted in 1905 which made it mandatory to read the Bible daily and/or to say the Lord's Prayer. Nominally the rules permitted the use of the Catholic Douay version as well as other versions. At the time Bill began his fight there was no provision for children to be excused from these exercises.

Bill's mother protested in his behalf to all the Baltimore school officials, from Vice-Principal to Superintendent of Schools, that these exercises violated the Constitution by establishing religion and destroying Bill's religious freedom. When the officials remained unmoved, the Murrays decided that Bill should go on strike, refusing to obey the compulsory education laws as a protest against enforced religious ceremonies. The "strike" remained unnoticed until Mrs. Murray herself brought it to the attention of the newspapers. Then, within two weeks, there were eighty-seven items about the situation in the Baltimore newspapers, and national publicity on radio and television.

Mrs Murray at this point lost the sympathy of many liberals because they thought that she was making use of her son in an unwise manner. They did not believe in deliberate truancy even in a just cause. But there is no doubt that the strike and the accompanying publicity paid off in more ways than one. Mrs. Murray received funds to take the case through the courts, and the publicity virtually forced Baltimore officials to amend their school rules to permit any child to be excused from religious ceremonies on the written request of parents.

Bill, after eighteen days of his "sit-out strike," went back to school. After much negotiation and delay he finally was permitted to absent himself from Bible-reading and the Lord's Prayer and still remain in the school as a pupil. Through attorney Leonard J. Kerpelman, Mrs. Murray took her case to the Maryland courts on much the same grounds advanced by other plaintiffs in the Regents' prayer and Schempp cases but in Mrs. Murray's case no testimony was taken. She was defeated promptly in the lowest Maryland court, but in the highest state court, although she was again defeated, she won a surprising minority opinion from this Court of Appeals, representing three of the seven judges. This was a tremendous moral victory when one considers the make-up of the Maryland judiciary.

Said the three dissenting justices, Chief Justice Brune, and Justices Henderson and Prescott: "There seems to be no substantial room for dispute that the reading of passages from the Bible and the recitation of the Lord's Prayer are Christian religious exercises. . . . [This] seems plainly to favor one religion and to do so against other religions and against non-believers in any religion."

The majority judges cautiously cited old cases and pointed out that until the Supreme Court had passed specifically on Bible-reading and the Lord's Prayer, they were justified in standing on old decisions "in this uncertain area." They dismissed the argument that Bill Murray was subject to psychological compulsion by saying:

The short answer to this claim is that the equality of treatment which the Fourteenth Amendment affords cannot and does not provide protection from the embarrassment, the divisiveness or the psychological discontent arising out of nonconformance with the mores of the majority.

Enter Florida and the South

It is a pity that when the Supreme Court finally came in 1963 to judgment day concerning Bible-reading and the Lord's Prayer in public schools, the most comprehensive challenge to current practice was not joined with the Schempp and Murray cases. This is—and was— the Dade County, Florida case, really a combination of two cases, one called the Chamberlin case and the other the Resnick case, both filed against the Board of Public Instruction of Dade County, Florida which includes the city of Miami.[7] The courts allowed the two cases to be consolidated, and we will treat them here as one.

This was the first case in American law to embrace practically all of those religious features now current in American public schools to which religious liberals object—prayer, Bible-reading, Christmas celebrations, religious symbols, baccalaureate programs, a religious census and religious tests for employment. The case, supervised by Leo Pfeffer of the American Jewish Congress, involved Florida parents who were Jewish, Unitarian and agnostic. In behalf of their children and all other parents similarly situated they challenged these practices as unconstitutional.

In the ultra-conservative religious atmosphere of Southern Florida the plaintiffs needed to be sturdy believers in their own rights of protest. Neither they nor their defense of the Constitution were popular. They were subjected to "many bigot phone calls" and much neighborhood badgering. Many eminent Protestant divines joined with the Dade County school authorities to fight against them in the courts. The local newspapers were consistently hostile.

Some 1,400 pages of testimony were taken in a trial of the issues in this case, and the whole controversy received national attention. In the end the plaintiffs won minor victories on some issues, but with respect to Bible-reading and the Lord's Prayer they were defeated by unanimous vote in the Florida Supreme Court in a decision which can only be reasonably interpreted as a flat defiance of the United States Supreme Court. Florida's highest court, describing the children involved as "unwitting victims of a quasi-political contest," and scoring the "sophistries of agnosticism," exposed its own fundamental philosophical outlook in the following paragraph:

For all practical purposes there are now in the world just two forms of government, loosely denominated Democracy and Communism. The vital difference between the two is that the Democracies accept religion and guarantee its free exercise, in one form or another, as part of the day-to-day lives of their people, whereas Communism has banished religion, except as it may be bootlegged in the dark and in hospitable corners. . . . typical of the American custom of meeting the other side more than half way, is the paradox of the appellee school board insuring the free exercise of religion while, by mandatory statute, it must teach the history, doctrines, objectives and technique of Communism. Thus the school board affords the atheists the freedom of hearing or not hearing the Bible read while it requires that all students, without choice, be taught the facts of Communism, the antithesis of the Bible.

What made the Florida Supreme Court's decision ominous was that all seven of its judges calmly disagreed with a long line of decisions on the separation of church and state already handed down by the United States Supreme Court, and made no attempt to gloss over their defiance. They might have evaded responsibility for defying the highest Court by pleading that certain of the issues raised had not yet been ruled upon by that Court. Instead they chose to meet the Supreme Court's analysis of the First Amendment head-on and substitute their own interpretation for that of the higher Court. In several places they excerpted lines from minority opinions which the majority had overruled; in other instances they calmly rejected the interpretation of the United States Constitution as clearly outlined by that agency which is auhorized to interpret it.

In the peculiar Florida atmosphere the plaintiffs felt gratified that they had been able to win a few concessions in the Circuit Court for Dade County. In this lower court, for the first time in any American court, the judge, J. Fritz Gordon, banned plays presented in public schools around the Christmas season concerning the birth of Jesus, and plays presented about Easter-time concerning the crucifixion of Jesus. This was done on the ground that they "could be termed religious teaching" on school property. Judge Gordon also banned religious movies in the public schools of the county as well as any sectarian comments on the Bible by the teachers. But, like the seven judges of Florida's highest court, he saw nothing unconstitutional about Bible-reading and prayer ceremonies in the schools of the county, although the two phenomena were often combined in services which both teachers and pupils called "the morning devotionals."

Judge Gordon saw nothing wrong in the Dade County practice of compelling each teacher when applying for a job to answer in writing on his application form the question: "Do you believe in God?" None of the plaintiffs in the case, he explained, were teachers.

Judicially the Florida Supreme Court received a swift rebuke and reversal by the United States Supreme Court at the time of the Schempp-Murray decision in June, 1963. In a brief *per curiam* brush off the Court, without even waiting for Florida papers replying to a *Jurisdictional Statement* from the plaintiffs, vacated the Florida judgment and sent it back for revision in accordance with the Court's sweeping ban of Bible-reading and the Lord's Prayer.

The fate of the plaintiffs in the Florida courts was consistent with the total picture of religion in public schools in the South as outlined by Professor Dierenfield in *Religion in American Public Schools.* The Dierenfield study had revealed that Southern school officials in countless cases ignored the interpretation of the separation of church and state promulgated by the Supreme Court. In reply to one of Professor Dierenfield's questions a school superintendent in North Carolina proudly outlined his plan for Bible instruction in the public schools of his city, as follows—and it should be remembered that this letter was written more than ten years after religious instruction had been made illegal in *all* American public schools by the decision of the Supreme Court in the McCollum case.

We have five full-time teachers of the Bible in the public schools on our staff. Three of them work in the high schools and teach pupils who elect the course, which is a one year course meeting daily and open to any senior high school student. Most of the pupils are either juniors or seniors.

In addition to these three, we have two teachers in the elementary schools who teach children in the fifth and sixth grades. These teachers are itinerant teachers and go to the classroom and take over a thirty-minute period. Children whose parents object to their being in the class are excused to go to the library or office or some other suitable place. There are a few Jews and Baptists and Catholics who do not remain in the room.

The salaries of these teachers are paid by the churches and by interested individuals, and the "Advisory Committee on the Teaching of the Bible in the Public Schools" works with the Board of Education in securing funds and in working with the teachers on the curriculum. The teachers are paid through the regular channels of our office, the money being turned into our office and therefore, the expenditure is equal to the income . . .

The teachers use a syllabus in the high schools course but the basis for the teaching is the Bible itself. Our high school teachers are very competent folks, well trained, and very enthusiastic people. The children are not forced to take the course, but numbers of them do. . . .[8]

It is not surprising that the *Columbia Law Review* in January, 1963 said that the McCollum decision banning religious instruction in American public schools, "has probably been as widely disobeyed as almost any holding the Court has ever handed down."

In this respect Texas is probably the most lawless state in the Union. Sectarian Bible classes for credit, taught by Protestant teachers, are very common in Texas high schools in spite of clear Supreme Court decisions that they are illegal. In at least two instances in recent years Texas Catholic priests have been refused the privilege of teaching Bible within public high schools in an attempt to counter-balance the one-sided character of Protestant teaching.

Dr. Earl Humble of the Southwest Baptist Theological Seminary of Dallas, in a Ph.D. thesis on religious practices in Texas schools, financed by both Baptist organizations and the Anti-Defamation League, has disclosed the fact that at least thirty Texas high schools have been teaching Bible and religion for credit with teachers on church payrolls and an attendance of more than 1,600 students; that at least 438 public schools have taken a religious census of their pupils upon registration and turned the facts over to local churches; and that 147 school teachers, on Monday mornings, have been checking the attendance of their pupils at Sunday schools on the previous Sundays.[9] Long prayers, usually delivered by Protestant ministers, are often broadcast over public address systems in high schools, and even football games are sometimes opened with prayer.

The Baptists of Texas have had an uneasy conscience about these practices for some time. Some of them have publicly criticized the policy of the schools. But the general sentiment in the state is pro-Bible, anti-Supreme Court, and fearfully hostile to anything that can be described as unbelief. Nominally allegiance to both God and the Bible is virtually mandatory in public office and in the public school system. "No religious test," says the Texas Constitution, "shall ever be required as a qualification to any office or public trust in this state; nor shall anyone be excluded from holding office on account of his religious sentiments, *provided he acknowledges the existence of a Supreme Being.*" (Italics supplied.) No school official, says the Texas school law, "shall directly or indirectly ask, indicate, or transmit orally or in writing the religion or religious affiliation of any person seeking employment or official position in the public schools of the State of Texas, *except to inquire of the applicant whether or not he or she believes in the existence of a Supreme Being.*" (Italics supplied.)

Argument and Decision

All these competing religious and secular traditions and forces came to the moment of truth on February 27 and 28, 1963 in the Supreme Court when the Schempp and Murray cases were

argued on two successive days before a packed court room with
long lines of would-be spectators waiting on the outside. If possible, the excitement was even greater than it had been in 1962.
This was a national, not a state, issue. Many observers considered
it the most important church-state confrontation in American legal
history. The great television networks were there to preserve what
they could for history. They were not allowed inside the courtroom, but they commandeered lawyers and litigants for comments
on the outside of the Court building. Later, after the decision, both
NBC and CBS devoted excellent, full-length evening programs to
the cases.

The lawyers for the plaintiffs were learned and eloquent,
particularly Henry Sawyer III of Philadelphia who represented the
Schempps. But it soon became apparent that eloquence was not
particularly necessary in this case. The questions from the bench
indicated that the justices knew what they wanted and that they
had individually and collectively given long weeks of consideration
to the arguments of counsel. They took over the case with gattling-
gun questions. Altogether there were 239 judicial interruptions in
four hours and twenty minutes of argument, which may have set
some kind of a record. The sparks flew, and occasionally they were
mixed with laughter. Justice Stewart in opposition frequently
clashed indirectly with Justice Black, the most inveterate defender
of Jefferson's wall.

The lawyers from Pennsylvania and Baltimore were distinctly
on the defensive through the two days. They were reduced—or
believed that they were reduced—by their compulsory respect for
the Court's past judgments to an absurd legal position. They
claimed that the primary purpose of the religious ceremonies they
were defending was to keep order and to establish the proper
moral climate in the classroom. They disclaimed or slurred over
the religious nature of the Bible and the Lord's Prayer as used in
Baltimore and Pennsylvania schools. Even Justice Stewart, who
was fundamentally in sympathy with the beleaguered lawyers,

could not stomach such an evasion. He broke in with a question: Why not try tranquillizers?

Justice Black demanded to know: "Is there any reason why, if you can have three minutes [for Bible-reading and the Lord's Prayer], you can't have forty?" Justice Warren tried to find out what counsel would recommend in a Hawaiian community which was 51 per cent Buddhist and 49 per cent Christian, particularly if the Christians wanted to walk out during the religious exercises.

The public waited, and the justices officially took almost four months to make up their minds for the June, 1963 decision. To all intents and purposes, however, the Schempp-Murray decision had been rendered in June, 1962 in the Regents' prayer case. The reasoning of the Court had not changed, and in both cases there was only one dissenter, Justice Potter Stewart. The two new justices, Arthur Goldberg and Byron White, went along with the old majority to affirm all the important theses in the Court's interpretation of church-state separation. The interdenominational character of the new decision was underscored when the opinion of the Court was written by Justice Tom Clark, a Texas Presbyterian, and supported in concurring opinions by Justice Goldberg, a Jew, and Justice Brennan, a Roman Catholic.[10]

Said Justice Tom Clark, speaking for the Court and outlawing all Bible-reading and use of the Lord's Prayer in American public schools as parts of a religious exercise:

The place of religion in our society is an exalted one, achieved through a long tradition of reliance on the home, the church and the inviolable citadel of the individual heart and mind. We have come to recognize through bitter experience that it is not within the power of government to invade that citadel, whether its purpose or effect be to aid or oppose, to advance or retard. In the relationship between man and religion, the State is firmly committed to a position of neutrality. Though the application of that rule requires interpretation of a delicate sort, the rule itself is clearly and concisely stated in the words of the First Amendment.

The Court, mindful, no doubt, of the public misunderstanding as well as the public uproar following the Regent's prayer decision, went out of its way this time to underscore its respect for the place of religion in American life. It conceded that the State "may not establish a 'religion of secularism' in the sense of affirmatively opposing or showing hostility to religion . . ." It declared that "one's education is not complete without a study of comparative religion or the history of religion and its relationship to the advancement of civilization. It certainly may be said that the Bible is worthy of study for its literary and historic qualities." Thus the Court gave implied sanction for the study of the Bible and religion "when presented objectively as part of a secular progam for education." And it was made clear that the service of military chaplains might be justified legally on the ground that otherwise "military personnel would be unable to engage in the practice of their faith."

In spite of these concessions, and maintaining a consistent pattern with them, the Court was emphatic in declaring that the "religious exercises" under attack in the Baltimore and Pennsylvania schools did not fall in any permissive area. They were clearly "in violation of the command of the First Amendment that the Government maintain strict neutrality."

As in the Regent's prayer case, Justice Douglas in his separate assent again emphasized the financial aspects of state support for any church activity. "Financing a church," he declared,

. . . either in its strictly religious activities or in its other activities is equally unconstitutional . . . the institution is an inseparable whole, a living organism, which is strengthened in any department by contributions from other than its own members. . . . It is not the amount of public funds expended; as this case illustrates, it is the use to which public funds are put that is controlling. . . . What may not be done directly may not be done indirectly lest the Establishment Clause become a mockery.

This was a body blow at the prevalent schemes of indirect financial support to parents now being suggested by various Catholic and some non-Catholic organizations, and it came with double force from a justice who had voted in 1947 in favor of the constitutionality of parochial school bus grants.

Unhappily the 76-page concurring opinion of Justice Brennan received very little attention in the press, partly bacause it came in a week of national storms over racial integration in many cities. Brennan, as the only Catholic on the Court, revealed a mastery of the law and the history of church-state relations in America which could only be described as lethal for those advocates of partial church-state union in his own church. He met the Catholic interpretation of the First Amendment head-on and refuted it. "I join fully in the opinion and the judgment of the Court," he said. Then he rejected the standard Catholic view that the First Amendment was meant only to prevent the establishment of a single church; he pointed out that "if anything the Lord's Prayer and the Holy Bible are more clearly sectarian" than the outlawed Regent's prayer and he quoted Theodore Roosevelt to the effect that in the interest of "absolutely nonsectarian schools" it is not the public's business "to have the Protestant Bible or the Catholic Vulgate or the Talmud read in these schools."

Like the other justices, Justice Brennan this time was careful to qualify the scope of his rejection of Bible-reading and the Lord's Prayer. The public must not read into the case extreme conclusions not covered by the Court. Brennan rejected the contention of "the school officials in these cases" that the invalidation of their practices implied the exclusion of "every vestige, however slight, of cooperation or accommodation between religion and government. . . . Our decision in these cases does not clearly forecast anything about the constitutionality of other types of interdependence between religious and other public institutions."

Dissent and Muted Uproar

Both the dissent in the Court by Justice Stewart and the dissent in Congress by indignant Congressmen were milder than the attack on the Regent's prayer decision in 1962. Stewart repeated much of his 1962 reasoning, but conceded that if particular versions of scriptures were prescribed in a school, "their validity under the Establishment Clause would be extremely doubtful." He asked that the Schempp and Murray lower-court decisions be remanded to gather more evidence as to whether there had been any actual coercion of students under the clause guaranteeing the free exercise of religion. He said that "a compulsory state educational system so structures a child's life that if religious exercises are held to be an impermissible activity in schools, religion is placed at an artificial and state-created disadvantage."

In Congress the adverse oratory was indignant but somewhat muted after the 1962 failure to produce broad support for a constitutional amendment. Senator Strom Thurmond called the new decision "another major triumph for the forces of secularism and atheism."[11] Senators Williams of Delaware, Carlson of Kansas, Bennett of Utah, Goldwater of Arizona, Allott of Colorado, Hartke of Indiana, Beall of Maryland and Johnston of South Carolina introduced or helped to sponsor resolutions looking toward a constitutional amendment that would permit Bible-reading and prayer in public schools. Some similar efforts were launched in the House.

Senator A. Willis Robertson of Virginia declared that the Court had said: "We will put all the rights in this country behind the few atheists who deny God and the Bible." Whereupon Senator Sparkman declared, referring to Senator Robertson: "I consider the Senator to be one of the great Bible scholars and religious leaders of the Nation. In fact, if the term is proper, I would say he is one of the greatest lay theologians there are, and great weight should be given to the opinions he is expressing."

The most ominous warning came from Senator Olin Johnston, South Carolina Baptist. He said:

Despite the Supreme Court ruling, I am urging schoolteachers and schools to continue the reading of the Bible and to continue praying in classrooms. There is no statutory provision to penalize the school officials for defying the Supreme Court. They can continue to pray and read the Bible in schools until a court injunction is issued in each individual and every case, restraining them from continuing the practice in defiance of the Supreme Court.

Senator Johnston's defiant attitude was echoed on the very day of the Supreme Court decision when the State Superintendent of Education of South Carolina announced that religious activities in the state's classrooms would continue as usual in spite of the Court's ruling.[12]

The official Catholic reaction was similar to that in 1962. Three American cardinals, in Rome for the election of Pope Paul VI, sent back their denunciations. Said Cardinal Spellman: "No one who believes in God, and I say believes in God, can approve such a decision." Cardinal McIntyre of Los Angeles again employed anti-Communist aspersions, saying that "our American heritage of philosophy, of religion and of freedom are being abandoned in imitation of Soviet philosophy, of Soviet materialism and of Soviet-regimented liberty." Even Cardinal Cushing, more temperate and more pro-administration than Cardinal McIntyre, angrily demanded an amendment to the Constitution permitting Bible-reading in public schools.[13]

These Catholic denunciations, however, were more than balanced by a shift in sentiment in American Protestantism toward support of the Court and its strict interpretation of Jefferson's wall. The Presbyterians had led the way in May, 1963 when the General Assembly of the United Presbyterian Church at Des Moines endorsed a statement declaring that religious observances should "never" be held in a public school or introduced into the public school as part of its program. The National Council of Churches faced the church-state issues in a General Board meeting in New York only a few days before the Court's Bible-reading decision. The atmosphere was tense when the Greek Orthodox Church, with 1,200,000 members, threatened to withdraw because a statement prepared for adoption by the Council's Division of Christian Education virtually upheld the anticipated decision of the Supreme Court on Bible-reading by saying: "Teaching for religious commitment is the responsibility of the home and the community of faith (such as the church or synagogue) rather than the public schools. ... Neither the church nor the state should use the public school to compel acceptance of any creed or conformity to any specific religious practice."[14]

Under the leadership of Henry P. Van Dusen of Union Theological Seminary opponents of the statement forced a few verbal changes in the original text, but the Council stood firm for its main principles by a vote of sixty-five to one, with one abstention.

As in the case of the Regents' prayer decision, the response of the American Jewish community was enthusiastic and almost unanimous. Probably 99 per cent of American Jews agreed with the editorial judgment of the *New York Times* upholding the religious neutrality of the public schools as defined by the Court. "Far from interfering with freedom of religion," said the *Times*, "the Supreme Court decision helps to guarantee it."[15] One of the oddities of the outcome of the case was that the scholarly verbal attack by Jewish organizations on the sectarian character of the Lord's Prayer proved unnecessary. The Court passed over the Lord's Prayer without raising the sectarian issue. The American Jewish Committee and the Anti-Defamation League of B'nai B'rith had filed a convincing *amicus* brief in the case, citing the *Universal Jewish Encyclopedia* to the effect that the Lord's Prayer "is a Christian rather than a Jewish prayer. In fact, it is probably the best known and most widely used Christian prayer." Presumably the Court agreed, but there was no need to establish this contention. It was enough to show that Pennsylvania and Maryland were carrying on *religious* exercises in schools supported with tax funds. The First Amendment did not merely ban *sectarian* religious exercises. Thus a long-lived legal illusion was laid to rest without any formal funeral.

CHAPTER 6

Tax Dollars for Church Schools?

The controversies over religion and education which we have
discussed in previous chapters are exclusively American issues, and
they are as much Protestant and Jewish as Catholic. The issue we
now approach is a world-wide one, based on a world policy of the
rulers of the Roman Catholic Church as expressed by many popes
and repeatedly underscored by many Catholic leaders in the United
States. The essence of the Catholic financial policy in education is
the claim that the Church, being the primary guardian of education for all its own people, and a supplementary guardian for *all*
education, is entitled as a matter of right to full subsidies out of
public treasuries for all the major costs of its schools.[1]

This is the most controversial religious issue in American society. It had also divided the people of Western and Southern Europe into warring camps for a century. It has split French society
into bitter clerical and anti-clerical factions and has resulted in
clerically stimulated riots in the streets of Belgium in which the
rioters have demanded more generous government appropriations
for Catholic schools. It has decimated the cultural life of the Netherlands and divided its educational life into three warring school
systems, Catholic, Protestant and public, and has segregated the
Protestant and Catholic people of Ireland into two educational
compartments, with 95 per cent of the Republic's children in priest-
managed schools supported by taxes and 5 per cent in the Protestant compartment also supported by taxes. The life of Scotland
has been compartmentalized almost as drastically, leaving the Catholic children in a 15 per cent bloc in the population with their publicly subsidized and religiously segregated schools, while the other
85 per cent remain in government schools with Protestant inci-

dental features. It is dividing the Australian people today in much the same way as it is dividing the American people.

Of course the policy of religious segregation and government subsidies for church schools in Europe is not wholly a Catholic policy. Its development in England, Scotland and the Netherlands, for example, is largely a Protestant responsibility. Many of the Protestant nations of Europe do not practice the separation of church and state as Americans understand that term. They finance sectarian schools out of tax funds or they build compulsory religion into national school systems. Sweden, for example, requires virtually all children, even the children of atheists, to take religious instruction in public schools, and the pattern is similar in other predominantly Protestant Scandinavian countries. In West Germany, which is still predominantly non-Catholic by a narrow margin, sectarian education is built into the state school systems and into public treasuries partly because the Adenauer regime insisted that the Vatican-Hitler Concordat of July 20, 1933 was still binding after the war on both national and state governments.[2]

As far as the United States is concerned, the sectarian financial issue is 99 per cent a Catholic issue. No substantial demand for public subsidies for sectarian schools is coming from any considerable Protestant or Jewish bloc in our society. Those few Protestant and Jewish leaders who go along with Catholic demands on the public treasury, or make parallel demands for themselves, are so unrepresentative that they can be disregarded.

Here is joined a Catholic versus American battle, with organized world Catholicism committed to a program and a philosophy of ecclesiastical education, supported out of public treasuries, while the law and tradition of the United States favor public support for public schools only. Probably a great many of the Catholic people of the United States favor the American tradition and do not go along with the financial demands of their Church's leaders; one Gallup poll revealed that 28 per cent of Catholic individuals who responded to questions opposed their own priests on the issue,[3] and it is well known that only about half of the Catholic children in the United States of elementary school age attend church schools.[4] But within the Catholic Church, because of its absolutist monarchical structure, the "Catholic" position on any subject is the position of the rulers of the Church, not necessarily the position of its members.

The issue created by the Catholic demand for tax dollars has been boiling under the surface of American life for at least 125 years. We have seen how it broke into the open as early as 1840 when Bishop John Hughes organized his Catholic political party in New York to secure public funds for his parochial schools. The issue entered American national politics in the 1930's when the Church abandoned its former policy of all-out opposition to federal aid and decided to ask federal subsidies for such fringe benefits as bus transportation and textbooks. From that point forward the Catholic pressure on Washington has steadily increased while, simultaneously, the range of Catholic financial demands has expanded. In 1949 Cardinal Spellman, in his famous exchange of unamenities with Mrs. Roosevelt and Representative Graham Barden solemnly assured the public that his Church sought only such fringe benefits as bus costs. "We are not asking for general public support of religious schools," he said. He denounced Representative Barden as a "new apostle of bigotry," supported by "disciples of discrimination" who were venting their "venom upon children" in a "sin as shocking as it is incomprehensible"—all because Barden's educational bill included no grants to parochial schools.[5] The press was extremely critical of Cardinal Spellman's abusive attack, but Congressmen were frightened by an avalanche of pro-Spellman mail and the Barden bill was finally pigeonholed by the Catholic chairman of a House committee in order to avoid the agony of a record vote.

In the 1950's the alleged limitation on Catholic demands to fringe benefits was quietly jettisoned, and by the time the first Catholic president reached the White House the Catholic hierarchy was ready to come out in the open with a demand for a full

proportional share in across-the-board support if Congress decided
to vote federal aid to public schools.

Spellman v. *Kennedy*

In spite of the long preparatory build-up in the 1940's and
the 1950's, the new all-out drive for direct financial support of the
central activities of Catholic schools in 1961 came as a distinct
shock to the public and to the new President. President Kennedy
had not believed that the leaders of his own Church would embarrass him so profoundly at the very beginning of his term in office.
Three days before he was inaugurated, Cardinal Spellman, acting
against the advice of the chief Catholic lobbyists in Washington,
issued a public demand in the name of distributive justice for an
equal share for his schools in any federal educational grants.[6] He
declared that to deny proportionately equal aid to Catholic schools
would amount to "economic compulsion," and he even implied
that it would amount to a denial of "that freedom of religion guaranteed by our country's Constitution." He did not even tip his
mitre in the direction of the Supreme Court's interpretation of that
Constitution as it applied to the separation of church and state.
Beneath the surface of the Cardinal's demand was the bland assumption that in interpreting the Constitution the Cardinal was
right and both the President and the Supreme Court were wrong.

The President was privately very angry and publicly very
much embarrassed. He had made a careful study of the law while
he was still a senator from Massachusetts, and had reached the perfectly natural conclusion that the words of the Supreme Court in
such cases as Everson, McCollum and Zorach made across-the-board
grants to ordinary sectarians schools clearly unconstitutional. He
had even gone beyond his other non-Catholic colleagues in accepting a strict line of demarcation between permissible and illegal
financial aid to church schools. When, in the year before he became
the Democratic candidate for the Presidency, his liberal colleagues
Wayne Morse of Oregon and Joseph Clark of Pennsylvania pro-

posed a "compromise" educational bill which included some loans to parochial schools for construction, Kennedy opposed the bill.

In spite of Spellman's plea, the new President, in his first educational message in February 1961, calmly proposed a federal expenditure of more than two billion dollars for public schools without a penny for across-the-board grants to parochial schools. He made no attempt to disguise his reason for excluding parochial aid. He said: "In accordance with the clear prohibition of the Constitution, no elementary or secondary school funds are allocated for constructing church schools or paying church school teachers' salaries."

There was nothing new about this attitude. His statement of principle in his educational message was a logical follow-up of his pledge at Houston during the 1960 campaign to preserve "the absolute separation of church and state," and his earlier statement to *Look* magazine expressing the belief that federal grants to church schools were unconstitutional.[7]

In spite of these ample previous warnings, the President's program produced a great outcry in the Catholic press. The National Catholic Welfare Conference, the National Council of Catholic Men, the Knights of Columbus and other Catholic groups poured into Washington the greatest barrage of vocal and written protest in recent years. It was the greatest church lobbying drive in our history. Said a writer in the *Catholic Reporter* of Kansas City: "Never before in U.S. history has the Church so effectively 'flexed her muscles in public.' "[8] Congressmen were flooded with form letters from parochial school children, often with the same misspelled words, and often including pictures of large families with a plea: "Can you ignore us?"

This tidal wave of Catholic protest was soon matched by an almost equal volume of Protestant, Jewish and unchurched opinion. Congressmen became aware that there was vehement opposition to Cardinal Spellman's point of view, and they hoped that the Cardinal's church would not be united behind him. But officially his Church backed him to the limit. On March 23, 1961 the administrative head of the Catholic bishops, Archbishop Karl Alter of Cincinnati, announced in the name of American Catholicism: "In the event that a federal aid program is enacted which excluded children in public schools, these children will be the victims of discriminatory legislation. There will be no alternative but to oppose such discrimination."[9] The words were slightly ambiguous but it was soon clear what they meant. They meant that the Catholic hierarchy would use its political power to block every general aid bill which did not admit its own schools on the ground floor.

Leading Protestants vigorously supported the young President against the hierarchy of his own Church. Indeed it was an amazing spectacle in political realignments which greeted Washington observers in Kennedy's first year. Anyone who had predicted it during the 1960 presidential campaign would have been greeted with jeers as a fantastically bad prophet. Baptist leaders who had opposed the entrance of a Catholic into the White House because of their fear that such a President would be subservient to Catholic school demands now rushed to Washington to assure President Kennedy that they honored him for keeping his Houston pledges. They explained that their apprehensions about the *hierarchy* were justified by the events, but that their estimate of the President's independence had been too pessimistic. The largest organization of American Protestantism, the National Council of Churches, representing about 39,000,000 Americans, re-iterated its former opposition to government grants to sectarian schools, and added new grounds of opposition.

We . . . do not consider it just or lawful that public funds should be assigned to support the elementary or secondary schools of any church. The assignment of such funds could easily lead additional religious or other groups to undertake full scale parochial or private education with reliance on tax support. This further fragmentation of general education in the United States would destroy the public school system or at least weaken it so gravely that it could not possibly adequately meet the educational needs of all the children of our growing society.[10]

The National Council even went so far as to oppose loans as well as grants to sectarian schools, special purpose grants, and any tax credits or tax forgiveness for parents of children in non-public schools at the elementary and high school levels. The Council was careful, however, to favor school lunches and medical service for parochial school children. Even Reinhold Niebuhr joined the chorus against grants to parochial schools, not on constitutional grounds but on the ground that: "We cannot afford this divisiveness in our education and in our national life."[11]

Meanwhile, all the leading Jewish organizations in the country had spoken out with emphasis against the Catholic financial demands. A tiny handful of Orthodox Jewish rabbis wanted public money for their own Jewish day schools, but they were clearly unrepresentative. Leo Pfeffer of the American Jewish Congress expressed the sentiments of American Judaism when, before a House committee in March 1961, he described the Catholic demand as "the most serious assault upon the wall of separation between church and state in the history of our nation."[12]

Senators Wayne Morse, Joseph Clark and Jacob Javits tried to break the religious deadlock in the Senate by stretching the National Defense Education Act of 1958—primarily an act for scholarships and special grants—to include $375,000,000 in construction loans for parochial and other private schools. A companion bill was introduced in the House. "The aim of Democratic managers of both measures," said John D. Morris in the *New York Times,* "is to satisfy Roman Catholic demands for some assistance to parochial schools as part of any general program of Federal aid to education."[13] Editorially the *Times* described it bluntly as a "ransom" deal. It was designed to buy up Catholic support for a general federal-aid program at the expense of the Constitution. Later the *Times* said:

Quite apart from the public school aid issue, approval by a House Education subcommittee of N.D.E.A. loans for parochial school facilities—even though such facilities are to be used only to teach non-religious subjects—is an evasion of the constitutional principle of the separation of church and state.

The "ransom" was paid in preliminary votes in both Senate and House, but then something quite unexpected happened. The Catholic Church refused to accept the terms of the deal. Cardinal Spellman was not satisfied with mere supplementary loans for Catholic school buildings. He and other church strategists evidently believed that to accept such loans instead of grants might "freeze" the position of Catholic schools in any future aid program, excluding them from any outright grants.

A more militant Catholic policy suddenly manifested itself in the House Rules Committee when a federal aid compromise package was presented. Representative James J. Delaney of Queens, New York, suddenly switched sides in that Committee and changed a potential eight-to-seven victory for the school compromise into an eight-to-seven defeat. Acting with vigorous support in the Catholic press and in his own heavily Catholic congressional district, he declared that he would not join his Democratic colleagues in sending any general aid bills to the House floor unless the entire aid program could be re-written to give some direct aid to parochial schools. Thereupon all federal aid bills died—with the exception of the traditional special aid bills, the usual grants for impacted (military) areas, and the extension of the National Defense Education Act. A $300,000,000 aid bill authorizing grants to colleges died with the Delaney veto. Later a general compromise failed in the House by a vote of 242 to 169.

Delaney was hailed as a hero in the Catholic press, and was re-elected in 1962 with ardent sectarian support. Said the Brooklyn *Tablet*: "We salute the sturdy Queens representative, his constituents and foes of bias everywhere for their sense of justice, love of fair play and courage of conviction."[14]

In vain, during this first great church-state conflict of the Kennedy regime, the *Washington Post* pleaded that "the Government must not, and cannot under the Constitution, intrude upon the teaching of religion. . . . Surely debate on the vital question of federal aid to education ought to begin with general recognition of the fact that this is forbidden territory."[15] *The New York Times* was equally emphatic in opposing Catholic demands, saying: "It would be an act of shortsightedness and folly for those who favor Federal aid to parochial schools to insist now on an 'all or nothing' approach, i.e. to say that unless parochial schools are included, they will work to defeat the whole program."[16] And the *St. Louis Post Dispatch* expressed the hope that "the cardinals and bishops will think better of a policy which seems to say 'public funds for our schools or for none.' "[17]

The Washington legislative patterns in 1962 and early 1963 were so similar to the pattern of 1961 that they do not need detailed descriptions here. The President's federal aid programs, under the able leadership of Senator Morse, passed the Senate but were defeated in the House, and it was Catholic or Catholic-inspired opposition, added to Republican and Southern conservatism, which spelled doom for those programs. Early in 1962 Cardinal Spellman, in an address before a Catholic group, declared that enactment of the administration's educational program would be a "terrible crime" and might mean the "eventual end" of parochial schools.[18] In September 1962 a college-aid "compromise," providing $2,345,000,000 to colleges, many of which were church colleges, perished largely because of the church-state issue. It had been offered partly as an inducement to win over Catholic and Catholic-oriented Congressmen. The National Education Association played a key role in this defeat when its executive secretary, William G. Carr, sent a telegram to all House members complaining that the provisions for church colleges "imperil America's traditional concept of separation of church and state."[19]

The 1962 election did not sufficiently alter the balance in Congress to affect the federal aid situation materially. Conservative Republicans plus conservative Democrats plus Congressmen from heavily Catholic districts continued to hold the balance of power over supporters of the President's program. Catholic Church leaders continued through 1962 to support an "entering wedge" piece of legislation proposed by Representative Delaney, a Junior G.I. Bill of Rights which would have appropriated about $1,700,000,000 in two years in the form of a $20 annual grant for each student in all elementary schools, public and private.[20] Under the Delaney plan the $20 grant for each public school student would be paid to his local school board; for each private school student the check would be given to his parents, to be endorsed over to the school he attended. It was argued that this scheme of indirect payment would avoid constitutional difficulties. The bill received almost no support outside the Catholic press, since it was regarded as a plain attempt to establish a precedent for further church grants. Its opponents pointed out that there was no real analogy between the G.I. Bill of Rights and Delaney's measure, since the G.I. grants were personal awards to veterans for past service, returnable in colleges of their choice. Mr. Delaney's proposed plan of grants was considered merely a subterfuge to achieve across-the-board grants to parochial schools by indirection.

When the President announced a great, new package plan for federal aid early in 1963, Monsignor Frederick G. Hochwalt, Director of the Department of Education of the National Catholic Welfare Conference, charged before a House Committee that the elementary school section of the new measure "discriminates against the private schools much in the same manner as other federal assistance proposals have done in the past at this level. To us these provisions as presently stated are totally unacceptable . . . the issues involve God-given as well as constitutional rights." Monsignor Hochwalt then proceeded to bolster the Catholic claims with impressive statistics. The Catholic schools have more than 5,000,000 students enrolled and they are growing at a rate even faster than the public schools. Later, the *National Catholic Almanac* for 1963 estimated that 14 per cent of the children in elementary and high schools in the United States were in the Catholic schools; that these Catholic schools had been constructed at an aggregate cost of approximately

7.7 billon dollars, and that they were maintained and operated at an annual cost of about 1.5 billon.[21] A supplementary reason for Catholic financial demands which is not often discussed in the non-Catholic press is that recruitment for non-salaried teaching nuns and brothers is declining proportionately and that the employment of substitute lay teachers is increasing parochial school costs at an alarming rate. Father Robert I. Gannon, former president of Fordham, declared at the Catholic University commencement in 1963: "Numerically our nuns are at a standstill; percentage-wise they are declining rapidly. So with our Brothers."

The whole financial structure of the Catholic school system rests upon these nuns and brothers.

Sectarian Dollars and the Consitution

The Delaney Junior G.I. Bill of Rights served to remind the public that the chief aim of Catholic strategy during the first three years of the Kennedy administration was to find a technique for by-passing the Constitution without a frontal attack on that instrument. Catholic leaders relied chiefly not on constitutional arguments but on appeals to sympathy. They evidently reasoned that if enough appealing human reasons were presented to change the public's attitude toward sectarian appropriations, a way would be found to circumvent the Court's strict interpretations of the wall of separation.

Although Catholic lawyers produced several closely reasoned and well-documented pleas for federal funds during this period, even Catholic laymen did not take these arguments too seriously in view of the stiffened Supreme Court attitude in education cases. In 1959, Father Neil G. McCluskey, education editor of *America,* had conceded in his *Catholic Viewpoint on Education* that "the Cathoilc laity and clergy are fully aware that direct basic support by the government to parochial schools is out of the question."[22] He gave as the principal reason for this awareness the fact that the Supreme Court would interpret such action as unconstitutional.

It was generally conceded that the constitutional case against tax appropriations to sectarian schools was stronger than the constitutional case against schoolroom prayer. Nevertheless, in view of the tremendous wave of propaganda in favor of financial grants to parochial schools, the administration felt obliged to issue a detailed document proving that such grants were, in fact, contrary to many Supreme Court decisions. The administration's "Memorandum on the Impact of the First Amendment to the Constitution upon Federal Aid to Education" was issued on March 28, 1961, and it admirably summed up the legal reasons why President Kennedy had declared grants to sectarian education unconstitutional. It obviously represented the opinions of both the President and his brother, Attorney General Robert Kennedy, although it was signed by Alanson W. Willcox, general counsel of the Department of Health, Education and Welfare.

The Kennedy lawyers had an easy task in preparing this Memorandum. The Supreme Court's opposition to across-the-board tax support for sectarian schools is about as clear as anything can be in the absence of a case directly in point. One reason why there has never been a direct Supreme Court decision on across-the-board grants is that no state has ventured to pass a bill providing such grants. There have been plenty of auxiliary financial concessions to such schools, but never in this century an across-the-board grant for central operations.

Every state in the Union now has a statute, constitutional provision, attorney general's opinion or court decision declaring in some fashion that such aid is unlawful.[23] There are, of course, special situations in which sectarian schools receive direct or indirect financial benefits from the government. One situation is that of "impacted" or military areas in which parents are deprived of their normal opportunity to secure educational free choice for their children. Another is the so-called "captive" school pattern of the Middle West in which several hundred public schools have been taken over by orders of teaching nuns with the connivance of Catholic boards, and the nuns placed upon the public payroll.[24] These "captive" schools are illegal but they have escaped legal penalties in many cases because they have adopted a legal fiction. They list themselves simultaneously in public directories as public schools and in Catholic directories as Catholic schools.

The administration's legal Memorandum went directly to the heart of the matter by citing the cases we have described in previous chapters, the Everson, McCollum and Zorach cases, in which the Court had repeatedly said that aid to religion was an unlawful establishment. It cited Black's famous sentence in the Everson case: "No tax in any amount, large or small, can be levied to support any religious activities or institutions, whatever they may be called, or whatever form they may adopt to teach or practice religion." This decision did not cover directly the question of tuition and building grants, since it concerned bus grants only, but the Memorandum pointed out: "The Supreme Court put transportation at the outer limits of the constitutionally permissible."

No fair-minded person could doubt that such a prohibition excluded from government largesse such plainly religious enterprises as parochial schools, whose primary reason for separate existence is the inculcation of religious faith. The Memorandum also quoted the famous line from the 1952 Zorach case: "Government may not finance religious groups nor undertake religious instruction nor blend secular and sectarian education."

Then the administration lawyers went farther than even the strict constructionists of the First Amendment had hoped for, and said, concerning general loans for sectarian elementary schools: "While we believe that loans constitute a less substantial assistance to religion than outright grants, we are persuaded by the decisions of the Supreme Court that this proposal is no less a form of support than grants, and is equally prohibited by the Constitution." That seemed to ban all attempts by the federal government to act as banker for parochial school development.

When the National Catholic Welfare Conference heard this sad news, its official spokesman, Monsignor Frederick G. Hochwalt, who had been advocating loans for Catholic school construction as an entering wedge for the larger Catholic financial program, switched back to grants with the statement: "If loans and grants are on the same constitutional basis, we are asking for grants." This quick strategic switch by a representative of the Church irked the *Washington Post* so much that it rebuked both the Monsignor and his backers:

The trouble with Monsignor Hochwalt's statement is that it seeks to brush away as of no consequence the very grave constitutional obstacles that stand in the way of both grants and loans to religious schools. These barriers were not raised by the legal staff of the Department of Health, Education and Welfare. The lawyers merely cited the Bill of Rights and numerous opinions of the Supreme Court to the effect that public funds may not be used to support religious institutions. This has been asserted so often and is so thoroughly grounded in the American tradition of separation of church and state that there is no longer any doubt about it.[25]

One of the most convincing points in the government's legal Memorandum against federal aid to sectarian schools was its citation of a little-known case from Vermont, the case of *Swart* v. *South Burlington*.[26] Although the decision of the Vermont Supreme Court in this case—a unanimous decision—had never been reviewed on its merits by the United States Supreme Court, it constituted an important precedent on the government's side.

This was a case in which Vermont, under an old statute, had allowed townships having no high schools of their own to pay tuition from their treasuries for their students who went to Catholic high schools in neighboring townships. The practice had been challenged by the state government, and later by the individual taxpayer in South Burlington who contended that this was an illegal use of his tax dollars under the Establishment Clause of the First Amendment. This case constituted the nearest approach in the history of the Supreme Court to that on-the-nose joining of financial issues which every lawyer in this field had been waiting for. In 1961, the Vermont Supreme Court, basing its decision squarely on the First Amendment and declaring the tuition payments illegal, said that "the same fundamental law which protects the liberty of a parent to reject the public system in the interest of his child's spiritual welfare, enjoins the state from participating in the religious education he has selected."

The United States Supreme Court decided that it was unnecessary to review the Vermont court's decision, so that decision stood as Vermont law. Since the *only* basic issue raised by the litigants in the case was the issue of no-establishment of religion under the First Amendment, the inference was very strong that the United States Supreme Court in deciding the case accepted the Vermont reasoning. Even the *Notre Dame Lawyer* conceded that this inference was probably correct.[27]

For the most part Catholic lawyers, in meeting the arguments of the administration Memorandum on the constitutionality of aid to parochial schools, fell back on tangential and historical claims. They could not find any solace in recent Supreme Court decisions. In effect, they produced a new doctrine of "educational freedom" which asserted that Catholic parents were being denied freedom when the government refused to pay for their schools.[28] As the *National Catholic Almanac* phrased it,

the denial of Federal aid to church-related schools constitutes an abridgment, because of economic hardship, of the freedom of parents to provide for the education of their children in schools of their choice. This abridgment of a basic freedom might result in practical denial of a right of the natural law guaranteed by the Constitution and explicitly stated by the United States Supreme Court in 1925.[29]

This was a garbled reference to the Pierce case in Oregon, decided in 1925, which gave Catholic schools the right to operate under the law. It gave them no claim whatever upon the public treasury. In fact, in the Oregon case, the Catholic schools were placed in exactly the same position as a private military school. Neither type of school was given any "right of the natural law" to collect tax funds for operating costs from the public.

As Professor Kurland has pointed out:

Probably the most abused citation in the construction of the first amendment is the case of *Pierce* v. *Society of Sisters*. The case raised no church-state issues. Indeed, no reference to the first amendment is made anywhere in the Court's opinion.... Thus does *Pierce* rest clearly on the protection of the business and property rights of the schools.[30]

Cardinal Spellman countered the government's legal Memorandum by claiming that it had loopholes for tax support[31] for "non-religious facilities of church-related schools" and that this split-level theory of non-religious aid might help "to resolve the present controversy." But the loop holes were far too small to accommodate the Cardinal's full program of across-the-board grants.

In recent years the immediate financial demands of Catholic leaders for tax support have varied from month to month while the underlying attitude toward the Constitution and the Supreme Court has remained reasonably constant. That underlying attitude was expressed by the *Catholic World* in an editorial in 1955 by its editor, Father John B. Sheerin. Father Sheerin described the wall-of-separation policy as a "pipe-dream," and added: "This wall of separation said to have been erected by the First Amendment exists only in the mind or rather the imagination of legal students smoking the opium of secularism." The editorial concluded with a primary demand for federal grants for Catholic school buildings, or "at least a remission of taxes for Catholic parents who want their children to possess the faith that has made America great and free."[32]

In working for more immediate goals the Catholic strategy has been more moderate than this editorial would imply. Demands for building costs are rarely mentioned. Indirect aid to parochial schools via the pocketbooks of parents is more commonly stressed. Many varieties of this indirect support have been suggested. Father Virgil Blum, a Jesuit writer, has favored money certificates or vouchers payable to parents, and also tax offsets or remissions.[33] Cardinal McIntyre of Los Angeles, a right-wing leader in his church, has championed a plan of awards to parents for church school costs. Catholic laymen, with the aid of a small number of non-Catholics, have formed a national propaganda organization called Citizens for Educational Freedom which supports and opposes candidates for public office according to their willingness to grant $450 per child per year to parents of children in non-public schools. Some of this organization's literature is openly hostile to "government-controlled education."

A very mild and modest form of indirect tax help has been suggested by scores of bills in Congress permitting income tax deductions for college tuition. Senator Abraham Ribicoff attracted national attention for one form of the concept in May 1963 by introducing two bills embodying the idea.[34] Under the first bill, parents would be permitted to deduct up to $1,500 in their income tax returns for each student attending college at their expense. Since the bill applied to all students in all colleges without any religious or non-religious conditions, the deduction would probably be constitutional. Senator Ribicoff introduced a second bill which would allow a deduction of only $100 per student for lower schools. This small deduction was regarded by most critics as only a device to break ground for more substantial tax grants to parochial schools at a later date.

Although there is much sympathy in Congress for the financial plight of parents of college students in an era of astronomically increasing costs, there does not seem to be any immediate prospect of success for any tax deduction or tax remission schemes. The Internal Revenue Service regards such schemes as too expensive, even in these days of deficit economies. Ribicoff's plan received little public support. Fred Hechinger of the *New York Times* noted that: "There is no indication that the Ribicoff proposals had any advance support from the Administration—even as a trial balloon. In all probability they were intended, not as a solution, but as an atmosphere sweetener."[35] Cardinal McIntyre of Los Angeles rejected the Ribicoff formula rather brusquely on the very day it was issued when he demanded a completely equal share for Catholic schools in any public grants. "There can't be any separation of church and state," he said," unless you want to be a Communist or a materialist—and if you want to, that's your privilege."

The Propaganda Battle

Cardinal McIntyre's explosive irrelevancy suggests that the dialectical battle over tax aid to parochial schools has become something quite alien to law and logic. It has become a propaganda race to establish an image in the public mind, an image of tolerance, minority rights and fair play. Catholic leaders are attempting to maneuver themselves in the public eye into the position of a persecuted minority which advocates equal educational rights for all children and which is being denied basic human rights.

Perhaps the most obvious fallacy in the whole maneuver is the claim that the Catholic minority is *the* American minority which somehow stands for the rights of all minorities. Actually our nation is a nation of many religious minorities and any special privilege given to one minority must be appraised in terms of its effect on all the other minorities. The Catholic minority is asking all other American minorities, including the 70,000,000 unchurched Americans, to help finance its own secession from the public school system, the only system designed for all Americans. Its claim is based upon the "separate but equal" doctrine for segregated schools—segregated by creed. Although the racial policy of the hierarchy has been magnificently liberal, its educational policy cannot escape the label of segregation. The famous *Washington Post* cartoonist Herblock put that thought in a cartoon in 1963 showing a "Religious School Lobbyist" marching up the Capitol steps with a large sign: "If the government doesn't support separate-but-equal schools for our children, it's guilty of DISCRIMINATION." At the side a Negro parent is standing with his child, looking on in utter bewilderment. He cannot understand the logic of men who oppose government grants for one type of segregated schools because they disbelieve in segregation and then ask tax dollars for their own religiously segregated system in the name of non-discrimination.

No one, of course, would deny that Catholic parents who pay government educational taxes and also parochial school tuition are deserving of public sympathy. Many of them are needy and their sacrifices in maintaining a dual, private school system are substantial. But the current campaign for their relief relies on several verbal clichés which do not truly represent the American situation. Those clichés usually employ eight key words and phrases whose meanings are self-evident: (1) monopoly; (2) discrimination; (3) double taxation; (4) independent schools; (5) freedom of choice in education; (6) partners in the American educational enterprise; (7) a public service; and (8) the non-religious part of Catholic schools. It may be worthwhile to make a kind of short-hand reply to these words and phrases.[36]

1. *Monopoly.* The Catholic Church is not threatened by any public school monopoly. No one of any importance in the United States is trying to put the Catholic schools out of business. They are expanding rapidly in perfect freedom, even more rapidly than the public schools, and their right to operate has been guaranteed by the Supreme Court.

2. *Discrimination.* There is no religious discrimination in the operation of the American public school system today, and there is no religious discrimination in limiting tax appropriations to that system. The system gives equal rights to all children, Catholics, Methodist, Jews and atheists. The invitation to Catholic parents to send their children to that system is given freely and without equivocation. If they choose to decline that invitation for personal and religious reasons, they have no basis for complaint. Many years ago the Greater Detroit Council of the CIO put this thesis very bluntly in a direct answer to those who were demanding tax support for sectarian schools: "The public education highway is the public school system, and if that is not good enough for you,

it is your privilege to build your own private education highway, but why should public funds be given to those who despise and ignore the public school system?"[37]

3. *Double taxation.* There is only one taxation system in the United States, that of the government. Under that system all citizens are taxed not as Catholics or Methodists or bachelors or parents but as citizens, in most cases according to their ability to pay. The contributions of Catholic parents to their Church for parochial schools are not taxes but voluntary contributions which no law obliges them to make. They can refrain from making those contributions at will, and send their children to America's free public schools. No one would think of charging that the wealthy parents who send their children to such private schools as Groton, Exeter and Lawrenceville are being subjected to double taxation because they choose not to send their children to public schools. But, if the Catholic claim of "double taxation" should be accepted, these wealthy parents would have the same right to public subsidies that Catholic parents have. There *would* be a new kind of double taxation if all citizens were compelled by law to pay for both the public schools and the schools belonging to the Catholic Church. This would introduce a new principle into American taxation, the compulsory support of religious institutions by the general taxpayer.

4. *Independent schools.* The Catholic schools are not independent. They are completely dependent and integral parts of the Catholic Church, often supported out of the same collection plate, and owned down to the last brick by religious orders or bishops without any control by the Catholic people who pay for them. They have no democratically chosen school boards and no democratic features in their machinery of control. As Justice Jackson said, after a summary of Catholic educational law in the Everson case: "I should be surprised if any Catholic would deny that the parochial school is a vital, if not the most vital, part of the Roman Catholic Church. . . . Catholic education is the rock on which the whole structure rests, and to render tax aid to its Church school is

indistinguishable to me from rendering the same aid to the Church itself."

5. *Freedom of choice in education.*   It is the public rather than the Catholic system of education which gives parents freedom of choice in education. Under the Catholic educational system the choice of schools is dictated by canon law, and it is limited to Catholic schools unless special permission is granted by a Catholic bishop. Canon 1374 of Catholic canon law reads:

> Catholic children may not attend non-Catholic, neutral or mixed schools, that is, those which are open to non-Catholics, and it pertains exclusively to the Ordinary [bishop] of the place to decide, in accordance with instructions of the Holy See, under which circumstances and with what precautions against the danger of perversion, attendance at such schools may be tolerated.

6. *Partners in the American educational enterprise.*   Catholic schools are not partners but rivals of the public school in the American educational enterprise. The people have no control over them except to require that they teach certain necessary subjects and maintain a minimum of attendance. Beyond that they are free to attack the public schools as "godless"—and they constantly do— and to urge the superior claims of the Church system, which they do as a matter of religious duty under their Church's law. In many localities they drain away so many pupils from the public school that the public school cannot function properly.

7. *A public service.*   It is true that Catholic schools perform some public service and that they save taxpayers several million dollars a year thereby. Many other private institutions also perform some public service tangentially without thereby establishing any claim to tax support. Churches perform a public service by helping to make men moral but, like the Catholic schools, their public service is incidental and subordinate to their religious function. If merely incidental public service were to entitle religious institutions to tax support, then virtually all church institutions could live off of the public treasury, and our nation would be taken back toward the church-state union of medieval Europe.

8. *The non-religious part of Catholic schools.* There is no part of the Catholic school program which is not directly connected with religion. According to papal instructions the Catholic schools must observe the rule that "every subject taught be permeated with Christian [Catholic] piety."[38] The atmosphere of each Catholic classroom, the religious symbols and paraphernalia, the close association with church buildings, the use of sectarian textbooks and the operation of the system by dedicated nuns combine to make any possible division between the religious and non-religious aspects of the Catholic schools quite chimerical. Since the Catholic Church and the Catholic school system constitute one financial entity, the flow of public revenue into one part of the system for "secular" activities would simply release a commensurate sum for wholly religious activities. Justice William O. Douglas put his finger on this vital point in his concurring opinion in the Schempp-Murray Bible-reading decision in 1963 when he said:

> Financing a church either in its strictly religious activities or in its other activities is equally unconstitutional, as I understand the Establishment Clause. Budgets for one activity may be technically separable from budgets for others. But the institution is an inseparable whole, a living organism, which is strengthened in proselytizing when it is strengthened in any department by contributions from other than its own members. . .
> What may not be done directly may not be done indirectly lest the Establishment Clause become a mockery.

The Narrow-Minded Society

This all-too-sketchy analysis of the agglomeration of desperation, artifice, and self-interest used to support Catholic appeals for financial help is not as important as another consideration, the social consequences of the adoption of a sectarian tax program in education. The possible addition of two to four billion dollars a year to the American tax bill is not the primary danger. Many students of the problem would consider two to four billions a year a bargain price to pay if by paying it the children of all creeds could be brought within the tolerant atmosphere of a community school system.

The two possible social consequences of Catholic victory in the drive for federal aid which justify the most serious apprehensions are (1) the increase of religious narrow-mindedness, and (2) the decimation of the public school in many localities if, as seems logical, the granting of subsidies to Catholic schools should lead ultimately to competing and subsidized Protestant and Jewish schools.

The first of these causes of apprehension is rarely discussed in the public press because of the reluctance of editors to strike directly at the content of Catholic education. This content is a basic factor in the situation and it is difficult to see how it can be eliminated from the discussion without prettifying the whole picture. The Catholic system creates narrow-mindedness not only through specifically narrow-minded and dogmatic teachings but also through the device of religious segregation itself. The Catholic child is withdrawn automatically during his formative years from that environment of tolerance and group cooperation which makes the public school "at once the symbol of our democracy and the most pervasive means for promoting our common destiny." (The words are those of Justice Frankfurter in the McCollum decision.) The Catholic demand for tax support means that non-Catholics are being asked to share in financing a system of separatism which automatically tends to breed religious antagonism.

No sensible person would contend that the narrow-mindedness of Catholic education is exclusive or unique among religions. A recent study of Protestant literature, *Faith and Prejudice* by Bernard E. Olson, has revealed a considerable residue of anti-Semitic and anti-Catholic bias in Protestant books. But the narrow partisanship of the Catholic school system is more socially significant than any similar phenomenon in the Protestant and Jewish world because the Catholic system is so large and because it is asking public tax support.

Space will not permit any detailed analysis here of the content of parochial school education—the character of Catholic text books has recently been exposed by George La Noue in the *Harvard Educational Review* (Summer, 1962), but nothing in Mr. La Noue's study is more flatly contrary to the principles of tolerant education than the traditional rule of Canon 1399 forbidding Catholics to read any book directly attacking Catholic doctrine. Catholic canon law is open for the whole world to read, and many of its provisions are wholly inappropriate for dissemination in any tax-supported school. Definite discriminatory practices against Protestants and Jews are taught as a matter of routine. The Catholic rules on mixed marriage may be taken as an illustration. Catholic high school students are taught that Canon 1060 "most severely forbids" them to marry a Protestant or a Jew, and that if they should receive special permission for such a mixed marriage, the marriage itself would be absolutely invalid under Canon 1061 unless the Protestant or Jewish party signed away the religion of all future children to the Catholic Church.[39]

These facts are relevant here only because non-Catholic taxpayers, who are the present victims of this discriminatory teaching, are being asked to pay for it in parochial schools supported by federal appropriations. One can imagine the public uproar if the Protestant counterpart of Catholic mixed marriage rules were disseminated in public, tax-supported high schools—if public high schools taught that (1) no Protestant could marry a Catholic or a Jew; (2) no Catholic marrying a Protestant or Jew by special permission could be considered legally married unless he were married by a Protestant clergyman and signed away the religion of all his children to Protestantism!

Even more serious than the apprehensions about government-financed narrow-mindedness are the apprehensions about the possible sectarian fragmentation of our whole educational life if government started to subsidize competing denominational school systems. At the present time most Protestants and Jews abjure all demands for separate Protestant and Jewish schools. They are committed to a public school concept in education. But could they resist the lure of public dollars if they saw a publicly subsidized Catholic system expanding rapidly and using its facilities for narrowly sectarian promotion?

George La Noue, in a recent study, "Public Funds for Parochial Schools?" made for the Department of Religious Liberty of the National Council of Churches, concluded that the use of tax funds for church-related schools would "severely damage, if not destroy, our public school system."[40] Dr. John C. Bennett of Union Seminary, a very friendly critic of Catholic schools, has said that "decisive encouragement of parochial schools through public financial aid would have a destructive effect on the public schools and on education generally. . . . I am told by those who have studied the matter most closely that we could not expect to have fewer than five or six systems of parochial schools competing for the resources of the community in the large or middle-sized cities. This would be divisive; it would be expensive; and it would mean that every system would be educationally weak."[41]

The experience of several nations of Western Europe indicates that such a picture of educational fragmentation and degeneration is not necessarily an illusion. It would seem that the logical policy to adopt to avoid such an eventuality in the United States is one of strict adherence to the basic principle: Public money for public schools only.

CHAPTER 7

Buses, Books and Teachers

Around the periphery of the major controversies in the religion-and-education field are many little controversies, seemingly trivial but crucial in significance. Should a nun be allowed to wear a distinctively religious costume in a public classroom? Should students graduating from a public high school be required to attend a religious baccalaureate service in order to secure their diplomas? Should taxpayers shoulder the cost of non-religious textbooks in parochial schools? Should they be required to pay for parochial school buses? How much religious emphasis should be permitted in Christmas and Easter celebrations in public schools?

More important even than these peripheral questions are the questions which involve both the financial wall between church and state and the ideological wall. Should sectarian colleges receive public grants when such grants are denied to schools at the lower level? Should state-supported colleges be permitted to use public money for religious activities?

Only two of these issues have received definitive treatment by the United States Supreme Court: the textbook problem and the transportation problem. As we shall see in a moment, the textbook answer is so out of line with present Supreme Court attitudes concerning the establishment of religion that it is likely to be reversed if a well-reasoned challenge is presented to the Court. And even the Court's five to four permissive ruling in favor of the constitutionality of transportation grants is in some danger because of shifting attitudes within the Court.

Local court decisions and local laws in regard to these big little issues are in a state of grand and variegated confusion. Wise authorities can be quoted on both sides of each controversy. There is no such thing as an "American policy" on costumed nuns, baccalaureate services, parochial textbooks, bus transportation, Christmas celebrations or college aid. Local law and local tradition rule the roost in such matters. Many educational leaders doubt the wisdom of setting up national standards and rules for such activities, but it is now too late to leave them to purely local determination, since the Supreme Court has ruled that all citizens in all localities are entitled to uniform national protection against established religion. If these practices can be proved to constitute such an unlawful establishment, they must go the way of Bible-reading and the Lord's Prayer.

In facing these peripheral issues, we will get little help from Congress. Congressmen not only lack the power to interfere in public school programs but they lack the desire to take a stand in so controversial a field. Ordinarily they avoid religious controversy as men avoid a plague, since there are almost no political rewards for integrity and courage in handling such matters.

The Two-Way College Issue

Of all these big little issues, the college aid issue is the most important. In the colleges a wide breach has already been made in the wall between religion and government, and the forces of church-state financial union are eager to march through. The commingling of church and state has become so traditional in many institutions of higher learning that it is taken for granted. Such commingling is constantly being used as a precedent for a similar break-through in the wall of separation at other educational levels. The typical argument runs: If church colleges can get away with public revenue and if state colleges can incorporate religious promotion into their programs, why should strict advocates of the separation of church and state demand an unjust double standard for lower schools?

The most popular counter-argument is that colleges are

above the compulsory school-age limit and their students are not, like the children in lower schools, part of a captive audience. They are mature enough to think for themselves and they should be given the option of studying about one of life's major phenomena, religion.

Two special facts make the demand for across-the-board government aid to church colleges particularly appealing. Although one half of the nation's high school graduates do not go on to college, there is a population explosion in the college field which is even more striking than the world population explosion. In the United States in 1960 there were about 3,610,000 students in colleges and universities; the figures jumped nearly 8 per cent in the following year, and it is now estimated that nearly 7,000,000 young Americans will be clamoring at college doors by 1970.[1] Meanwhile, tuition costs at many colleges have more than doubled in the 1950's. Also the financial wall between church and state at the federal level has been partially circumvented for many years by such special-grant legislation as loans for college housing, grants from the National Science Foundation, the National Defense Education Act for scholarships, etc. The total annual federal provisions for higher education run to about two and one-half billion dollars. About 20 per cent of every dollar spent by colleges and universities in the country comes from federal sources. The private colleges, including many church colleges, probably get about 16 per cent of their operating funds from special federal grants of one sort or another. And no part of the program of commingled, borderline church-state expenditure has ever been successfully challenged in the Supreme Court. Added to these special facts is the historical fact that a large number of our greatest private, non-sectarian universities began as church colleges, and some of them still maintain a nominal denominational connection.

The persuasive force of these special factors was apparent in the second session of the Eighty-seventh Congress in 1962 when college aid bills passed both houses and went down to final defeat in an inter-house squabble over details of the program. The church-state issue played a part in the defeat, but both houses accepted a formula for church-state separation in college aid which blurred the dividing line between religion and government.[2] The bills provided that grants and loans could not be used for divinity schools, chapels or rooms devoted primarily to religious instruction, but no one discussed the coercive religious practices in sectarian colleges. No one asked who would police the buildings of church colleges to determine which rooms were used for religion. No one asked how much money would be released for religion by grants to secular activities. No one on the floor of either house of Congress raised the question whether compulsory chapels and compulsory courses in religion at denominational colleges should not disqualify such institutions for federal aid. The same administration lawyers who had found in the Constitution clear prohibitions against loans and grants to sectarian schools at the elementary level found no serious constitutional objections to a college-aid program, although they did concede that grants might be more questionable legally than loans.

"The constitutional principles are obviously the same," said the administration lawyers, "whether the subject is elementary and secondary education or higher education, but the factual circumstances surrounding the application of the principles are dramatically different. The reasons are largely historical."[3] Among the "dramatically different" college circumstances cited by the administration lawyers were the absence of state compulsion for enrollment at the college level, the fact that free education is not available to all college students, and the fact that in colleges "the connection between religion and education is less apparent, and that religious indoctrination is less pervasive in a sectarian college curriculum."

The administration lawyers might have cited in defense of federal aid to church colleges an equally persuasive precedent, namely that many of our largest state universities have, without serious challenge, adopted programs of state expenditure for religion.[4] The programs have gone far beyond scientific courses in

Comparative Religion, the Philosophy of Religion and the Psychology of Religion, all of which subjects, if taught with genuine scholarship, may be accepted as normal parts of a public university's curriculum. A School of Religion at the State University of Iowa has been going beyond such scholarly impartiality for some 35 years—at public expense. The University of Michigan has had an Office of Religious Affairs since 1956, which at one time employed four clergymen with tax funds. Their function was to "coordinate" and stimulate the activities of twenty-two student religious foundations in the campus community. There have been no court rulings in this borderline church-state territory of tax-supported religion at state universities except one old (1891) Illinois case which permitted the continuation of compulsory chapel at the state university.[5] An Illinois student was expelled for refusing to attend chapel, and his expulsion was sustained by the state's highest court. Today compulsory chapels have been generally abandoned at public institutions—the United States armed forces academies constitute the major exceptions—but there is still a very large amount of religious coercion within sectarian colleges of all denominations, and these institutions are asking for across-the-board appropriations without offering to abandon any of their coercive features.

Every Catholic college in America ordinarily requires Catholic students to take courses in Catholicism,[6] not independent, analytical courses in Catholicism but courses which can only be described as indoctrination. (Non-Catholic students are excused from such requirements.) The twenty-eight Jesuit universities in the country, which have taken the lead in demanding across-the-board grants from the federal government, not only have this coercive requirement for all Catholic students on their rolls but they also delegate ownership and control over the institutions to inner boards composed entirely of members of the Jesuit Order, who are subject to removal at will by higher ecclesiastical authorities for purely theological reasons. There is no attempt to disguise this rigidly denominational character of Jesuit institutions. Says the catalogue of Cincinnati's Xavier University in describing the auxilary aids to Catholic faith promoted on the campus:

Xavier University uses various means of promoting a sincere Catholic way of living in its students. Too numerous for catalogue listing, they permeate classroom and general campus atmosphere. From the elaborate celebration of Mass to a quiet visit in Bellarmine Chapel, student life is vibrant with that simple devotion characteristic of Christian principles.[7]

Although many colleges which are described in public records as "Protestant" have only a courtesy connection with Protestantism, and do not require any indoctrination for their Protestant students, there are some exceptions.

Baylor University in Waco, Texas (Southern Baptist) still requires chapel attendance for four semesters as a condition for graduation. Brigham Young University in Utah, claiming to be "the largest church-related institution of higher learning in the United States," has built Mormonism into the curriculum as completely as Notre Dame has built in Catholicism. (At Notre Dame 98 per cent of the students are Roman Catholics and must therefore take courses in Catholicism.) Westminster College in Fulton, Missouri, calling itself "the only Protestant liberal arts college for men west of the Mississippi," operating under Presbyterian ownership and control, requires six hours of Bible in the Department of Bible and Religion, whose four professors are all Protestant clergymen. "The courses in this department," says the college catalogue, "are designed to provide students with adequate knowledge of the religious content, literary form, and historical background of the Bible in order that they may have an appreciation of its truth, and be challenged by its message."[8]

No sensible person doubts the legal right of such sectarian institutions to operate at private expense but it is difficult to see how a consistent policy of church-state separation can be maintained when (1) some state universities are permitted to use tax funds for large-scale promotion of religion, and (2) direct, across-the-board federal grants are being proposed—with fair prospects of success—for wholly sectarian colleges which maintain an evangelistic atmosphere and which impose on most of their students compulsory courses in their own religion exclusively, not scholarly or impartial courses in comparative religion. If this is not forbidden state aid to religion under the First Amendment as interpreted by the Supreme Court, then ordinary words have lost their ordinary meanings. The Supreme Court has not made the Bill of Rights applicable by age groups. It has not sanctioned aid to religion at the adult level. Fundamentally there is no more reason for tax-supported religious *promotion* by a state university than for tax-supported religious promotion at a public high school.

If and when the Supreme Court reaches a long overdue decision on the wall of separation in college life, it is to be hoped that it will reject the superficial and inadequate Congressional ban on divinity schools and chapel buildings, and lay down a more specific and comprehensive rule barring across-the-board grants to (1) any college owned or controlled by a religious organization, or (2) any college which requires any of its students to take courses in a sectarian faith.

Buses and Textbooks

Considering the relatively small amount of money involved in the battle, no controversy in the field of religion and education has caused so much acrimony as the controversy over tax appropriations for bus transportation for parochial schools. Perhaps the leaders of the Catholic Church thought that when they had cleared the federal constitutional hurdle in 1947 with a five to four permissive decision in favor of tax appropriations for buses, the rest of the battle would soon be over. Actually the tide has begun to turn the other way in recent years. Today only sixteen of the fifty states have anything like state-wide programs for tax-supported buses for parochial schools, and many of these states limit transportation rather strictly to the bus routes used by public school buses. Catholics have recently won the battle for bus transportation in many parts of Maine, but they have lost legal battles in Alaska, Wisconsin, Kentucky and Oklahoma.

The struggle for free, non-religious textbooks for parochial schools has been much more limited than the bus struggle in spite of the fact that grants of textbooks for such schools received Supreme Court clearance seventeen years earlier than the clearance given to bus grants. The battle in this field has attracted relatively little attention, and today it is usually estimated that only three states can be counted as textbook-grant states, Mississippi, Louisiana and New Mexico. Rhode Island, with a Catholic population of more than 60 per cent, has recently been added to the endowed textbook states, but the law faces a court test. Oregon has been lost by the endowed textbook forces by a court decision.

The appropriation of public money for such fringe benefits as school buses and non-religious textbooks is not always determined by the size of the Catholic bloc in the population. Sometimes it depends upon the accidents of history, the wording of old state constitutions and laws, or the courage (or lack of courage) of a state attorney general. The sixteen states which now grant public funds for bus transportation to parochial schools stretch clear across the country, and they have no consistent ethnic or religious pattern. The chief centers of Catholic population have been appropriating public funds for parochial school buses for a long time, but there are some overwhelmingly non-Catholic states which also follow the same pattern. Here are the sixteen bus states with their Roman Catholic percentages in parentheses. The percentages are taken from the National Catholic Almanac of 1963. California (21.8) ; Colorado (18.8) ; Connecticut (45.9) ; Illinois (29.8) ; Indiana (13.9) ; Kansas (13.3) ; Louisiana (34.1) ; Maryland (21.6) ; Massachusetts (51.8) ; Michigan (25.5) ; New Hampshire (36.9) ; New Jersey (40.8) ; New Mexico (39.2) ; New York (35.3) ; Oregon (12.1) ; Rhode Island (60.7) .

The primary reason for coupling bus grants and textbook aid

in any discussion is that they are both fringe benefits and they are both being defended by the same legal theory, the so-called child-benefit theory put forward by the five-man majority of the Supreme Court in the 1947 Everson bus case. According to that theory, there is nothing in the First and Fourteenth Amendments to prevent certain types of safety and welfare appropriations for the benefit of a child as distinct from the religious school which he attends. The child can be split in two for purposes of legal distinction. When his body is taken to school in a public bus he is merely a child being treated as child, entitled to all those safety and welfare measures granted to all children. Bus grants for his transportation are therefore not an establishment of religion. When he arrives at the parochial school, he has become part of a religious institution which is not entitled to any direct "aid to religion."

The essence of the child benefit theory as expressed by Justice Black in the Everson decision lay in these words:

It is undoubtedly true that children are helped to get to church schools. There is even a possibility that some of the children might not be sent to the church schools if the parents were compelled to pay their children's bus fares. . . . Moreover, state-paid policemen, detailed to protect children going to and from church schools from the very real hazards of traffic, would serve much the same purpose and accomplish much the same result as state provisions intended to guarantee free transportation which the state deems to be best for the children's welfare. . . .

The State contributes no money to the schools. It does not support them. Its legislation, as applied, does no more than provide a general program to help parents get their children, regardless of their religion, safely and expeditiously to and from accredited schools.[9]

This child benefit theory has been subjected to a strong counter-attack in American courts for more than a decade. Several of the four dissenting justices in the Everson case itself, while expressing great sympathy for Catholic children facing modern traffic perils, scored the majority theory as a fiction which might serve as a dangerous precedent for more complete establishment of religion through school programs. Justice Rutledge, supported in dissent by three other justices, declared: "For me ... the feat is impossible to select so indispensable an item [as transportation] from the composite of total costs, and characterize it as not aiding, contributing to, promoting or sustaining the propagation of beliefs ..." Justice Jackson in dissent argued that, in using the analogy between police services and bus grants, the majority had ignored institutional religious tests involved. "A policeman," he said, "protects a Catholic, of course—but not because he is a Catholic; it is because he is a man and a member of our society." He argued that the bus grants in the Everson case were not a true parallel to such services since they were grants specifically to children attending Catholic schools. He might have added that similar logic would justify state expenditures for bus transportation of children going to Sunday school.

Since then several state courts have criticized the child benefit theory in bus transportation even more pointedly, and some have overruled it when their own constitutions and statutes gave state judges an option to disagree. Of course the Supreme Court ruling in the Everson case applied only to the federal Constitution and did not prevent any state court from interpreting its constitution and laws more strictly. Tax grants for sectarian buses are in special peril because several of the 16 states now permitting such grants have never reviewed all the issues involved in their highest courts.

In general, the opposing state judges have based their opposition to parochial school bus grants on the theory that the payment of bus costs is, after all, tax support for religious schools no matter how carefully it is dressed up as a mere personal safety grant for the child. They have rejected the child benefit theory as an artifice.

The Supreme Court of Washington, two years after the Everson case, "respectfully" described sectarian bus grants as illegal "support" of sectarian education under the Washington state constitution.[10] Missouri followed suit in 1953.[11] In 1961 the Alaska Supreme Court, listing eight court decisions as contrary to the child benefit theory, rejected the theory for itself and outlawed the Alaska bus statute.[12] In 1962 the Wisconsin Supreme Court, in outlawing free bus rides for Catholic school children as "merely a convenience to assist them in attending a parochial school," declared that "the weight of authority since the Everson case is clearly against the constitutionality of providing publicly financed transportation and related aids to non-public school children."[13] Incidentally, this Wisconsin Supreme Court indicated how expensive modern bus transportation has become—$64 per pupil per year for that state.

The Supreme Court of Oregon in 1962 put its finger on the essential weakness of the child benefit theory by saying: "The difficulty with this theory is . . . that unless it is qualified in some way it can be used to justify the expenditure of public funds for every educational purpose, because all educational aids are of benefit to the people."[14] Much earlier the Oklahoma Supreme Court had pointed out that "practically every proper expenditure for school purposes aids the child."[15]

These defeats of Catholic bus demands in state courts have been partly offset by a stormy victory in Maine. Early in 1957 about 900 Catholic parents with children in the parochial schools of Augusta threatened to "dump" these children on the public schools by a "pressure invasion" unless local authorities gave them tax funds for transportation. The "pressure invasion" was called off abruptly when the public school authorities blandly announced that they would do their best to accept the invaders, but eventually, after a long and bitter battle through the Maine courts and the Maine legislature, a law was passed in 1961 authorizing the use of tax funds for sectarian school transportation at local option. Several Maine cities promptly approved such local expenditures.[16]

More extensive demonstrations by Catholic parents and children in Missouri in May, 1963 failed to persuade the Missouri legislature to permit parochial students to ride on public buses in that state.[17] The demonstrations took the form of parades and mass "sit-in" enrollments in the public schools in many cities and towns throughout the state. Some local public schools were swamped by the influx of new students "enrolling" at the end of the academic year, but school officials did not make the mistake of turning away any students. They made it clear that if Catholic parents actually wanted to transfer their children to public schools the children would be welcomed even though it would cost the taxpayers sixteen times as much to educate a Catholic child in a public school as it would to transport him to a Catholic school. Since the Catholic population of Missouri is not more than 17 per cent of the total, it is not likely that even the most militant drive by church interests will defeat the legislative opposition.

The acrimony in these bus battles has been increased by the misuse of the Supreme Court's minor and permissive concession in the Everson bus case. Critics of Catholicism had been warning the public that the bus demand was merely an entering wedge in a larger program of tax demands and that any concession would be inflated and used as a precedent for more concessions. The prophecy was rather dramatically fulfilled in the ensuing campaign.

In 1955 the child benefit theory, which the Court had limited strictly to a personal benefit for the child, was seized upon by the *Catholic World* in an open letter to President Eisenhower saying that "in the matter of erecting new school buildings, it's obvious that American children are entitled to the benefit of public welfare legislation regardless of race, creed or color. That was the decision of the United States Supreme Court in February 1947, upholding a New Jersey statute providing free bus transportation for children attending Catholic schools. American youth, whether Catholic, Protestant or Jewish, have a right to be educated in school buildings that have decent physical facilities."[18] A leading Catholic writer in this field, Father Virgil C. Blum, announced the theory that the classification of children "into those who attend government schools and those who do not attend such schools" is "an arbitrary discrimination" which "violates the First and Fourteenth Amendments."[19] On the basis of his reasoning the chief Catholic chain newspaper in the country, the *Register*, headlined a front-page story: "Says U.S. Constitution Bars Restrictions on School Bus Rides."[20]

These claims, of course, constitute a fantastic misrepresentation of the Constitution and the Supreme Court's interpretation of it. The distinction between public and private institutions in respect to financial rights is too well grounded in legal tradition to need any detailed defense. The Supreme Court in the Everson case said that the state "cannot exclude *individual* Catholics, Lutherans, Mohammedans, Baptists, Jews, Methodists, Non-believers, Presbyterians, or the members of any other faith, because of their faith, or the lack of it, from receiving the benefits of public welfare legislation," but the justices went out of their way in the very next sentence to say that "we do not mean to intimate that a state could not provide transportation only to children attending public schools." The Court clearly left the option to local school authorities. In pursuance of the long-established distinction between public and private facilities, more than two-thirds of the states still limit their transportation expenditures to public schools.

Meanwhile, the new and more rigid line taken by the Supreme Court in the Bible-reading and prayer cases raises the question whether all tax grants for sectarian transportation may not ultimately be declared unconstitutional. The announced reversal of his position on the question by Justice Douglas in his separate opinion in the Regents' prayer case was significant. He had cast the deciding vote for parochial buses in the Everson case. But it is also significant that in 1961 when some Connecticut taxpayers challenged a Connecticut bus law which relied upon the reasoning in the Everson case, the Supreme Court refused to review the Connecticut court's approval of that law.[21] This probably means that the Court will let sleeping dogs lie, and leave further quarrels on this subject to the states.

Not so in the case of tax grants for non-religious textbooks in sectarian schools. The alleged constitutionality of such grants rests upon such a flimsy foundation that it is likely to be destroyed by any serious court challenge. The Oregon Supreme Court set the probable pattern of future developments in this field when it outlawed expenditures for such purposes in 1962, and the Supreme Court of the United States refused to review its conclusions. The Oregon court pointed out that "such books are an integral part of the educational process" and added that

... we are unable to see any substantial distinction between the furnishing of textbooks and the furnishing of blackboards, desks, laboratory instruments. ... Defendants argue that the denial of the use of free textbooks to pupils solely because they attend parochial schools would constitute a violation of the equal protection clause of the Fourteenth Amendment. The argument is without merit. The classification which excludes such pupils from the state's bounty is not only reasonable, it is commanded by the constitution itself.[22]

Tax appropriations for textbooks in sectarian schools have been considered constitutional under the United States Constitution since 1930, under a decision in a Louisiana case which can only be described as a judicial fluke. The opinion of the Court allowing the state of Louisiana to lend books to private schools did not even mention the First Amendment or the possible establishment of religion. It accepted the child benefit theory as sufficiently persuasive in the case of textbook grants to bridge the gap between private schools and the public treasury, but it completely ducked the church-state issues involved.[23] The reasoning has been outdated by later Supreme Court opinions.

Meanwhile a study of textbooks used in parochial schools, made at the request of the National Council of Churches by George R. La Noue and published in the *Harvard Educational Review,* has proved that religion is integrated into virtually all parochial school texts, even into textbooks in science, languages and mathematics.[24] Many great textbook publishing firms have established separate Catholic divisions in order to guarantee denominational treatment of all subjects in accord with sectarian standards. Such sponsored books are called "impartial" factually,

but they are heavily loaded with doctrinal illustrations and em
phases. To finance such books at public expense is, to use the
analogy of the Oregon Supreme Court, no different in principle
from furnishing blackboards and desks.

Baccalaureate Services, Christmas, and Nuns

Two things that baccalaureate services, Christmas celebra
tions, and nuns have in common is that they embarrass public
school authorities and they occupy a kind of no-man's land in
church-state law. Since they are unquestionably religious in nature,
they raise the doubt that they belong in a public school system
when that system is officially committed to religious neutrality.

The baccalaureate service presents the most trivial of these
problems, but it has become quite annoying to school administrators, especially in New England. When America was a near-Protes-
tant country in its orientation, the local parson could deliver the
sermon-address to the public high school seniors with no thought
of offending Catholic and Jewish parents. It was taken for granted
that this sermon-address would be religious, rather solemn, spotted
with homely humor and advice, accompanied by Protestant hymns,
and capped with a fervent Protestant prayer. The only point in
having a baccalaureate service separate from graduation exercises
was to give this added religious emphasis—the word baccalaureate
is defined as "a religious service usually connected with commencement ceremonies."

Professor Dierenfield's study indicates that about 87 per cent
of American high schools still have a baccalaureate service, and
only in New England, with its large Catholic population, has there
been any significant abstention from the baccalaureate tradition.[25]
Most baccalaureate services are now voluntary affairs, held on
school premises rather than in churches.

Until recently the attack on the baccalaureate idea has been
almost wholly a Catholic attack with small religious liberal groups

joining in. The attack seems doubly justified when, as occasionally happens, students in a public high school graduating class are actually denied their diplomas for failure to attend a baccalaureate service held in a church to which they do not belong. This was the case, for example, in Moundsville, West Virginia in 1957 when twenty-two Roman Catholic students were denied a public award of their diplomas as graduating seniors in a public high school because they refused to attend a baccalaureate sermon by a Presbyterian minister in a Methodist church.[26] Both the American Civil Liberties Union and Glenn Archer of POAU made sharp protests, contending that the religious freedom of the Catholic seniors had been illegally impaired. After the public uproar, the seniors were quietly given their diplomas in private.

The Catholic rule on the subject of baccalaureate services is quite specific and it has been widely publicized by at least two American bishops in recent years, Archbishop William O. Brady of St. Paul, Minnesota, and Bishop Daniel J. Feeney of Portland, Maine. Archbishop Brady, in 1958, deplored the "attempt to crown the final days of the secular academic year with a religious sugar coating," and declared that a local baccalaureate service should be held in a "purely public place," not in the Catholic church or in any other church.[27] He forbade his priests and people to have anything to do with sectarian baccalaureate services.

In Maine, Bishop Feeny was even more specific. He used many of the same phrases in defense of the separation of church and state in education which were later used in the non-Catholic attack on Bible-reading and prayer in public schools. "Public authorities," he said, "may not use their power to oblige those legally subject to them to attend religious services in violation of conscience. . . . It is well to remember that New England today is not the New England of the Puritans, of the union of church and state that held sway from its early settlement until well after the revolutionary period."[28] Several Maine towns thereafter did away with their baccalaureate services altogether.

The educational authorities of New York State have ruled

baccalaureate services illegal under the First Amendment, and they are undoubtedly correct in their legal reasoning. But the state courts of most other states have ducked the issue whenever possible and left the determination to local school authorities. In the Dade County, Florida cases which we have already discussed, a Florida circuit court reached the amazing conclusion that there was no evidence of "religious teaching" in the voluntary baccalaureate services considered, although their religious character was quite self-evident.[29] The most logical solution for this embarrassing issue would seem to be that adopted by a Minneapolis high school a solemn "dedication service" at the time of commencement, with no particular religious features and a speaker who delivers a moral address without sectarian overtones. As one Minnesota official has said, this "keeps the seniors together" during the graduation festivities, and at the same time it gives them some thoughts about the meaning of a life dedicated to service.

Christmas and Easter celebrations in public schools pose a serious problem for Jewish parents, and they have been repeatedly challenged in recent years in those cities which have a large concentration of Jewish citizens. The New York and Boston areas, particularly, have seen several lively disputes about Christian features in Christmas celebrations in public schools.

We have already discussed some aspects of the Christmas and Easter problem in summing up the findings of Florida courts in the Dade County cases. In those cases a Southern judge agreed to enjoin the presentation in Florida public schools of religious programs observing Christmas, Easter and Hanukkah. This was considered a substantial victory by the leaders of the American Civil Liberties Union and the American Jewish Congress who had sponsored the action. But, since no national verdict on the subject has been handed down by the Supreme Court, the great majority of American public schools continue to celebrate Christmas, and a smaller majority have Easter celebrations also.[30] No one knows how much doctrinal religion is injected into these celebrations, along with general good will, a fondness for amateur theatricals and a love of traditional carols.

From a strict Jewish point of view any mention of Jesus in song or story as the Lord and Messiah, any assertion of his miraculous birth, and especially any dramatization of the crucifixion which puts major responsibility for his death on the Jews is an affront to Jewish sensitivity. The unfortunate psychological effect of Christmas on Jewish public school children is constantly being emphasized in Jewish protests, and often non-Jewish leaders join in the protests. Robert W. Lynn in an editorial in a Protestant journal, *Christianity and Crisis,* has told of a Protestant minister who, in discussing the problem with a parishioner, phrased the basic question in this way: "How would you feel if your child were required to sing that Jesus is *not* our Savior?"[31]

The Jewish feeling against Christian ceremonials at Christmas, even against Christmas trees in public schools, was dramatically brought to national attention in December, 1962, in Sharon, Massachusetts, a Boston suburb which has a Jewish majority. Four Sharon principals of public schools decided to have no Christmas trees in their schools for the Christmas season, and their right to make such local policy decisions was sustained by the school superintendent of Sharon, Herman Richardson. One thousand Sharon citizens petitioned for a reversal of the policy and staged a stormy public protest meeting with national television coverage. A letter from the wife of a soldier in Germany, published in the *Jewish Advocate,* summarized the bitter feeling engendered by the episode among some devout Christians: "My husband is serving in the United States Army now in Germany and I wonder what for. I had thought for God and Country. You have no idea how much things like this help the Communists."[32] Sharon's school superintendent resigned early in 1963, ostensibly for purely personal reasons.

The bitterness involved in such disputes will continue to plague many other school officials for a long time. The controversy has spread clear across the country, and in some localities it has involved rightist political undertones. In general, both Protestant and Catholic leaders tend to oppose the Jewish position, particularly on celebrations limited to Christmas trees and the singing of carols. Christmas, they contend, is a national holiday of good will and it is too much to ask Christian parents and children to abandon the celebration of such a holiday in public schools. On Christmas Eve, 1962, the *Wall Street Journal* said in a bitter satirical editorial article inspired by the incidents in Sharon, Massachusetts:

> What is this nonsense about closing down the state-supported public schools for ten days, letting teachers waste their time and youth escape the rigors of education? By what Constitutional justification, may we ask, does the President of the United States tolerate the wreaths of holly in Government offices and excuse employees from showing up promptly at 8:30 on Christmas morn? ... In fact, how can we have Christmas as a national holiday at all?[33]

When twenty-eight residents of Ossining, New York, went to court in 1958 to force the removal of a Nativity Crèche from a local high school lawn, they were defeated by a lower court ruling which held that the influence of religious symbolism during the Christmas season was inescapable, and that friendly gestures between church and state at the Christmas season were quite permissible.

In the present American mood this policy is likely to prevail in most parts of the United States for a long time. A "compromise" solution has been suggested, the celebration in the public schools of both Christmas and the Jewish Hanukkah at about the same time. Such a compromise is not acceptable to Jewish parents because, as the American Jewish Committee has phrased it, "Hanukkah is not central to Judaism; indeed Jewish children are not required to absent themselves from school on this holiday."[34] Moreover, Jews who believe sincerely in the separation of church and state do not wish to add a Jewish violation to a Christian violation in order to save face.

The question of whether costumed nuns should be allowed to teach in public schools is another of those puzzling moral issues that has been left hanging in the middle of local jurisprudence. The Supreme Court has never even discussed the problem. Libertarians have recognized that no Catholic should be barred from public school teaching simply because he is a Catholic. But what about an elaborate sectarian costume? The American Civil Liberties Union has taken the position that the mere wearing of a religious costume should not in itself bar anybody.

The trouble with this purist formula, which is quite correct in the abstract, is that a nun's costume never occurs *in vacuo*. It is almost always part of a process of the take-over of a public school by a religious order, with the resulting operation of the school under a Mother Superior or other official of the order in cooperation with a Catholic-dominated school board in a predominantly Catholic town. Anyone who studies the teacher directories of those states which now permit the employment of teaching nuns—perhaps 20 states and about 2,000 nuns—will see that nuns teach in public schools in groups, not individually, and that they virtually never appear as teachers except in situations in which a sister is actual director of the school.[35] The familiar legend is repeated again and again in state catalogues and directories: Smithtown School, Sr. Mary Joseph, Principal; Sr. Catherine Esther; Sr. Mary Matthew; Helen Broderick; Josephine Clark; John Billings. Probably the three last names are the names of lay teachers of music, art and physical education who come into the school an hour or two a week. The school is described as having an equal number of "lay" and religious teachers, although 95 per cent of the teaching is done by the nuns of the "mother" religious order, and all the regular teachers are recruited from the order.

This technique of sectarian take-over of a public school is the real problem involved in the employment of nun teachers. It occurs usually in small towns in the Middle West, and sometimes in the Southwest. It is most common in such states as Kansas, Indiana, Ohio, Kentucky and Colorado; and it has occurred in New Mexico, Wisconsin and Missouri. In Kansas alone there are more than 50 "public" schools staffed primarily by nuns. In almost all cases some auxiliary sectarian features can be discovered in the educational activities in such schools—catechism classes, religious statues, Catholic tracts, and the marshalling of the pupils each morning across the church yard to the adjoining Catholic church for Mass—but these overt and illegal features are usually suspended when a lawsuit is threatened by indignant non-Catholic parents.

Occasionally the non-Catholic parents give up and permit two school systems to exist in a town side by side, one Catholic and one public, both supported out of the public treasury. This is the picture in two Middle Western towns I have studied: Jasper, Indiana and Hays, Kansas. More often the small town with the "captive" school and nun teachers becomes a one-school town, and Protestant and Jewish parents move out. Occasionally a whole group of "captive" schools and their teaching nuns are forced to move off the public payroll and return to the Catholic payroll as parochial schools. In a long and dramatic controversy in Wisconsin in the 1950's the state authorities eliminated tax appropriations for fourteen captive schools in which the nun teachers had been using sectarian textbooks and other sectarian devices.[36]

Frequently these nun-directed schools are listed simultaneously in the public school directories as public schools and in the *National Catholic Directory* as parochial schools. In Hays, Kansas, for example, the two Catholic schools which have been ironed into the public treasury are listed in the public school directory as "Jefferson West" and "Jefferson East" while their real names, carved in stone on the outside, are "St. Joseph's School" and "Immaculate Heart of Mary School." A non-geographical system of pupil placement has been worked out for these two "Catholic public" schools, permitting Catholic children in any part of the city to be assigned to them, whereas Protestant and Jewish children are assigned to the nearest genuinely public school.[37]

The most famous captive schools in America existed in the 1940's in and around Dixon, New Mexico. In barring the nuns from further teaching in public schools, the Supreme Court of

New Mexico found that "there is no separation between the Roman Catholic Church and the State of New Mexico" in some twenty-five schools, all taught by nuns in distinctive garb. The school buses arrived at 8:30, and Catholic religion was taught until 9. Contracts were made with the Mother Superior of a religious order to hire nuns from that order for not less than five years. Non-Catholic children in bad weather had no place to go and "were of necessity required to attend [Catholic] religious instruction." "In short," said the New Mexico Supreme Court, "New Mexico had a Roman Catholic school system supported by public funds within its public school system." Concerning the costumes of the nuns, the court said: "Not only does the wearing of religious garb and insignia have a propagandizing effect for the church, but by its very nature it introduced sectarian religion into the school."[38]

One Missouri lower court went even farther in condemning the practices of nun teachers in public schools. It declared that the nuns

... by the very nature of the obligations of their oaths of obedience ... place themselves beyond the control of civil authorities (except where agreeable to their superiors) ... that said nuns and each of them by their oaths cease to exist as free citizens ... the Court finds that, regardless of the garb which said nuns may wear, that the sisters of the highly esteemed, benevolent and charitable religious orders may not lawfully be employed as teachers in any free public schools.[39]

Much of the reasoning of those state judges who oppose the employment of nuns in public schools goes back to a dissenting opinion in an old (1894) Pennsylvania case, where the dissenting judge pointed out that it was not their religion which should disqualify teaching nuns but the accompaniments of their religion. He said:

It is the introduction into the schools, as teachers, of persons

who are, by their striking and distinctive ecclesiastical robes, necessarily and constantly asserting their membership in a particular
church, and in a religious order within that church.... No
priest or bishop in full canonical dress more plainly declares his
church....

With faces averted from the world they have renounced;
wearing their peculiar robes, which tell of their church, their order
and their subordination to the guidance of their ecclesiastical
superiors; using their religious names, and addressed by the des-
ignated "sister" ... They cannot, or they will not, attend teachers'
institutes.... They do not attend public examinations.... If in
some neighboring borough the several departments of the public
school should be filled by Episcopal clergymen as teachers, who
should appear only in their canonical robes, and with their prayer
books suspended from their necks, and if Catholic parents of
children entitled to admission into the school should appeal to the
courts for relief for their children from the presence and influence
of ecclesiastics who insisted upon keeping the name of their church,
and their relation to it, before the minds of their pupils, I should
no more doubt their right to such relief than I can doubt the right
of the plaintiffs in this case.[40]

The recent drift of court decisions at the state level, however,
has been much less severe than this dissenting comment in the old
Pennsylvania case. Today, although teaching in religious garb is
outlawed in New York, Oregon, Iowa and Nebraska, and most of
the states have no nuns teaching in public schools, the judicial
tendency is toward a permissive attitude toward costumes and a
simultaneously strict prohibition against religious instruction by
such costumed nuns. Such split-level judicial attitudes put the
burden of proof on non-Catholic parents to prove that the local
public schools are being used unconstitutionally when they are
operated by costumed nuns. Usually in a small and overwhelmingly Catholic community it is virtually impossible to get such proof
and to oust those nuns who have overstepped the wall of separation
between church and state. It should be remembered that the
Catholic Church itself does not consider sectarian teaching in a
public classroom either morally wrong or constitutionally illegal,

and its tacit approval of current procedure fortifies both the nuns and local Catholic officials.

Beyond these big little issues lie a number of very important issues which can be considered either as auxiliary problems or as partial steps toward a solution of the religion-and-education controversy. Let us turn to them now.

CHAPTER 8

Truth and Consequences

In a sense there are no solutions to these fundamental church-state controversies. As long as men hold fast with deep conviction to their ideas of God, prayer, the scriptures and the church, they will disagree about the relationship of the state to those concepts and the part to be played by public and private schools as instructors of religion. This is no reproach to religion but a proof of its vitality. Men do not bother to quarrel about the things they consider unimportant. As long as religion endures and is considered vital by men, some continuing controversy about its relation to the schools is as certain as the rising and the setting of the sun.

In a pluralistic society, however, there must be a *modus vivendi* for church and state in the schools, a mechanism for accommodation and compromise enabling men to reduce controversy to a minimum and to get on with the business of education in reasonable peace. What are the prospects for accommodation and compromise in the areas we have discussed? What are the solutions and semi-solutions and false solutions which confront those who honestly seek a rational separation of church and state with the full maintenance of religious freedom?

The Threat of Constitutional Amendment

The least acceptable "solution" for the whole controversy is a constitutional amendment overruling the Supreme Court and altering the basic national policy of church-state separation in education. If the terms of such an amendment were sufficiently drastic, they might take America back more than a century to the period when our new public schools were fighting for life against sectarian encroachments.

When forty-nine legislative proposals designed to amend the Constitution were introduced in Congress within a few weeks after the Regents' prayer decision in the summer of 1962, it seemed for a time that a mass movement was under way to change the national tradition. The brief Senate hearings on these amendments were engineered in such a way by Senator James O. Eastland of Mississippi as to give the appearance of an overwhelming movement against the Supreme Court in favor of amending the Constitution. No compensatory hearings were held in the House. At the beginning of the Eighty-eighth Congress in 1963, the flood of proposed amendments continued, and it was increased after the Bible-reading decision in June, 1963.

There can be no doubt that there is a movement today to amend the Constitution, and it must be taken seriously, but it has less than an even chance of success for many special reasons. The forces supporting proposed amendments are badly divided. The mechanism of amending the Constitution is so difficult and cumbersome that it discourages advocates of change. Finally, neither the chief leaders of American Catholicism nor of Protestantism seem prepared to wage an all-out battle for an amendment of the Constitution. The statement by the National Council of Churches of June 7, 1963, already summarized, puts that Protestant organization on record at least by inference as supporting the Constitution interpreted by the Supreme Court. The Council would be particularly opposed to any amendment of the Constitution which might shift American policy in the direction of financial aid to parochial schools. Although Cardinals Spellman, Cushing and McIntyre launched their bitter attack on the Supreme Court's Bible-reading decision in June, 1963, the Jesuits, who are the shrewdest political tacticians of Catholicism, do not agree with them.

The Jesuit magazine *America*, shortly before the Bible-reading decision, came out with a warning against any movement

for amendment which might grow out of the passions of adverse
feeling, declaring that "for all practical purposes, the First Amend
ment's religion clauses ought to be regarded as unamendable."
The editors reminded their readers that Catholics have often been
accused of paying "only lip service to the separation of Church and
State," and argued: "In the atmosphere of suspicion that still sur
rounds us, we should gain little and lose much by identifying our
selves with an effort to change the text of the First Amendment
however good our motives or sound our interpretation of religious
liberty."[1]

An old, and now rather decrepit, movement to amend the
Constitution in the direction of official recognition of Christianity
has been going on since 1946. Its goal is called the Christian
Amendment and its headquarters are in Pittsburgh. Although this
Christian Amendment does not mention education as such, it
would recognize "the authority and law of Jesus Christ" as su
preme in the nation and its adoption would undoubtedly be used
as a justification for religious teaching in public schools. It has
been introduced in Congress no less than forty times, and in 1954,
before its full implications were apparent, it was actually approved
by the Senate Judiciary Committee. In 1961 it was reintroduced by
nine Congressmen,[2] but at the present time it has no considerable
support even in the churches. In 1959 it was voted down fifty nine
to one as "pretension" by the General Board of the National
Council of Churches.

Of the forty-nine sample suggestions for constitutional
amendments proposed in the flurry of opposition to the Regents
prayer decision in 1962, the types which seem to have the best
chance of success are those which confine themselves to permissive
prayer and Bible-reading. The governor's resolution of July 1962
calling for a pro-prayer constitutional amendment, confined its
appeal to voluntary prayer. The 1962 national convention of the
American Legion similarly called for a constitutional amendment
permitting voluntary spoken prayer, and many of the resolutions
introduced into Congress restricted their demands to this one item.

In the Eighty-seventh Congress Senators Eastland, Johnston, McClellan and Talmadge combined to support a proposed amendment which would have sanctioned "prayers or the reading of the Bible as part of the program of any public school or other public place in the United States." For good measure, they threw in a provision giving each state the unimpeded right to determine "its own public policy on questions of decency and morality." This legislative combination represented Southern reaction both to the Regents' prayer decision and to another decision handed down on the same "awful day" in 1962 permitting three magazines with a homosexual slant to continue publication. In the Eighty-eighth Congress the coalition of senators mentioned in Chapter 5, headed by Senator Williams of Delaware, presented a proposed amendment which contained a modified form of the Eastland idea without the provisions concerning indecent literature. It confined itself to schools, and read:

> Nothing contained in this Constitution shall be construed to prohibit the authority administering any school, school system, or educational institution supported in whole or in part from any public funds from providing for the participation by the students thereof in any periods of Bible reading or nonsectarian prayer if such participation is voluntary.[3]

Far more dangerous from the point of view of believers in church-state separation is the amendment proposed by a distinguished religious liberal, Episcopal Bishop James A. Pike of California, who is both a lawyer and a clergyman. Pike almost monopolized the headlines resulting from the 1962 Senate hearings on prayer amendments. He took the position that the First Amendment was never intended to do more than banish preference for a single state church, that the Supreme Court had been wrong for years in its decisions in the McCollum and other cases, and that Congress and the states should correct the Court by re-writing the First Amendment to bring it back to its "original" meaning. His proposed new wording read: "Congress shall make no law respect-

ing the recognition as an established church of any denominatio
sect or organized religious association."⁴ Bishop Pike's reasonir
was strikingly similar to that of Justice Reed in his dissent in tl
McCollum case. Reed had argued that the Establishment Claus
"may have been intended by Congress to be aimed only at a stat
church" and that its prohibition might be restricted to "purposefu
assistance directly to the church itself or to some religious group c
organization doing religious work of such a character that it ma
fairly be said to be performing ecclesiastical functions."

The legal arguments against the conceptions of Bishop Pik
and Justice Reed have already been summarized in previous chaj
ters. Reed was voted down eight to one. The Court has repeatedl
taken the position that multiple establishments of religion by man
sects, either within or outside the public schools, do not lose thei
illegal character merely by proliferation. It has recognized that
church school may unlawfully establish religion as explicitly as
church by building religion into the curriculum. Bishop Pike'
proposed amendment would open the public schools to outrigh
religious propaganda by various sects so long as the state did no
recognize any particular church as preferred.

It is probable also that the Pike amendment, if added to th
Constitution, would be used to support the contention that finan
cial aid could be given to all religious schools on a non-preferentia
basis. Bishop Pike is not personally in favor of such a program, bu
his proposal would seem to invite a general, non-preferential fed
eral aid bill preceded by a self-righteous disclaimer denying an
intent to recognize or establish any single church or denomination
Pike's suggestion was hailed with great enthusiasm by one sectior
of the Catholic press, and Father John P. Leary, S.J., president o
Gonzaga University, supplemented it with more specific wording
"The saying of commonly accepted prayers in public schools anc
government assemblies or the indirect assistance to religiou:
groups who serve the commonwealth in areas of specifically tem
poral concern shall in no way be considered a breach of the Firs
Amendment."⁵

What are the chances that a campaign for the Pike amendment might succeed? No prophet can answer the question confidently. Any campaign for such an amendment would be extremely bitter, and it would divide America along religious lines as it has never been divided before. Probably it would end in defeat. The American people enjoy hurling occasional brickbats at a Supreme Court decision but they also have enormous respect for the Court's authority in the American scheme of government. They would be very reluctant to reverse a Supreme Court finding under religious pressure.

More important, the machinery of constitutional change is so cumbersome that many citizens—including all those politicians who wish to avoid religious controversy—would hesitate to embark on the long weary road to amendment. It is true that Article V of the Constitution provides a clumsy mechanism for amendment which might partially bypass Congress. But ordinarily two-thirds of both Houses would have to agree on one version of any proposed amendment and, finally, three-fourths of all the state legislatures would have to ratify it. It should be remembered that it took nineteen years to secure an income-tax amendment to the Constitution after the Supreme Court outlawed the income tax act of 1894, and no religious animosities were involved in that struggle.

Four Middle Ways

Bishop Pike called his plan for drastic overhauling of the First Amendment a "middle way." Its adoption would, in fact, involve a reversal of constitutional policy, and it should be considered an extremist remedy, although the good bishop himself is by no means an extremist.

There are, however, several intermediate and compromise adjustments between church and state in education which deserve to be defined as middle ways. They constitute attempts to give some incidental status to religion in public schools or some indirect financial help to church schools without violating the Supreme Court's interpretation of the First Amendment. They are released time, dismissed time, shared time and moral guidance without religious indoctrination. All of these different formulas are being tried in various parts of the United States today, and all of them may be considered legal within the limits of the federal Constitution if they are carefully administered in good faith under state statutes. Probably they should not be considered as solutions for the religion-and-schools controversy so much as halting and experimental attempts to arrive at some kind of compromise between the strict separationists and the advocates of religious indoctrination.

Before listing these four compromise adjustments, it should be pointed out that another remedy is frequently advocated as a compromise in this controversy, the plan for teaching *about* religion in public schools without any attempt to use such teaching for purposes of indoctrination. Actually there has never been any widespread objection to some teaching *about* religion in public schools if such teaching could be fitted into the curriculum as part of a scholarly review of other cultural features in man's environment. The Bible as literature and religion as history are acceptable and suitable parts of common education. Justice Tom Clark, speaking for the Court in the 1963 Bible-reading decision, made this perfectly clear when he said:

It certainly may be said that the Bible is worthy of study for its literary and historic qualities. Nothing we have said here indicates that such study of the Bible or of religion, when presented objectively as part of a secular program of education, may not be effected consistent with the First Amendment.

The trouble with the suggestion that teaching *about* religion is an acceptable remedy for religious controversy is that America does not have teachers trained to teach about religion in an impartial way, and if they achieved the difficult goal of impartiality in a public classroom, the advocates of partisan faith would descend upon them like hungry wolves. They would be condemned for failure to give due reverence to cherished orthodoxies. The last thing in the world that the average advocate of orthodox religion wants in the public schools is a candid, comparative analysis of various faiths without preference or advocacy. He would consider any mildly derogatory statement about his own creed and church wholly unacceptable in a public school.

At the present time there are probably only two classes of teachers competent to teach an impartial class *about* religion in American public schools, the professional university teachers of comparative religion, who are not ordinarily available for elementary schools, and the teachers of the Ethical Culture schools, whose deviations from orthodoxy would be considered quite unacceptable to theological conservatives. Robert W. Lynn, in a 1962 article in *Christianity and Crisis*, favored the concept of education about religion in the public schools but conceded that: "It would require unusual scholarly competence, better teacher training and an unprecedented degree of interfaith cooperation in the local community." He cited the illustration of a Midwestern city in the middle 1950s where the Roman Catholic, Jewish and Protestant clergymen tried to draw up a syllabus for teaching about religion in their public schools. What would they say about Martin Luther? "Beyond the simplest biographical data," says Dr. Lynn, "they were able to agree only upon the supposed fact that Brother Martin was the father of the modern public school!"[6]

The following four "middle ways" deserve four separate chapters because of their importance, but they must be condensed thus:

1. *Released time.* Released-time classes *away from* public school buildings—that is the only kind now legal in the United States—go back to Gary, Indiana in 1913. They have been constitutional under the First Amendment since the Supreme Court gave them clearance in 1952 by a vote of six to three. In those states where some legal provision has been made for them, now forty-eight of the fifty states, the majority of students and school officials do not avail themselves of the opportunities provided by the sys-

tem. Recent estimates indicate that only about 30 per cent of the public school systems in the United States use released time, and within these systems a very large proportion of the students never go near the released-time classes.[7]

The usual released-time practice, optional with local school boards, is to excuse all pupils whose parents request it for one hour a week at the end of one school day, permitting those pupils who elect it to go to a separate building to be taught religion by a teacher of their own faith who is paid, if at all, by a religious denomination or council of churches and not by the taxpayers. The public school receives a record of the attendance of each pupil at each religious class and assumes responsibility for supervising the pupils who have been left behind in the public classroom.

This released-time system is favored officially by the chief organizations of American Protestantism and Catholicism. The National Council of Churches has established a separate Department of Weekday Religious Education to promote and extend it, while the Roman Catholic Church, the chief beneficiary of the system in many large cities, is definitely enthusiastic about the plan as a second-choice substitute for attendance at its own schools. The system, however, has encountered widespread opposition in some Protestant circles, in the Jewish community and among Unitarians and religious liberals in general. School officials regard it as a cultural and administrative nightmare.

Several cities have recently abandoned the plan after years of experimentation with it partly because of the very limited use of the system and partly because it tends to disrupt school procedure and leave the stay-in-school pupils little constructive work to do while their confreres are attending religious classes. Many school officials also consider the separate classification of pupils by religion, even for only one hour a week, unfortunately divisive. According to Professor Dierenfield's study, more than twice as many public school officials oppose the scheme as favor it, and more than one-fourth of them regard it as "a waste of time."[8] It can scarcely be called an overwhelming success when less than 7 per cent of American public school pupils make use of it.

Nevertheless, with all its faults, the released-time plan may be considered a safety valve in the present explosive situation. It may not be pedagogically sound or socially desirable—which is the view of this writer—but it does provide some answer to those critics of the public school who claim that the system is godless. God is available at least one hour a week outside of public school buildings under authentic devotional auspices if local laws permit. If the churches do not accept the challenge and opportunity, they have only themselves to blame. Since 1912, the Mormons in Utah and adjoining states have demonstrated that one form of the system can be made into a very effective adjunct of public high school education. They have constructed part-time seminaries adjoining public high schools for released-time or dismissed-time classes—depending upon the permissiveness of local laws.[9] The 425 Mormon part-time seminaries, staffed by trained religious teachers of their own, usually teach religion one hour a day. There is nothing to prevent other American religious groups from adopting the same pattern as a substitute for a separate parochial system.

2. *Dismissed time.* This is often confused with released time, but the two phenomena are different because dismissed time involves no formal cooperation with government beyond the agreement to dismiss the whole public school at a certain time, leaving attendance at religious classes entirely unpoliced and optional. The dismissed-time concept, which originally developed in France with a whole day of dismissed time each week, is usually carried out by public schools in the United States by the shortening of one day in the week by one hour.

Even strict advocates of the separation of church and state in education usually have no objection to dismissed time; in fact, they regard it as the only surely constitutional formula for off-premises, week-day religious training. It meets the constitutional objections of the three justices who protested so strenuously against released time in the 1952 Zorach case on the ground that, as Justice Jackson put it in his dissent: "This released time program is founded upon a use of the State's power of coercion . . . the public school serves as a temporary jail for a pupil who will not go to church." Justice Frankfurter added in his dissent:

The deeply devisive controversy aroused by the attempts to secure public school pupils for sectarian instruction would promptly end if the advocates of such instruction were content to have the school "close its doors or suspend operation"—that is dismiss classes in their entirety, without discrimination—instead of seeking to use the public schools as the instrument for security of attendance at denominational classes.

3. *Shared time.* This is now the white-haired boy of all suggestions to "settle" religion-and-schools controversies. It has received tremendous and rather undiscriminating publicity in American journals during the past two years. Essentially it is a compromise formula designed to break the Washington deadlock over federal aid to education, conferring an indirect benefit on Catholic parochial schools by inviting their students to come to the public schools for some non-religious studies. The assumption behind the formula is that Catholic leaders who oppose federal aid may be mollified if "we give them something for their schools" in this indirect way.

The scheme, as usually advanced, is designed to give Catholic pupils special training in public schools in such subjects as science, languages and industrial arts, leaving other subjects to parochial classrooms. The concept has been enthusiastically received in the Catholic press, and has also won the endorsement of many leading Protestants. Early in 1963 the National Catholic Education Association estimated that shared-time arrangements would be permissible under the statutes of 21 states, illegal in 10 states, and of uncertain status in 4 more.[10]

The shared-time concept is not new; it has been in operation in some states for more than 45 years although it has not excited much public attention until recently. This is partly because it has been rather strictly limited to a few hours a week, usually bunched in one afternoon, and confined to such occasional subjects as cooking and shop work. Hartford, Connecticut, for example, has been receiving nearly 1,000 pupils from the eighth and ninth grades of parochial schools for a two-hour period once a week for instruction in home economics and industrial arts at a current estimated cost of about $2,000 in tax funds.[11] The most widely advertised plan for extending the concept is that in operation near Pittsburgh where eleventh-grade pupils at St. Thomas high school in Braddock spend their mornings in the Catholic school and do some afternoon work at the Forbes Trail Technical school—a public institution—in Monroeville.

The plan has some advantages in those cities where it would be mechanically feasible. It would bring into the public schools on a part-time basis many students who are now culturally isolated in a narrowly dogmatic atmosphere. (That is one reason, perhaps, why many Catholic educators are suspicious of it, since their Canon Law calls for sectarian isolation.) Probably this community sharing would be a good thing for interfaith relationships. It would undoubtedly ease the financial burden of Catholic parents. The *Washington Post* has rightly said that "it deserves careful and sympathetic study as a possible way out of the religious controversy that has blocked federal aid to public schools."[12]

At the present time, unfortunately, the idea of shared time is being over-sold as a general solution to the whole religion-and-schools controversy. At best it would only modify the tense situation provisionally and conditionally. There is no indication that its adoption would halt the Catholic drive for more complete federal aid for a separate parochial system. On the contrary, the concession to Catholic demands would undoubtedly be used as additional "confirmation" of the justice of the claim that Catholic schools are full "partners" in the American educational enterprise, and so entitled to the same financial consideration as public schools.

The administrative problems involved in adjusting public school and parochial school schedules would be truly herculean. One official of the National Education Association described the plan in 1963 as "a can of worms." The squirming difficulties are obvious. Would the arrival in a public school of 100 extra Catholic students to study French involve the hiring of a number of extra teachers? Of extra rooms? What if the Catholic students insisted that the only free time for French in their schedule was late afternoon? What would the Catholic bishop say—and the public superintendent do—if one of the French teachers in the public school happened to be entirely competent but anti-clerical? If the biology teacher honestly favored the concept of evolution and said so? If the science teacher hinted that the menace of over-population had a scientific solution in birth control? Perhaps the most searching question of all is tangential: If shared time is simply a bona fide plan for helping parochial schools solve their financial problems while preserving their religious values, why should not Catholic authorities be content with an extended released- or dismissed-time arrangement, similar to the Mormon arrangement in Utah, giving their pupils more thorough religious instruction than is now given but permitting them to enroll for all other subjects in the public schools?

Such questions inevitably raise the issue of the constitutionality of the shared-time plan. At first blush the concept seems perfectly acceptable under the federal Constitution if the parochial school students fully assent to the discipline and schedules of public school officials. (Some state constitutions and statutes exclude the concept.) There is nothing specific in the First Amendment or in the Supreme Court cases about that amendment to exclude the idea of attendence of parochial students at public schools on a part-time basis. They are American children, entitled under the law to enroll free at any public school. The real questions concerning constitutionality arise when the details of administration and practice are considered.

Would it be possible to administer a cooperative arrangement of this sort without commingling secular and sectarian affairs in a way forbidden by the Court? In practice would not sectarian school officials be given some veto power over public school arrangements? Would not the final result be that "aid to religion" by indirection which the Court has forbidden in other manifestations? Certainly the Catholic Church would be a great financial gainer from the whole arrangement, and the American taxpayer would foot the extra bill. The Court might declare the arrangement unconstitutional under the theory championed by Justice Frankfurter in his concurring opinion in the McCollum case that there is a "requirement to abstain from fusing functions of Government and of religious sects."

For the time being all one can say about such questions is that their answer depends largely on how shared time is administered. It offers some hope of satisfactory adjustments on the frontier of church and state in some communities. Simultaneously it raises administrative and constitutional difficulties which might in the end make the adjustments between church and state in education more unmanageable than ever.

4. *Moral guidance without religious indoctrination.* This remedy has been tried in many cities with the help of officially published handbooks, textbooks and teaching aids devoted to "Moral and Spiritual Values." In the opinion of their administrators, more than 99 per cent of American public schools teach some moral values, more or less formally, and there is no substantial opposition from local communities.[13] The rub comes when "moral" becomes "spiritual." Even the most distinguished philosophers and theologians cannot agree on the line of demarcation between those two entities. Great public controversies over the proper distinction between moral teaching and religious faith in the public schools have broken out all the way from New York City to San Diego.

When an Educational Policies Commission sponsored jointly by the National Education Association and the American Association of School Administrators put out a nine-point program in 1951 called "Moral and Spiritual Values in the Public Schools," its one mildly affirmative reference to religion: "Teaching about religion as an important fact in our culture," provoked immediate questioning.[14] When the Board of Superintendents of New York

City in June 1955 called on the public schools to "reinforce the program of the home and the church in strengthening belief in God," the opposition from the Jewish community and from religious liberals was virtually unanimous. Said the New York Teachers Guild: "It would introduce religious controversy into the schools in such a way as to be divisive and to excite old animosities and prejudices. . . . It is the function of the public schools to foster critical thinking. It is the prerogative of the home and the church to inculcate faith." The New York Board of Superintendents quickly retreated, and the next policy statement on schools and moral teaching omitted all reference to God.

Although strictly non-theological moral training is legally acceptable in public schools, the results of the moral guidance formula in practice seem to indicate that it is not an answer to the religion-and-schools controversy but only one form of introducing the controversy. After moral guidance has been adopted as a formula, the most difficult question still remains: What is the logical dividing line between permissible moral values and the unconstitutional promotion of religion?

Moral guidance in public schools without religious indoctrination is being assailed almost as vigorously by religious conservatives as religious indoctrination is being questioned by religious liberals. The liberals want all indoctrination excluded; many orthodox leaders, both Protestant and Catholic, assert that true moral guidance without religion is impossible. The Catholic bishops of the United States in their statement on secularism in 1952 said:

> To teach moral and spiritual values divorced from religion and based solely on social convention, as these men [secularists] claim to do, is not enough. Unless man's conscience is enlightened by the knowledge of principles that express God's law, there can be no firm and lasting morality. . . . Without religious education, moral education is impossible.[15]

About the same time Jerome Nathanson, a leader of the Ethical Culture Society, summed up the opposing argument about religion and moral guidance. Scoring the theology "which denies that man is adequate to the tasks confronting him" and protesting against "the menacing inroads which organized religion is trying to make on our public-school system," he said: "We have only to look around us, to say nothing of examining the historical record, to learn that there is absolutely no necessary relation between organized religion and morality."[16]

Controversy and Truth

The sentence used by the Teacher's Guild in its attack on the New York City Board of Superintendents raises the most fundamental issue in the whole controversy: "It is the function of the public schools to foster critical thinking." If this thesis is sound, then religion cannot be introduced into American public schools without facing critical analysis, and if the analysis results in judgments hostile to orthodox beliefs, the result may be utterly unacceptable to a large part of the population. In any case, if American public school teachers are true to their moral obligation to present life as it is to their students, they cannot avoid the great controversies involving the truth of religious documents and religious claims. Thus far they have been able to avoid such controversies in most school systems by using the ignoble, ostrich-like device of "no comment" when the Bible is read in public classrooms or when any controversial religious question comes up for classroom discussion. Their enforced silence in the whole area of religion is not only contrary to all the highest principles of good pedagogy but it is also a continuing affront to their freedom of speech.

As far as the federal government is concerned, the question of the use of the Bible in religious exercises in public schools was legally settled when Justice Tom Clark, on June 17, 1963, read the Court's decision in the Schempp-Murray case outlawing such use. But the intellectual and moral issues still remain in American life, and unless they are met squarely the public may ultimately be persuaded to reverse the Court by a constitutional amendment or nullify the Court's prohibition by local disobedience. The issues involve truth in teaching and the integrity of that "critical thinking" which the Teacher's Guild championed.

If religion is to be taught in public schools through the Bible —and it would be unrealistic to act on any other assumption—two controversies about Christian truth and faith cannot be avoided. One is very minor, the differing claims of Protestants and Catholics over the true versions of the Christian scriptures. The other is a major issue in our culture, the clash between literal and conditional acceptance of the historical content of the Bible. On each of these fronts, if Christianity insists on bringing its teaching into public classrooms, a confrontation with modern scholarship seems inevitable.

The conflict over Catholic and Protestant versions of the Bible is so trivial that it is hard for most men of the present day to remember that only a few centuries ago both Catholics and Protestants were burned at the stake for espousing the "wrong" version. And it is hard to remember also that the great Philadelphia riots of 1844 centered on this issue. Today the climate of denominational biblical discussion in the United States is equable, and quarrels over biblical versions seem to most people rather silly. There is some talk of a "common Bible" acceptable to both Protestants and Catholics. It is true that the Catholic Douay version has 72 books, while the Protestant King James version has only 66. Protestants have demoted to the lower level of the Apocrypha several books that Catholics have accepted into the canon of the Old Testament; the Catholic and Protestant versions of the New Testament are almost the same.[17] The revised Protestant Bibles are probably more accurate than the early Catholic Bibles, but there is little difference in accuracy and, by strict scholarly standards, there are many inaccuracies in both versions. If it were legal, the reading of the Bible in public schools could easily be confined to passages acceptable to both Catholics and Protestants.

One obstacle to Protestant-Catholic agreements in biblical controversies is that the rule of the Catholic Church in its Canon Law against Protestant Bibles is abruptly arbitrary. According to Canon 1399 no Catholic may possess, read, sell or give away a non-Catholic version of the Bible without special priestly permission.[18] This law was issued in 1918 and its drastic character has been re-emphasized several times since then by the Popes.

Although American Protestants do not denounce as sinful the reading of Catholic Bibles, they are distinctly partial to Protestant biblical sources, often without being aware of it. They serenely take for granted the pre-eminence of the King James version in those public schools where Bible-reading has been practiced. They are rarely conscious that the King James version, in both Old Testament and New Testament, contains passages which are anti-Semitic or heavily weighted in favor of Christian prophecy. There was a slightly startled look on the faces of some Protestant spectators in the Supreme Court in February, 1963 when one justice brought out the fact that the ascription to King James in the front of the King James Bible is distinctly anti-Catholic, expressing the opinion of the translators that "we shall be traduced by Popish persons at home or abroad, who therefore will malign us," and charging that these persons desire to keep the people "in ignorance and darkness."

The way out of the senseless controversy over Protestant and Catholic versions of the Bible may come through the Second Vatican Council which, under the genial leadership of the late Pope John XXIII, instituted in 1962 several gestures of amity toward "the separated brethren" and at the same time gave the Bible very great prominence as the basic document of faith for all Christians. There is hope that Pope Paul VI will continue the trend toward reasonable adjustments.

But in our present pluralistic society it would be idle to describe any Catholic-Protestant agreement on a common Bible as a "way out" of any religion-and-schools controversy. There is something much more serious on the dialectical horizon than the ancient and rather petty quarrel between Catholics and Protestants over their respective versions. It is the controversy over the actual truth or falsehood of the contents of the Bible.

To begin with, this controversy involves, in any use of *any* Christian Bible, very serious discrimination against Jewish parents and children. The Bible as a whole, as the testimony in the Schempp case revealed, could never be acceptable to devout Jews since it includes the New Testament, and the New Testament abounds in disparaging comments about Jewish religious leaders and in Christian doctrinal assertions which are wholly unacceptable to those of the Jewish faith.

Some states have recognized the Jewish-Christian difficulties in the use of the Bible. The State of Maine has tried to soften the impact involved in New Testament readings by adding to its *Suggested Bible Readings for Maine Public Schools* a few passages from talmudic literature, totalling about three pages. But the state's approved list of readings from the New Testament includes the entire range of sectarian Christian history from the magical features surrounding the birth of Jesus through the miracles of Jesus to the crucifixion, the resurrection and the ascension. It is not surprising that in 1958 the Jewish members of the Maine State Board of Character Education and Bible Study declined to join their Protestant and Catholic associates in endorsing the list of New Testament readings.[19]

Equally serious ideological controversies between Christian Bible conservatives and Christian theological liberals are involved in the use of the Bible in public classrooms. The Bible literalists are well represented by such Protestant leaders as Billy Graham, who declared in 1963 at a Texas Baptist Conference: "If the Bible says that Jonah swallowed the whale, let's accept it and believe it; or, if the Bible says that two plus two is five, let's believe it. Brethren, let's get on with the job of proclaiming the Gospel."[20]

It is impossible to say what proportion of American Christians today accept so literal a point of view in regard to the Bible but it is certain that they number several millions. Probably most of the Protestants affiliated with the National Council of Churches would not go so far in across-the-board acceptance. The Protestant groups affiliated directly or indirectly with the National Association of Evangelicals, claiming several million Americans, are committed substantially to the Billy Graham view. They list as the No. 1 item in their statement of faith: "We believe the Bible to be the inspired, the only infallible, authoritative word of God."[21] They condemn to "the resurrection of damnation" all those who "do not accept the Bible as God's word." Most American Protestant groups tend to accept the Bible as vital for salvation but not infallible.

At the present time few public school teachers are caught in the controversy between the Bible literalists and the Bible liberals because their policy has been, essentially, to surrender to the literalists. That is to say, the teachers, by reading all passages from the Bible, good or bad, with equal solemnity and reverence, have imparted to their pupils the impression that all the biblical material used is literally true. This impression has been fostered by the practice of omitting from schoolreading lists those passages in the Bible that are most violent, most immoral or most obscene. But the reading lists always contain many passages that are considered unscientific by the liberals.

Both literalists and liberals agree that the Bible is one of the world's important books, that it contains much of beauty and moral exaltation, and that children should be familiar with it as part of their education. But the literalists tend to regard the Bible as one unified book written under divine and inerrant guidance while the liberals regard it as two libraries of uneven material whose parts should not be treated as equally valuable.

Of course the criticism of the unquestioning use of the Bible as fact is not confined to left-wing theologians. Many leaders of Protestant thought hold this same view. Early in 1963 the highest ranking Episcopalian in the world—some would say that he is the non-Catholic counterpart of the Pope—Dr. Michael Ramsey, Archbishop of Canterbury, asked in a lecture at the University of London:

> Did the Biblical miracles really happen? If history matters for Christianity, the rigors of historical criticism must be faced to the full. It is important to apply historical criticism to the narratives about the miracles.
>
> When this is done, it may be found to be probable that there were some unhistorical accreditations to the narratives. It may be that some of the miracle stories can be given naturalistic explanations. It may be that the stories of demonic possession are explicable as stories of psychiatric disorder.[22]

Shortly before the Archbishop of Canterbury made this statement, two eminent British scholars, including the professor of Bible Criticism at the University of Glasgow, announced that by using a new type of electronic computer research they had reached the conclusion that only four of the fourteen epistles in the New Testament now attributed to St. Paul were actually written by him: Romans, I and II Corinthians, and Galatians.[23]

Such revelations of new information concerning the Bible have been going on for more than a century, shattering the older image of the book as a unified summary of history. The most severe criticisms have centered upon the story of creation in the first chapter of Genesis, a story which happens to be one of the most popular readings for public school children. This Genesis story, picturing God as making the world in six daily installments, with the land and the sea and the animals coming before man, and the whole process being completed some time about four centuries before the Christian era, is challenged by almost all the latest discoveries in archeology, geology and astronomy. The story is full of poetry and majestic beauty, but is it true? The liberals argue that even if the Genesis "days" are construed as epochs, the facts are hopelessly incorrect and that it profanes the integrity of the teaching profession for teachers to pass on such tales to children without comment as if they were literally true.

Science tells school children that the earth is perhaps two billion years old, that life appeared here perhaps five hundred million years ago, and that some present-day photographic plates are recording data from light beams which took off from some place in outer space two billion years ago. Science also tells the children that human beings are not descended from two progenitors who lived in any garden anywhere, and that man probably came into existence by a process of evolution from animal forms of life. It is especially inappropriate, say the liberals, to take the Pentateuch as authentic history, written by Moses, when leading Jewish scholars have reached a contrary view, rejecting what Rabbi Lewis Browne called "the historicity of the rock-splitting, Pentateuch-writing, priest-loving Moses of tradition . . . [as] quite obviously a piece of propagandist fiction concocted by the priesthood of a later day."[24]

When the liberals wish to embarrass the literalists even more, they insist that school children should be told that the Bible is not wholly a moral book, that it pictures the God of the Old Testament as a God living at a level far below that of the Geneva Convention, and that the Old Testament even contains many obscene passages, ranging from the story of Lot's incest with his own daughters to Tamar's seduction of her father-in-law. Mark Twain, speaking through Satan, has recently proclaimed posthumously in his *Letters from the Earth,* what he thought of the morality of both Moses and the Old Testament God. The gist of his favorite passage about the Israelites who obeyed God's order to destroy the Midianites is as follows—from chapter 31 of Numbers:

And they warred against the Midianites, as the Lord commanded Moses; and they slew all the males . . . took all the women of Midian captives . . . burnt all their cities . . . took all the spoil . . . they brought the captives, and the prey, and the spoil unto Moses and Eleazar the priest . . . and Moses was wroth. . . . Have ye saved all the women alive? . . . kill every male among the little ones; and kill every woman that hath known man by lying with him. But all the women-children, that have not known a man by lying with him, keep alive for yourselves.

It is not within the purpose of this book to analyze in detail the shades of rightness and wrongness in the literalist and liberal positions concerning the Bible. But it is impossible to avoid the conclusion that the cleavage between these two positions is so fundamental that it is bound to lead to bitter controversy as long as the Bible is used in public schools. In the Puritan communities of Massachusetts in the seventeenth century The Book was accepted as literally accurate in all particulars, largely because sound textual criticism had not yet developed. Today the great majority of biblical scholars, Protestant, Catholic and Jewish, whatever they may think of the validity of certain passages in the Bible, accept the analytical historical methods of Bible study which began to blossom in the middle of the nineteenth century and which have completely transformed the view of the Bible as a static and error-less work.

Meanwhile, the children who have been listening to Bible readings in American public schools have not been permitted to receive the benefit of any of this new learning. They have been receiving a flat, undiscriminating mixture of exalted poetry, general Judeo-Christian moral aspiration, incorrect history and outdated savagery in morals, all produced in a tone of reverent acceptance which creates the impression that the savage and the sacred are equally acceptable to civilized persons. To some extent they have been asked to keep one foot in the twentieth century and another foot in the never-never land of ancient superstition.

"Completely Neutral"

Justice Hugo Black, in opposing public school released-time classes in the Zorach case in 1952, used a phrase which may be aptly employed as a kind of moral epilogue to all that has been said in *Religion and the Schools*. In speaking of the purpose of the authors of the First Amendment he said: "Now as then, it is only by wholly isolating the state from the religious sphere and compelling it to be completely neutral that the freedom of each and every denomination and of all unbelievers can be maintained."

Justice Black was speaking, of course, primarily of public schools, since the procedure in public schools was the gravamen of the Zorach case. He was not asking that American life itself be isolated from religion. As his later opinions made clear, he had no intention of using the Constitution to eliminate even the most foolish manifestation of religious freedom or those peripheral religious features that have clustered around state ceremonials. He was interested primarily in dis-establishing formal religion from the vital center of America's most important institution, the public school, because he agreed with Madison and Jefferson that government power should not be commingled with institutional religious power and that free men should not be subjected to any involuntary assessment to maintain religion. Particularly, he felt that "unenthusiastic" children should not be subjected to what he described as "the pressure of this state machinery."

That Justice Black's philosophy of complete neutrality in the public schools is not necessarily one of anti-religion or secularism scarcely needs to be said. Or it should not need to be said if men would use words with accuracy and integrity. But dialectical struggles over religion rarely employ fighting words with complete accuracy. In the dictionaries a secular school is one "not under church control." A secularist, on the other hand, is a person "who rejects every form of religious faith and worship." The "complete neutrality" championed by Justice Black does not reject any form of religious faith and worship; on the contrary, it is based on the widest possible application of the greatest possible free enterprise for all religions. On its negative side it is concerned merely with the location of faith and worship within the state apparatus, supported by the power of government. Black is concerned with the total damage to personal liberty resulting from such a relationship in a pluralistic society such as ours.

Probably at least three-fourths of the angry exchanges in the religion-and-schools controversy could be eliminated if protagonists on both sides would keep in mind this clear distinction between "secular" and "secularist." The secular school—not under church control—has been for more than a century the most distinctively American thing in the American way of life. It distinguishes the American way of life from the mixed religious and secular patterns of European church-state education, where controversy and division have been so much more pronounced than they have been in this country, and where, incidentally, the education of the common people has been much more neglected.

Such a comment brings us back to the most fundamental reason why our nation needs to maintain the separation of church and state in education. The consequences of a contrary policy are potentially so tragic in our pluralistic society. Quarrels over dogma —and they are inevitable if religion is imported into public classrooms—are sure to detract from the reputation and accomplishments of the public school, and equally sure to detract from the honorable place accorded to religion in our national life. If the worst happens and the struggle over prayer, Bible-reading and tax grants to sectarian schools results in the establishment of several competing denominational school systems, the resultant fragmentation will be a cultural disaster of the first magnitude.

In 1952, while he was president of Harvard, James B. Conant challenged the whole philosophy of educational separatism, including religious separatism, by saying that "a dual system serves and helps to maintain group cleavages" in our society. "We do not have," he said, "an established church. To my mind, our schools should serve all creeds. The greater the proportion of our youth who attend independent schools, the greater the threat to our democratic unity. Therefore, to use taxpayers' money to assist such a move is, for me, to suggest that American society should use its own hand to destroy itself."[25]

The "threat to our democratic unity" through internal religious strife in the public school system is almost as great as the potential threat involved in separate, competing systems of schools, divided according to creed. The creedless public school, open with-

out discrimination to all, is the natural training school for tolerance. About six out of seven of our children are educated in such
schools and their attitudes toward the public school itself and
toward children of other faiths will determine the school's place
in our future society and the future of tolerance as the American
norm.

That place cannot be maintained by a purely negative attitude toward the separation of church and state in education. It is
clear from past experience that the Supreme Court ruling in this
area will not be self-enforcing. The Court's decision in 1963 was
only a week old before several state officials announced that they
would defy it or that they would act on the assumption that
"voluntary" religious exercises may still be conducted as usual.
This subversive inactivity must be met with a determined and
concerted counterdrive by all those citizens who believe in the
Constitution and in Jefferson's wall of separation.

The United States, more than any other great nation of the
world, has accepted the thesis that education is the function of the
state, to be exercised through local governments controlled by the
people. One corollary of the thesis is that such education should be
non-religious—not anti-religious—and that the promotion of religion should be left primarily to the church and the home. The
fundamental thesis cannot be maintained in a pluralistic society if
state schools are committed to any religious faith or creed, since
such commitment discriminates against the adherents of other
faiths and the adherents of no faith. In such a milieu a friendly
neutrality toward all faiths, committed specifically to no faith,
seems to be the only practical policy for a democratic government.

There is in this design no derogation of religion if it takes its
proper place in our society. It may suffuse, inspire and inform the
whole body politic. That voluntary, suasive place is its natural
place, or, to use Justice Black's words, its "holy field." And he
amplified that thought in a historic paragraph: "State help to
religion injects political and party prejudices into a holy field. It
too often substitutes force for prayer, hate for love, and persecution

for persuasion. Government should not be allowed, under cover of the soft euphemism of 'co-operation', to steal into the sacred area of religious choice."

Appendix I

The Regents' Prayer Decision

(*Engel* v. *Vitale*, 370 U.S. 421 [1962]) (June 25, 1962)

MR. JUSTICE BLACK delivered the opinion of the Court.

The respondent Board of Education of Union Free School District No. 9, New Hyde Park, New York, acting in its official capacity under state law, directed the School District's principal to cause the following prayer to be said aloud by each class in the presence of a teacher at the beginning of each school day:

"Almighty God, we acknowledge our dependence upon Thee, and we beg Thy blessings upon us, our parents, our teachers and our country."

This daily procedure was adopted on the recommendation of the State Board of Regents, a governmental agency created by the State Constitution to which the New York Legislature has granted broad supervisory, executive, and legislative powers over the State's public school system.[1] These state officials composed the prayer which they recommended and published as a part of their "Statement on Moral and Spiritual Training in the Schools," saying: "We believe that this Statement will be subscribed to by all men and women of good will, and we call upon all of them to aid in giving life to our program."

Shortly after the practice of reciting the Regents' prayer was adopted by the School District, the parents of ten pupils brought this action in a New York State Court insisting that use of this official prayer in the public schools was contrary to the beliefs, religions, or religious practices of both themselves and their children. Among other things, these parents challenged the constitutionality of both the state law authorizing the School District to direct the use of prayer in public schools and the School District's regulation ordering the recitation of this particular prayer on the ground that these actions of official governmental agencies violate that part of the First Amendment of the Federal Constitution which commands that "Congress shall make no law respecting an establishment of religion"—a command which was "made applicable to the State of New York by the Fourteenth Amendment of the said Constitution." The New York Court of Appeals, over the dissents of Judges Dye and Fuld, sustained an order of the lower state courts which had upheld the power of New York to use the Regents' prayer as a part of the daily procedures of its public schools so long as the schools did not compel any pupil to join in the prayer over his or his parents' objection.[2] We granted certiorari to review this important decision involving rights protected by the First and Fourteenth Amendments.[3]

We think that by using its public school system to encourage recitation of the Regents' prayer, the State of New York has adopted a practice wholly inconsistent with the Establishment Clause. There can, of course, be no doubt that New York's program of daily classroom invocation of God's blessings as prescribed in the Regents' prayer is a religious activity. It is a solemn avowal of divine faith and supplication for the blessings of the Almighty. The nature of such a prayer has always been religious, none of the respondents has denied this and the trial court expressly so found:

> "The religious nature of prayer was recognized by Jefferson and has been concurred in by theological writers, the United States Supreme Court and State courts and administrative officials, including New York's Commissioner of Education. A committee of the New York Legislature has agreed.
>
> "The Board of Regents as *amicus curiae,* the respondents and intervenors all concede the religious nature of prayer, but seek to distinguish this prayer because it is based on our spiritual heritage. . . ."[4]

The petitioners contend among other things that the state laws requiring or permitting use of the Regents' prayer must be struck down as a violation of the Establishment Clause because that prayer was composed by governmental officials as a part of a governmental program to further religious beliefs. For this reason, petitioners argue, the State's use of the Regents' prayer in its public school system breaches the constitutional wall of separation between Church and State. We agree with that contention since we think that the constitutional prohibition against laws respecting an establishment of religion must at least mean that in this country it is no part of the business of government to compose official prayers for any group of the American people to recite as a part of a religious program carried on by government.

It is a matter of history that this very practice of establishing governmentally composed prayers for religious services was one of the reasons which caused many of our early colonists to leave England and seek religious freedom in America. The Book of Common Prayer, which was created under governmental direction and which was approved by Acts of Parliament in 1548 and 1549,[5] set out in minute detail the accepted form and content of prayer and other religious ceremonies to be used in the established, tax-supported Church of England.[6] The controversies over the Book and what should be its content repeatedly threatened to disrupt the peace of that country as the accepted forms of prayer in the established church changed with the views of the particular ruler that happened to be in control at the time.[7] Powerful groups representing some of the varying religious views of the people struggled among themselves to impress their particular views upon the Government and obtain amendments of the Book more suitable to their respective notions of how religious services should be conducted in order that the official religious establishment would advance their particular religious beliefs.[8] Other groups, lacking the necessary political power to influence the Goverment on the matter, decided to leave England and its established church and seek freedom in America from England's governmentally ordained and supported religion.

It is an unfortunate fact of history that when some of the very groups which had most strenuously opposed the established Church of England found themselves sufficiently in control of colonial governments in this country to write their own prayers into law, they passed laws making their own religion the official religion of their respective colonies.[9] Indeed, as late as the time of the Revolutionary War, there were established churches in at least eight of the thirteen former colonies and established religions in at least four of the other five.[10] But the successful Revolution against English political domination was shortly followed by intense opposition to the practice of establishing religion by law. This opposition crystallized rapidly into an effective political force in Virginia where the minority religious groups such as Presbyterians, Lutherans, Quakers and Baptists had gained such strength that the adherents to the established Episcopal Church were actually a minority themselves. In 1785-1786, those opposed to the

established Church, led by James Madison and Thomas Jefferson
who, though themselves not members of any of these dissenting
religious groups, opposed all religious establishments by law on
grounds of principle, obtained the enactment of the famous "Vir
ginia Bill for Religious Liberty" by which all religious groups were
placed on an equal footing so far as the State was concerned.[1]
Similar though less far-reaching legislation was being considered
and passed in other States.[12]

By the time of the adoption of the Constitution, our history
shows that there was a widespread awareness among many Ameri
cans of the dangers of a union of Church and State. These people
knew, some of them from bitter personal experience, that one of
the greatest dangers to the freedom of the individual to worship in
his own way lay in the Government's placing its official stamp of
approval upon one particular kind of prayer or one particular
form of religious services. They knew the anguish, hardship and
bitter strife that could come when zealous religious groups strug
gled with one another to obtain the Government's stamp of
approval from each King, Queen, or Protector that came to tempo
rary power. The Constitution was intended to avert a part of this
danger by leaving the government of this country in the hands of
the people rather than in the hands of any monarch. But this
safeguard was not enough. Our Founders were no more willing to
let the content of their prayers and their privilege of praying
whenever they pleased be influenced by the ballot box than they
were to let these vital matters of personal conscience depend upon
the succession of monarchs. The First Amendment was added to
the Constitution to stand as a guarantee that neither the power
nor the prestige of the Federal Government would be used to
control, support or influence the kinds of prayer the American
people can say—that the people's religions must not be subjected
to the pressures of government for change each time a new political
administration is elected to office. Under that Amendment's prohi
bition against governmental establishment of religion, as rein
forced by the provisions of the Fourteenth Amendment, govern
ment in this country, be it state or federal, is without power to
prescribe by law any particular form of prayer which is to be used
as an official prayer in carrying on any program of governmentally
sponsored religious activity.

There can be no doubt that New York's state prayer program
officially establishes the religious beliefs embodied in the Regents'

prayer. The respondents' argument to the contrary, which is largely based upon the contention that the Regents' prayer is "non-denominational" and the fact that the program, as modified and approved by state courts, does not require all pupils to recite the prayer but permits those who wish to do so to remain silent or be excused from the room, ignores the essential nature of the program's constitutional defects. Neither the fact that the prayer may be denominationally neutral, nor the fact that its observance on the part of the students is voluntary can serve to free it from the limitations of the Establishment Clause, as it might from the Free Exercise Clause, of the First Amendment, both of which are operative against the States by virtue of the Fourteenth Amendment. Although these two clauses may in certain instances overlap, they forbid two quite different kinds of governmental encroachment upon religious freedom. The Establishment Clause, unlike the Free Exercise Clause, does not depend upon any showing of direct governmental compulsion and is violated by the enactment of laws which establish an official religion whether those laws operate directly to coerce nonobserving individuals or not. This is not to say, of course, that laws officially prescribing a particular form of religious worship do not involve coercion of such individuals. When the power, prestige and financial support of government is placed behind a particular religious belief, the indirect coercive pressure upon religious minorities to conform to the prevailing officially approved religion is plain. But the purposes underlying the Establishment Clause go much further than that. Its first and most immediate purpose rested on the belief that a union of government and religion tends to destroy government and to degrade religion. The history of governmentally established religion, both in England and in this country, showed that whenever government had allied itself with one particular form of religion, the inevitable result had been that it had incurred the hatred, disrespect and even contempt of those who held contrary beliefs.[13] That same history showed that many people had lost their respect for any religion that had relied upon the support of government to spread its faith.[14] The Establishment Clause thus stands as an expression of principle on the part of the Founders of our Constitution that religion is too personal, too sacred, too holy, to permit its "unhallowed perversion" by a civil magistrate.[15] Another purpose of the Establishment Clause rested upon an awareness of the historical fact that governmentally established religions and religious persecutions go hand in hand.[16] The Founders knew that only a few years after the Book of Common Prayer became the only accepted form of religious services in the established Church of England, an Act of Uniformity was passed to compel all Englishmen to attend those services and to make it a criminal offense to conduct or attend religious gatherings of any other kind[17]—a law which was consistently flouted by dissenting religious groups in England and which contributed to widespread persecutions of people like John Bunyan who persisted in holding "unlawful [religious] meetings . . . to the great disturbance and distraction of the good subjects of this kingdom. . . ."[18] And they knew that similar persecutions had received the sanction of law in several of the colonies in this country soon after the establishment of official religions in those colonies.[19] It was in large part to get completely away from this sort of systematic religious persecution that the Founders brought into being our Nation, our Constitution, and our Bill of Rights with its prohibition against any governmental establishment of religion. The New York laws officially prescribing the Regents' prayer are inconsistent with both the purposes of the Establishment Clause and with the Establishment Clause itself.

It has been argued that to apply the Constitution in such a way as to prohibit state laws respecting an establishment of religious services in public schools is to indicate a hostility toward religion or toward prayer. Nothing, of course, could be more wrong. The history of man is inseparable from the history of religion. And perhaps it is not too much to say that since the beginning of that history many people have devoutly believed that "More things are wrought by prayer than this world dreams of.' It was doubtless largely due to men who believed this that there grew up a sentiment that caused men to leave the cross-currents of officially established state religions and religious persecution in Europe and come to this country filled with the hope that they could find a place in which they could pray when they pleased to the God of their faith in the language they chose.[20] And there were men of this same faith in the power of prayer who led the fight for adoption of our Constitution and also for our Bill of Rights with the very guarantees of religious freedom that forbid the sort of governmental activity which New York has attempted here. These men knew that the First Amendment, which tried to put an end to governmental control of religion and of prayer, was not written to destroy either. They knew rather that it was written to quiet well-justified fears which nearly all of them felt arising out of an awareness that governments of the past had shackled men's tongues to make them speak only the religious thoughts that government wanted them to speak and to pray only to the God that government wanted them to pray to. It is neither sacrilegious nor antireligious to say that each separate government in this country should stay out of the business of writing or sanctioning official prayers and leave that purely religious function to the people themselves and to those the people choose to look to for religious guidance.[21]

It is true that New York's establishment of its Regents' prayer as an officially approved religious doctrine of that State does not amount to a total establishment of one particular religious sect to the exclusion of all others—that, indeed, the governmental endorsement of that prayer seems relatively insignificant when compared to the governmental encroachments upon religion which were commonplace 200 years ago. To those who may subscribe to the view that because the Regents' official prayer is so brief and general there can be no danger to religious freedom in its governmental establishment, however, it may be appropriate to say in the words of James Madison, the author of the First Amendment:

"[I]t is proper to take alarm at the first experiment on our liberties. . . . Who does not see that the same authority which can establish Christianity, in exclusion of all other Religions, may establish with the same ease any particular sect of Christians, in exclusion of all other Sects? That the same authority which can force a citizen to contribute three pence only of his property for the support of any one establishment, may force him to conform to any other establishment in all cases whatsoever?"[22]

The judgment of the Court of Appeals of New York is reversed and the cause remanded for further proceedings not inconsistent with this opinion.

Reversed and remanded.

Mr. Justice FRANKFURTER took no part in the decision of this case.

Mr. Justice WHITE took no part in the consideration or decision of this case.

MR. JUSTICE DOUGLAS, concurring.

It is customary in deciding a constitutional question to treat
it in its narrowest form. Yet at times the setting of the question
gives it a form and content which no abstract treatment could do.
The point for decision is whether the Government can constitutionally finance a religious exercise. Our system at the federal and
state levels is presently honeycombed with such financing.[23] Nevertheless, I think it is an unconstitutional undertaking whatever
form it takes.

First, a word as to what this case does not involve.

Plainly, our Bill of Rights would not permit a State or the
Federal Government to adopt an official prayer and penalize anyone who would not utter it. This, however, is not that case, for
there is no element of compulsion or coercion in New York's
regulation requiring that public schools be opened each day with
the following prayer:

> "Almighty God, we acknowledge our dependence upon Thee,
> and we beg Thy blessings upon us, our parents, our teachers
> and our Country."

The prayer is said upon the commencement of the school day,
immediately following the pledge of allegiance to the flag. The
prayer is said aloud in the presence of a teacher, who either leads
the recitation or selects a student to do so. No student, however, is
compelled to take part. The respondents have adopted a regulation which provides that "neither teachers nor any school authority shall comment on participation or non-participation ... nor
suggest or request that any posture or language be used or dress
be worn or be not used or not worn." Provision is also made for
excusing children, upon written request of a parent or guardian,
from the saying of the prayer or from the room in which the prayer
is said. A letter implementing and explaining this regulation has
been sent to each taxpayer and parent in the school district. As I
read this regulation, a child is free to stand or not stand, to recite
or not recite, without fear of reprisal or even comment by the
teacher or any other school official.

In short, the only one who need utter the prayer is the
teacher; and no teacher is complaining of it. Students can stand
mute or even leave the classroom, if they desire.[24]

McCollum v. *Board of Education,* 333 U. S. 203, does not
decide this case. It involved the use of public school facilities for

religious education of students. Students either had to attend religious instruction or "go to some other place in the school building for pursuit of their secular studies. . . . Reports of their presence or absence were to be made to their secular teachers." *Id.,* at 209. The influence of the teaching staff was therefore brought to bear on the student body, to support the instilling religious principles. In the present case, school facilities are used to say the prayer and the teaching staff is employed to lead the pupils in it. There is, however, no effort at indoctrination and no attempt at exposition. Prayers of course may be so long and of such a character as to amount to an attempt at the religious instruction that was denied the public schools by the *McCollum* case. But New York's prayer is of a character that does not involve any element of proselytizing as in the *McCollum* case.

The question presented by this case is therefore an extremely narrow one. It is whether New York oversteps the bounds when it finances a religious exercise.

What New York does on the opening of its public schools is what we do when we open court. Our Marshal has from the beginning announced the convening of the Court and then added "God save the United States and this honorable court." That utterance is a supplication, a prayer in which we, the judges, are free to join, but which we need not recite any more than the students need recite the New York prayer.

What New York does on the opening of its public schools is what each House of Congress[25] does at the opening of each day's business.[26] Reverend Frederick B. Harris is Chaplain of the Senate; Reverend Bernard Braskamp is Chaplain of the House. Guest chaplains of various denominations also officiate.[27]

In New York the teacher who leads in prayer is on the public payroll; and the time she takes seems minuscule as compared with the salaries appropriated by state legislatures and Congress for chaplains to conduct prayers in the legislative halls. Only a bare fraction of the teacher's time is given to reciting this short 22-word prayer, about the same amount of time that our Marshal spends announcing the opening of our sessions and offering a prayer for this Court. Yet for me the principle is the same, no matter how briefly the prayer is said, for in each of the instances given the person praying is a public official on the public payroll, performing a religious exercise in a governmental institution.[28] It is said that the element of coercion is inherent in the giving of this prayer.

If that is true here, it is also true of the prayer with which this Court is convened, and with those that open the Congress. Few adults, let alone children, would leave our courtroom or the Senate or the House while those prayers are being given. Every such audience is in a sense a "captive" audience.

At the same time I cannot say that to authorize this prayer is to establish a religion in the strictly historic meaning of those words.[29] A religion is not established in the usual sense merely by letting those who chose to do so say the prayer that the public school teacher leads. Yet once government finances a religious exercise it inserts a divisive influence into our communities.[30] The New York court said that the prayer given does not conform to all of the tenets of the Jewish, Unitarian, and Ethical Culture groups. One of petitioners is an agnostic.

"We are a religious people whose institutions presupposes a Supreme Being." *Zorach* v. *Clauson,* 343 U. S. 306, 313. Under our Bill of Rights free play is given for making religion an active force in our lives.[31] But "if a religious leaven is to be worked into the affairs of our people, it is to be done by individuals and groups, not by the Government." *McGowan* v. *Maryland,* 366 U. S. 420, 563 (dissenting opinion). By reason of the First Amendment government is commanded "to have no interest in theology or ritual" (*id.,* at 564), for on those matters "government must be neutral." *Ibid.* The First Amendment leaves the Government in a position not of hostility to religion but of neutrality. The philosophy is that the atheist or agnostic—the nonbeliever—is entitled to go his own way. The philosophy is that if government interferes in matters spiritual, it will be a divisive force. The First Amendment teaches that a government neutral in the field of religion better serves all religious interests.

My problem today would be uncomplicated but for *Everson* v. *Board of Education,* 330 U. S. 1, 17, which allowed taxpayers' money to be used to pay "the bus fares of parochial school pupils as a part of a general program under which" the fares of pupils attending public and other schools were also paid. The *Everson* case seems in retrospect to be out of line with the First Amendment. Its result is appealing, as it allows aid to be given to needy children. Yet by the same token, public funds could be used to satisfy other needs of children in parochial schools—lunches, books, and tuition being obvious examples. Mr. Justice Rutledge stated in dissent what I think is durable First Amendment philosophy:

> "The reasons underlying the Amendment's policy have not vanished with time or diminished in force. Now as when it was adopted the price of religious freedom is double. It is that the church and religion shall live both within and upon that freedom. There cannot be freedom of religion, safeguarded by the state, and intervention by the church or its agencies in the state's domain or dependency on its largesse. Madison's Remonstrance, Par. 6, 8. The great condition of religious liberty is that it be maintained free from sustenance, as also from other interferences, by the state. For when it comes to rest upon that secular foundation it vanishes with the resting. *Id.,* Par. 7, 8. Public money devoted to payment of religious costs, educational or other, brings the quest for more. It brings too the struggle of sect against sect for the larger share or for any. Here one by numbers alone will benefit most, there another. That is precisely the history of societies which have had an established religion and dissident groups. *Id.* Par. 8, 11. It is the very thing Jefferson and Madison experienced and sought to guard against, whether in its blunt or in its more screened forms. *Ibid.* The end of such strife cannot be other than to destroy the cherished liberty. The dominating group will achieve the dominant benefit; or all will embroil the state in their dissensions. *Id.* Par. 11." *Id.,* pp. 53-54.

What New York does with this prayer is a break with that tradition. I therefore join the Court in reversing the judgment below.

MR. JUSTICE STEWART, dissenting.

A local school board in New York has provided that those pupils who wish to do so may join in a brief prayer at the beginning of each school day, acknowledging their dependence upon God and asking His blessing upon them and upon their parents, their teachers, and their country. The Court today decides that in permitting this brief non-denominational prayer the school board has violated the Constitution of the United States. I think this decision is wrong.

The Court does not hold, nor could it, that New York has interfered with the free exercise of anybody's religion. For the state courts have made clear that those who object to reciting the prayer must be entirely free of any compulsion to do so, including any "embarrassments and pressures." Cf. *West Virginia State Board of Education* v. *Barnette*, 319 U. S. 624. But the Court says that in permitting school children to say this simple prayer, the New York authorities have established "an official religion."

With all respect, I think the Court has misapplied a great constitutional principle. I cannot see how an "official religion" is established by letting those who want to say a prayer say it. On the contrary, I think that to deny the wish of these school children to join in reciting this prayer is to deny them the opportunity of sharing in the spiritual heritage of our Nation.

The Court's historical review of the quarrels over the Book of Common Prayer in England throws no light for me on the issue before us in this case. England had then and has now an established church. Equally unenlightening, I think, is the history of the early establishment and later rejection of an official church in our own States. For we deal here not with the establishment of a state church, which would, of course, be constitutionally impermissible, but with whether school children who want to begin their day by joining in prayer must be prohibited from doing so. Moreover, I think that the Court's task, in this as in all areas of constitutional adjudication, is not responsibly aided by the uncritical invocation of metaphors like the "wall of separation," a phrase nowhere to be found in the Constitution. What is relevant to the issue here is not the history of an established church in sixteenth century England or in eighteenth century America, but the history of the religious traditions of our people, reflected in countless practices of the institutions and officials of our government.

At the opening of each day's Session of this Court we stand, while one of our officials invokes the protection of God. Since the days of John Marshall our Crier has said, "God save the United States and this Honorable Court."[32] Both the Senate and the House of Representatives open their daily Sessions with prayer.[33] Each of our Presidents, from George Washington to John F. Kennedy, has upon assuming his Office asked the protection and help of God.[34]

The Court today says that the state and federal governments are without constitutional power to prescribe any particular form of words to be recited by any group of the American people on any subject touching religion.[35] The third stanza of "The Star-Spangled Banner," made our National Anthem by Act of Congress in 1931,[36] contains these verses:

> "Blest with victory and peace, may the heav'n rescued land
>   Praise the Pow'r that hath made and preserved us a
>   nation!
> Then conquer we must, when our cause it is just,
>   And this be our motto 'In God is our Trust.' "

In 1954 Congress added a phrase to the Pledge of Allegiance to the Flag so that it now contains the words "one Nation *under* God, indivisible, with liberty and justice for all."[37] In 1952 Congress enacted legislation calling upon the President each year to proclaim a National Day of Prayer.[38] Since 1865 the words "IN GOD WE TRUST" have been impressed on our coins.[39]

Countless similar examples could be listed, but there is no need to belabor the obvious.[40] It was all summed up by this Court just ten years ago in a single sentence: "We are a religious people whose institutions presuppose a Supreme Being." *Zorach* v. *Clauson,* 343 U. S. 306, 313.

I do not believe that this Court, or the Congress, or the President has by the actions and practices I have mentioned established an "official religion" in violation of the Constitution. And I do not believe the State of New York has done so in this case. What each has done has been to recognize and to follow the deeply entrenched and highly cherished spiritual traditions of our Nation —traditions which come down to us from those who almost two hundred years ago avowed their "firm reliance on the Protection of Divine Providence" when they proclaimed the freedom and independence of this brave new world.[41]

I dissent.

NOTES

[1] See New York Constitution, Art. V, § 4; New York Education Law, §§ 101, 120 *et seq.*, 202, 214-219, 224, 245 *et seq.*, 704, and 801 *et seq.*

[2] 10 N. Y. 2d 174, 176 N. E. 2d 579. The trial court's opinion, which is reported at 18 Misc. 2d 659, 191 N. Y. S. 2d 453, had made it clear that the Board of Education must set up some sort of procedures to protect those who objected to reciting the prayer: "This is not to say that the rights accorded petitioners and their children under the 'free exercise' clause do not mandate

(Footnote 2—continued.)

safeguards against such embarrassments and pressures. It is enough on this score, however, that regulations, such as were adopted by New York City's Board of Education in connection with its released time program, be adopted, making clear that neither teachers nor any other school authority may comment on participation or nonparticipation in the exercise nor suggest or require that any posture or language be used or dress be worn or be not used or not worn. Nonparticipation may take the form either of remaining silent during the exercise, or if the parent or child so desires, of being excused entirely from the exercise. Such regulations must also make provision for those nonparticipants who are to be excused from the prayer exercise. The exact provision to be made is a matter for decision by the board, rather than the court, within the framework of constitutional requirements. Within that framework would fall a provision that prayer participants proceed to a common assembly while nonparticipants attend other rooms, or that nonparticipants be permitted to arrive at school a few minutes late or to attend separate opening exercises, or any other method which treats with equality both participants and nonparticipants." 18 Misc. 2d, at 696, 191 N. Y. S. 2d, at 492-493. See also the opinion of the Appellate Division affirming that of the trial court, reported at 11 App. Div. 2d 340, 206 N. Y. S. 2d 183.

    3 368 U. S. 924.

    4 18 Misc. 2d, at 671-672, 191 N. Y. S. 2d, at 468-469.

    5 2 & 3 Edward VI, c. 1, entitled "An Act for Uniformity of Service and Administration of the Sacraments throughout the Realm"; 3 & 4 Edward VI, c. 10, entitled "An Act for the abolishing and putting away of divers Books and Images."

    6 The provisions of the various versions of the Book of Common Prayer are set out in broad outline in the Encyclopedia Britannica, Vol. 18 (1957 ed.), pp. 420-423. For a more complete description, see Pullan, The History of the Book of Common Prayer (1900).

    7 The first major revision of the Book of Common Prayer was made in 1552 during the reign of Edward VI, 5 & 6 Edward VI, c. 1. In 1553, Edward VI died and was succeeded by Mary who abolished the Book of Common Prayer entirely. 1 Mary, c. 2. But upon the accession of Elizabeth in 1558, the Book was restored with important alterations from the form it had been given by Edward VI. 1 Elizabeth, c. 2. The resentment to this amended form of the Book was kept firmly under control during the reign of Elizabeth but, upon her death in 1603, a petition signed by more than 1,000 Puritan ministers was presented to King James I asking for further alterations in the Book. Some alterations were made and the Book retained substantially this form until it was completely suppressed again in 1645 as a result of the successful Puritan Revolution. Shortly after the restoration in 1660 of Charles II, the Book was again reintroduced, 13 & 14 Charles II, c. 4, and again with alterations. Rather than accept this form of the Book some 2,000 Puritan ministers vacated their benefices. See generally Pullan, The History of the Book of Common Prayer (1900), pp. vii-xvi; Encyclopedia Britannica (1957 ed.), Vol. 18, pp. 421-422.

    8 For example, the Puritans twice attempted to modify the Book of Common Prayer and once attempted to destroy it. The story of their struggle to modify the Book in the reign of Charles I is vividly summarized in Pullan, History of the Book of Common Prayer, at p. xiii: "The King actively supported

(Footnote 8—continued.)

those members of the Church of England who were anxious to vindicate its Catholic character and maintain the ceremonial which Elizabeth had approved. Laud, Archbishop of Canterbury, was the leader of this school. Equally resolute in his opposition to the distinctive tenets of Rome and of Geneva, he enjoyed the hatred of both Jesuit and Calvinist. He helped the Scottish bishops, who had made large concessions to the uncouth habits of Presbyterian worship, to draw up a Book of Common Prayer for Scotland. It contained a Communion Office resembling that of the book of 1549. It came into use in 1637, and met with a bitter and barbarous opposition. The vigour of the Scottish Protestants strengthened the hands of their English sympathisers. Laud and Charles were executed, Episcopacy was abolished, the use of the Book of Common Prayer was prohibited."

[9] For a description of some of the laws enacted by early theocratic governments in New England, see Parrington, Main Currents in American Thought (1930), Vol. 1, pp. 5-50; Whipple, Our Ancient Liberties (1927), pp. 63-78; Wertenbaker, The Puritan Oligarchy (1947).

[10] The Church of England was the established church of at least five colonies: Maryland, Virginia, North Carolina, South Carolina and Georgia. There seems to be some controversy as to whether that church was officially established in New York and New Jersey but there is no doubt that it received substantial support from those states. See Cobb, The Rise of Religious Liberty in America (1902), pp. 338, 408. In Massachusetts, New Hampshire and Connecticut, the Congregationalist Church was officially established. In Pennsylvania and Delaware, all Christian sects were treated equally in most situations but Catholics were discriminated against in some respects. See generally Cobb, The Rise of Religious Liberty in America (1902). In Rhode Island all Protestants enjoyed equal privileges but it is not clear whether Catholics were allowed to vote. Compare Fiske, The Critical Period in American History (1899), p. 76 with Cobb, The Rise of Religious Liberty in America (1902), pp. 437-438.

[11] 12 Hening, Statutes of Virginia (1823), 84, entitled "An Act for establishing religious freedom." The story of the events surrounding the enactment of this law was reviewed in Everson v. Board of Education, 330 U. S. 1, both by the Court, at pp. 11-13, and in the dissenting opinion of Mr. Justice Rutledge, at pp. 33-42. See also Fiske, The Critical Period in American History (1899), pp. 78-82; James, The Struggle for Religious Liberty in Virginia (1900); Thom, The Struggle for Religious Freedom in Virginia: The Baptists (1900) ; Cobb, The Rise of Religious Liberty in America (1902), pp. 74-115, 482-499.

[12] See Cobb, The Rise of Religious Liberty in America (1902), pp. 482-509.

[13] "[A]ttempts to enforce by legal sanctions, acts obnoxious to so great a proportion of Citizens, tend to enervate the laws in general, and to slacken the bands of Society. If it be difficult to execute any law which is not generally deemed necessary or salutary, what must be the case where it is deemed invalid and dangerous? and what may be the effect of so striking an example of impotency in the Government, on its general authority." Memorial and Remonstrance against Religious Assessments, II Writings of Madison 183, 190.

[14] "It is moreover to weaken in those who profess this Religion a pious confidence in its innate excellence, and the patronage of its Author; and to foster in those who still reject it, a suspicion that its friends are too conscious of

(Footnote 14—continued.)

its fallacies, to trust it to its own merits.... [E]xperience witnesseth that eccle-siastical establishments, instead of maintaining the purity and efficacy of Reli-gion, have had a contrary operation. During almost fifteen centuries, has the legal establishment of Christianity been on trial. What have been its fruits? More or less in all places, pride and indolence in the Clergy; ignorance and servility in the laity; in both, superstition, bigotry and persecution. Enquire of the Teachers of Christianity for the ages in which it appeared in its greatest lustre; those of every sect, point to the ages prior to its incorporation with Civil policy." *Id.*, at 187.

[15] Memorial and Remonstrance against Religious Assessments, II Writings of Madison, at 187.

[16] "[T]he proposed establishment is a departure from that generous pol-icy, which, offering an asylum to the persecuted and oppressed of every Nation and Religion, promised a lustre to our country, and an accession to the number of its citizens. What a melancholy mark is the Bill of sudden degeneracy? Instead of holding forth as asylum to the persecuted, it is itself a signal of persecution. ... Distant as it may be, in its present form, from the Inquisition it differs from it only in degree. The one is the first step, the other the last in the career of intolerance. The magnanimous sufferer under this cruel scourge in foreign Re-gions, must view the Bill as a Beacon on our Coast, warning him to seek some other haven, where liberty and philanthropy in their due extent may offer a more certain repose from his troubles." *Id.*, at 188.

[17] 5 & 6 Edward VI, c. 1, entitled "An Act for the Uniformity of Service and Administration of Sacraments throughout the Realm." This Act was re-pealed during the reign of Mary but revived upon the accession of Elizabeth. See note 7, *supra*. The reasons which led to the enactment of this statute were set out in its preamble: "Where there hath been a very godly Order set forth by the Authority of Parliament, for Common Prayer and Administration of Sacraments to be used in the Mother Tongue within the Church of *England,* agreeable to the Word of God and the Primitive Church, very comfortable to all good People desiring to live in Christian Converastion, and most profitable to the Estate of this Realm, upon the which the Mercy, Favour and Blessing of Almighty God is in no wise so readily and plenteously poured as by Common Prayers, due using of the Sacraments, and often preaching of the Gospel, with the Devotion of the Hearers: (1) And yet this notwithstanding, a great Number of People in divers Parts of this Realm, following their own Sensuality, and living either without Knowledge or due Fear of God, do wilfully and damnably before Almighty God abstain and refuse to come to their Parish Churches and other Places where Common Prayer, Administration of the Sacraments, and Preaching of the Word of God, is used upon *Sundays* and other Days ordained to be Holydays."

[18] Bunyan's own account of his trial is set forth in A Relation of the Im-prisonment of Mr. John Bunyan, reprinted in Grace Abounding and The Pil-grim's Progress (Brown ed. 1907), at 103-132.

[19] For a vivid account of some of these persecutions, see Wertenbaker, The Puritan Oligarchy (1947).

[20] Perhaps the best example of the sort of men who came to this country for precisely that reason is Roger Williams, the founder of Rhode Island, who has been described as "the truest Christian amongst many who sincerely desired

(Footnote 20—continued.)

to be Christian." Parrington, Main Currents of American Thought (1930), Vol. 1, at p. 74. Williams, who was one of the earliest exponents of the doctrine of separation of church and state, believed that separation was necessary in order to protect the church from the danger of destruction which he thought inevitably flowed from control by even the best-intentioned civil authorities: "The unknowing zeale of *Constantine* and other Emperours, did more hurt to *Christ Jesus* his Crowne and Kingdome, then the raging fury of the most bloody *Neroes.* In the *persecutions* of the later, *Christians* were sweet and fragrant, like spice pounded and beaten in morters: But those *good* Emperours, persecuting some erroneous persons, *Arrius, &c.* and advancing the professours of some Truths of Christ (for there was no small number of *Truths* lost in those times) and maintaining their *Religion* by the materiall Sword, I say by this meanes *Christianity* was *ecclipsed,* and the Professors of it fell asleep...." Williams, The Bloudy Tenent, of Persecution, for cause of Conscience, discussed, in A Conference betweene Truth and Peace (London, 1644) , reprinted in Naragansett Club Publications, Vol. III, p. 184. To Williams, it was no part of the business or competence of a civil magistrate to interfere in religious matters: "[W]hat imprudence and *indiscretion* is it in the most common affaires of Life, to conceive that *Emperours, Kings* and *Rulers* of the earth must not only be qualified with *politicall* and *state abilities* to *make* and *execute* such *Civill Lawes* which may concerne the common *rights, peace* and *safety* (which is worke and businesse, load and burthen enough for the ablest shoulders in the Commonweal) but also furnished with such *Spirituall* and heavenly *abilities to* governe the *Spirituall* and *Christian Commonweale....*" Id., at 366. See also *id.,* at 136-137.

[21] There is of course nothing in the decision reached here that is inconsistent with the fact that school children and others are officially encouraged to express love for our country by reciting historical documents such as the Declaration of Independence which contain references to the Deity or by singing officially espoused anthems which include the composer's professions of faith in a Supreme Being, or with the fact that there are many manifestations in our public life of belief in God. Such patriotic or ceremonial occasions bear no true resemblance to the unquestioned religious exercise that the State of New York has sponsored in this instance.

[22] Memorial and Remonstrance against Religious Assessments, II Writings of Madison 183, at 185-186.

[23] "There are many 'aids' to religion in this country at all levels of government. To mention but a few at the federal level, one might begin by observing that the very First Congress which wrote the First Amendment provided for chaplains in both Houses and in the armed services. There is compulsory chapel at the service academies, and religious services are held in federal hospitals and prisons. The President issues religious proclamations. The Bible is used for the administration of oaths. N. Y. A. and W. P. A. funds were available to parochial schools during the depression. Veterans receiving money under the 'G. I.' Bill of 1944 could attend denominational schools, to which payments were made directly by the government. During World War II, federal money was contributed to denominational schools for the training of nurses. The bentfits of the National School Lunch Act are available to students in private as well as public schools. The Hospital Survey and Construction Act of 1946 specifically made money available to non-public hospitals. The slogan 'In God We Trust' is used by the

(Footnote 23—continued.)
Treasury Department, and Congress recently added God to the pledge of allegiance. There is Bible-reading in the schools of the District of Columbia, and religious instruction is given in the District's National Training School for Boys. Religious organizations are exempt from the federal income tax and are granted postal privileges. Up to defined limits—15 per cent of the adjusted gross income of individuals and 5 per cent of the net income of corporations—contributions to religious organizations are deductible for federal income tax purposes. There are limits to the deductibility of gifts and bequests to religious institutions made under the federal gift and estate tax laws. This list of federal 'aids' could easily be expanded, and of course there is a long list in each state." Fellman, The Limits of Freedom (1959), pp. 40-41.

[24] West Point Cadets are required to attend chapel each Sunday, Reg., c. 21, § 2101. The same requirement obtains at the Naval Academy (Reg., c. 9, § 0901, (1) (a)), and at the Air Force Academy except First Classmen. Catalogue, 1962-1963, p. 110. And see Honeywell, Chaplains of the United States Army (1958); Jorgensen, The Service of Chaplains to Army Air Units, 1917-1946, Vol I (1961).

[25] The New York Legislature follows the same procedure. See, e.g., Vol. 1, N. Y. Assembly Jour., 184th Sess., 1961, p. 8; Vol. 1, N. Y. Senate Jour., 184th Sess., 1961, p. 5.

[26] Rules of the Senate provide that each calendar day's session shall open with prayer. See Rule III, Senate Manual, S. Doc. No. 2, 87th Cong., 1st Sess. The same is true of the Rules of the House. See Rule VII, Rules of the House of Representatives, H. R. Doc. No. 459, 86th Cong., 2d. Sess. The Chaplains of the Senate and of the House receive $8,810 annually. See 75 Stat. 320, 324.

[27] It would, I assume, make no difference in the present case if a different prayer were said every day or if the ministers of the community rotated, each giving his own prayer. For some of the petitioners in the present case profess no religion.

The Pledge of Allegiance, like the prayer, recognizes the existence of a Supreme Being. Since 1954 it has contained the words "one nation *under God,* indivisible, with liberty and justice for all." 36 U. S. C. 172. The House Report, recommending the addition of the words "under God" stated that those words in no way run contrary to the First Amendment but recognize "only the guidance of God in our national affairs." H. R. Rep. No. 1693, 83d Cong., 2d Sess., p. 3. And see S. Rep. No. 1287, 83d Cong., 2d Sess. Senator Ferguson, who sponsored the measure in the Senate, pointed out that the words "In God We Trust" are over the entrance to the Senate Chamber. 100 Cong. Rec. 6348. He added:

"I have felt that the Pledge of Allegiance to the Flag which stands for the United States of America should recognize the Creator who we really believe is in control of the destinies of this great Republic.

"It is true that under the Constitution no power is lodged anywhere to establish a religion. This is not an attempt to establish a religion; it has nothing to do with anything of that kind. It relates to belief in God, in whom we sincerely repose our trust. We know that America cannot be defended by guns, planes, and ships alone. Appropriations and expenditures for defense will be of value only if the God under whom we live believes that we are in the right. We should at all times recognize God's province over the lives of our people and

(Footnote 27—continued.)

over this great Nation." *Ibid.* And see 100 Cong. Rec. 7757 *et seq.* for the debates in the House.

The Act of March 3, 1865, 13 Stat. 517, 518, authorized the phrase "In God We Trust" to be placed on coins. And see 17 Stat. 427. The first mandatory requirement for the use of that motto on coins was made by the Act of May 18, 1908, 35 Stat. 164. See H. R. Rep. No. 1106, 60th Cong., 1st Sess.; 42 Cong. Rec. 3384 *et seq.* The use of the motto on all currency and coins was directed by the Act of July 11, 1955, 69 Stat. 290. See H. R. Rep. No. 662, 84th Cong., 1st Sess.; S. Rep. No. 637, 84th Cong., 1st Sess. Moreover, by the Joint Resolution of July 30, 1956, our national motto was declared to be "In God We Trust." 70 Stat. 732. In reporting the Joint Resolution, the Senate Judiciary Committee stated:

"Further official recognition of this motto was given by the adoption of the Star-Spangled Banner as our naitonal anthem. One stanza of our national anthem is as follows:

'O, thus be it ever when freemen shall stand
Between their lov'd home and the war's desolation:
Blest with vict'ry and peace may the heav'n rescued land
Praise the power that hath made and preserved us a nation!
Then conquer we must when our cause it is just,
And this be our motto—"In God is our trust."
And the Star-Spangled Banner in triumph shall wave
O'er the land of the free and the home of the brave.'

"In view of these words in our national anthem, it is clear that 'In God we trust' has a strong claim as our national motto." S. Rep. No. 2703, 84th Cong., 2d Sess., p. 2.

[28] The fact that taxpayers do not have standing in the federal courts to raise the issue (*Frothingham* v. *Mellon,* 262 U. S. 447) is of course no justification for drawing a line between what is done in New York on one hand and on the other what we do and what Congress does in this matter of prayer.

[29] The Court analogizes the present case to those involving the traditional Established Church. We once had an Established Church, the Anglican. All baptisms and marriages had to take place there. That church was supported by taxation. In these and other ways the Anglican Church was favored over the others. The First Amendment put an end to placing any one church in a preferred position. It ended support of any church or all churches by taxation. It went further and prevented secular sanction to any religious ceremony, dogma, or rite. Thus, it prevents civil penalties from being applied against recalcitrants or nonconformists.

[30] Some communities, including Washington, D. C., have a Christmas tree purchased with the taxpayers' money. The tree is sometimes decorated with the words "Peace on earth, goodwill to men." At other times the authorities draw from a different version of the Bible which says "Peace on earth to men of goodwill." Christmas, I suppose, is still a religious celebration, not merely a day put on the calendar for the benefit of merchants.

[31] Religion was once deemed to be a function of the public school system. The Northwest Ordinance, which antedated the First Amendment, provided in Article 3 that "Religion, morality, and knowledge being necessary to good government and the happiness of mankind, schools and the means of education shall forever be encouraged."

[32] See Warren, The Supreme Court in United States History, Vol. 1, 469.
[33] See Rule III, Senate Manual, S. Doc. No. 2, 87th Cong., 1st Sess. See Rule VII, Rules of the House of Representatives, H. R. Doc. No. 459, 86th Cong., 2d Sess.
[34] For example:

On April 30, 1789, President George Washington said:

"... it would be peculiarly improper to omit in this first official act my fervent supplications to that Almighty Being who rules over the universe, who presides in the councils of nations, and whose providential aids can supply every human defect, that His benediction may consecrate to the liberties and happiness of the people of the United States a Government instituted by themselves for these essential purposes, and may enable every instrument employed in its administration to execute with success the functions allotted to His charge. In tendering this homage to the Great Author of every public and private good, I assure myself that it expresses your sentiments not less than my own, nor those of my fellow-citizens at large less than either. No people can be bound to acknowledge and adore the Invisible Hand which conducts the affairs of men more than those of the United States.

.   .   .   .   .

"Having thus imparted to you my sentiments as they have been awakened by the occasion which brings us together, I shall take my present leave; but not without resorting once more to the benign Parent of the Human Race in humble supplication that, since He has been pleased to favor the American people with opportunities for deliberating in perfect tranquillity, and dispositions for deciding with unparalled unanimity on a form of government for the security of their union and the advancement of their happiness, so His divine blessing may be equally *conspicuous* in the enlarged views, the temperate consultations, and the wise measures on which the success of this Government must depend."

On March 4, 1797, President John Adams said:

"And may that Being who is supreme over all, the Patron of Order, the Fountain of Justice, and the Protector in all ages of the world of virtuous liberty, continue His blessing upon this nation and its Government and give it all possible success and duration consistent with the ends of His providence."

On March 4, 1805, President Thomas Jefferson said:

"I shall need, too, the favor of that Being in whose hands we are, who led our fathers, as Israel of old, from their native land and planted them in a country flowing with all the necessaries and comforts of life; who has covered our infancy with His providence and our riper years with His wisdom and power, and to whose goodness I ask you to join in supplications with me that He will so enlighten the minds of your servants, guide their councils, and prosper their measures that whatsoever they do shall result in your good, and shall secure to you the peace, friendship, and approbation of all nations."

On March 4, 1809, President James Madison said:

"But the source to which I look ... is in ... my fellow-citizens, and in the counsels of those representing them in the other departments associated in the care of the national interests. In these my confidence will

(Footnote 34—continued.)

under every difficulty be best placed, next to that which we have all been encouraged to feel in the guardianship and guidance of that Almighty Being whose power regulates the destiny of nations, whose blessings have been so conspicuously dispensed to this rising Republic, and to whom we are bound to address our devout gratitude for the past, as well as our fervent supplications and best hopes for the future."

On March 4, 1865, President Abraham Lincoln said:

Fondly do we hope, fervently do we pray, that this mighty scourge of war may speedily pass away. Yet, if God wills that it continue until all the wealth piled by the bondsman's two hundred and fifty years of unrequited toil shall be sunk, and until every drop of blood drawn with the lash shall be paid by another drawn with the sword, as was said three thousand years ago, so still it must be said "the judgments of the Lord are true and righteous altogether."

"With malice toward none, with charity for all, with firmness in the right as God gives us to see the right, let us strive on to finish the work we are in, to bind up the nation's wounds, to care for him who shall have borne the battle and for his widow and his orphan, to do all which may achieve and cherish a just and lasting peace among ourselves and with all nations."

On March 4, 1885, President Grover Cleveland said:

"And let us not trust to human effort alone, but humbly acknowledging the power and goodness of Almighty God, who presides over the destiny of nations, and who has at all times been revealed in our country's history, let us invoke His aid and His blessing upon our labors."

On March 5, 1917, President Woodrow Wilson said:

"I pray God I may be given the wisdom and the prudence to do my duty in the true spirit of this great people."

On March 4, 1933, President Franklin D. Roosevelt said:

"In this dedication of a Nation we humbly ask the blessing of God. May He protect each and every one of us. May He guide me in the days to come."

On January 21, 1957, President Dwight D. Eisenhower said:

"Before all else, we seek, upon our common labor as a nation, the blessings of Almighty God. And the hopes in our hearts fashion the deepest prayers of our whole people."

On January 20, 1961, President John F. Kennedy said:

"The world is very different now. . . . And yet the same revolutionary beliefs for which our forebears fought are still at issue around the globe—the belief that the rights of man come not from the generosity of the state, but from the hand of God.

.   .   .   .

"With a good conscience our only sure reward, with history the final judge of our deeds, let us go forth to lead the land we love, asking His blessing and His help, but knowing that here on earth God's work must truly be our own."

[35] My brother DOUGLAS says that the only question before us is whether government "can constitutionally finance a religious exercise." The official chap-

(Footnote 35—continued.)

lains of Congress are paid with public money. So are military chaplains. So are state and federal prison chaplains.

[36] 36 U. S. C. § 170.

[37] 36 U. S. C. § 172.

[38] 36 U. S .C. § 185.

[39] 13 Stat. 517, 518; 17 Stat. 427; 35 Stat. 164; 69 Stat. 290. The current provisions are embodied in 31 U. S. C. §§ 324, 324a.

[40] I am at a loss to understand the Court's unsupported *ipse dixit* that these official expressions of religious faith in and reliance upon a Supreme Being "bear no true resemblance to the unquestioned religious exercise that the State of New York has sponsored in this instance." See p. ——, *supra*, n. 21. I can hardly think that the Court means to say that the First Amendment imposes a lesser restriction upon the Federal Government than does the Fourteenth Amendment upon the States. Or is the Court suggesting that the Constitution permits judges and Congressmen and Presidents to join in prayer, but prohibits school children from doing so?

[41] The Declaration of Independence ends with this sentence: "And for the support of this Declaration, with a firm reliance on the Protection of Divine Providence, we mutually pledge to each other our Lives, our Fortunes and our sacred Honor."

Appendix II

The Bible-Reading and Lord's Prayer Decision

(*Abington* v. *Schempp* and *Murray* v. *Curlett*) (June 17, 1963)

MR. JUSTICE CLARK delivered the opinion of the Court.

Once again we are called upon to consider the scope of the provision of the First Amendment to the United States Constitution which declares that "Congress shall make no law respecting an establishment of religion or prohibiting the free exercise thereof. . . ." These companion cases present the issues in the context of state action requiring that schools begin each day with readings from the Bible. While raising the basic questions under slightly different factual situations, the cases permit of joint treatment. In light of the history of the First Amendment and of our cases interpreting and applying its requirements, we hold that the practices at issue and the laws requiring them are unconstitutional under the Establishment Clause, as applied to the states through the Fourteenth Amendment.

I.

The Facts in Each Case: No. 142. The Commonwealth of Pennsylvania by law, 24 Pa. Stat. § 15-1516, as amended, Pub. Law 1928 (Supp. 1960) Dec. 17, 1959, requires that "At least ten verses from the Holy Bible shall be read, without comment, at the opening of each public school on each school day. Any child shall be excused from such Bible reading, or attending such Bible reading, upon the written request of his parent or guardian." The Schempp family, husband and wife and two of their three children, brought suit to enjoin enforcement of the statute, contending that their rights under the Fourteenth Amendment to the Constitution of the United States are, have been, and will continue to be violated unless this statute be declared unconstitutional as violative of these provisions of the First Amendment. They sought to enjoin the appellant school district, wherein the Schempp children attend school, and its officers and the Superintendent of Public Instruction of the Commonwealth from continuing to conduct such readings and recitation of the Lord's Prayer in the public schools of the district pursuant to the statute. A three-judge statutory District Court for the Eastern District of Pennsylvania held that the statute is violative of the Establishment Clause of the First Amendment as applied to the States by the Due Process Clause of the Fourteenth Amendment and directed that appropriate injunctive relief issue. 201 F. Supp. 815.[1] On appeal by the District, its officials and the Superintendent, under 28 U. S. C. § 1253, we noted probable jurisdiction. 371 U. S. 807.

The appellees Edward Lewis Schempp, his wife Sidney, and their children, Roger and Donna, are of the Unitarian faith and are members of the Unitarian Church in Germantown, Philadelphia, Pennsylvania, where they, as well as another son, Ellory, regularly attend religious services. The latter was originally a party but having graduated from the school system *pendente lite* was voluntarily dismissed from the action. The other children attend the Abington Senior High School, which is a public school operated by appellant district.

On each school day at the Abington Senior High School between 8:15 and 8:30 a. m., while the pupils are attending their home rooms or advisory sections, opening exercises are conducted pursuant to the statute. The exercises are broadcast into each room in the school building through an intercommunications system and are conducted under the supervision of a teacher by students attending the school's radio and television workshop. Selected students from this course gather each morning in the school's workshop studio for the exercises, which include readings by one of the students of 10 verses of the Holy Bible, broadcast to each room in the building. This is followed by the recitation of the Lord's Prayer, likewise over the intercommunications system, but also by the students in the various classrooms, who are asked to stand and join in repeating the prayer in unison. The exercises are closed with the flag salute and such pertinent announcements as are of interest to the students. Participation in the opening exercises, as directed by the statute, is voluntary. The student reading the verses from the Bible may select the passages and read from any version he chooses, although the only copies furnished by the school are the King James version, copies of which were circulated to each teacher by the school district. During the period in which the exercises have been conducted the King James, the Douay and the Revised Standard versions of the Bible have been used, as well as the Jewish Holy Scriptures. There are no prefatory statements, no questions asked or solicited, no comments or explanations made and no interpretations given at or during the exercises. The students and parents are advised that the student may absent himself from the classroom or, should he elect to remain, not participate in the exercises.

It appears from the record that in schools not having an intercommunications system the Bible reading and the recitation of the Lord's Prayer were conducted by the home-room teacher,[2] who chose the text of the verses and read them herself or had students read them in rotation or by volunteers. This was followed by a standing recitation of the Lord's Prayer, together with the Pledge of Allegiance to the flag by the class in unison and a closing announcement of routine school items of interest.

At the first trial Edward Schempp and the children testified as to specific religious doctrines purveyed by a literal reading of the Bible "which were contrary to the religious beliefs which they held and to their familial teaching." 177 F. Supp. 398, 400. The children testified that all of the doctrines to which they referred were read to them at various times as part of the exercises. Edward Schempp testified at the second trial that he had considered having Roger and Donna excused from attendance at the exercises but decided against it for several reasons, including his belief that the children's relationships with their teachers and classmates would be adversely affected.[3]

Expert testimony was introduced by both appellants and appellees at the first trial, which testimony was summarized by the trial court as follows:

"Dr. Solomon Grayzel testified that there were marked differences between the Jewish Holy Scriptures and the Christian Holy Bible, the most obvious of which was the absence of the New Testament in the Jewish Holy Scriptures. Dr. Grayzel testified that portions of the New Testament were offensive to

Jewish tradition and that, from the standpoint of Jewish faith, the concept of Jesus Christ as the Son of God was 'practically blasphemous.' He cited instances in the New Testament which, assertedly, were not only sectarian in nature but tended to bring the Jews into ridicule or scorn. Dr. Grayzel gave as his expert opinion that such material from the New Testament could be explained to Jewish children in such a way as to do no harm to them. But if portions of the New Testament were read without explanation, they could be, and in his specific experience with children Dr. Grayzel observed, had been, psychologically harmful to the child and had caused a divisive force within the social media of the school.

"Dr. Grayzel also testified that there was significant difference in attitude with regard to the respective Books of the Jewish and Christian Religions in that Judaism attaches no special significance to the reading of the Bible *per se* and that the Jewish Holy Scriptures are source materials to be studied. But Dr. Grayzel did state that many portions of the New, as well as of the Old, Testament contained passages of great literary and moral value.

"Dr. Luther A. Weigle, an expert witness for the defense, testified in some detail as to the reasons for and the methods employed in developing the King James and the Revised Standard Versions of the Bible. On direct examination, Dr. Weigle stated that the Bible was non-sectarian. He later stated that the phrase 'non-sectarian' meant to him non-sectarian within the Christian faiths. Dr. Weigle stated that his definition of the Holy Bible would include the Jewish Holy Scriptures, but also stated that the 'Holy Bible' would not be complete without the New Testament. He stated that the New Testament 'conveyed the message of Christians.' In his opinion, reading of the Holy Scriptures to the exclusion of the New Testament would be a sectarian practice. Dr. Weigle stated that the Bible was of great moral, historical and literary value. This is conceded by all the parties and is also the view of the court." 177 F. Supp. 398, 401-402.

The trial court, in striking down the practices and the statute requiring them, made specific findings of fact that the children's attendance at Abington Senior High School is compulsory and that the practice of reading 10 verses from the Bible is also compelled by law. It also found that:

> "The reading of the verses, even without comment, possesses a devotional and religious character and constitutes in effect a religious observance. The devotional and religious nature of the morning exercises is made all the more apparent by the fact that the Bible reading is followed immediately by a recital in unison by the pupils of the Lord's Prayer. The fact that some pupils, or theoretically all pupils, might be excused from attendance at the exercises does not mitigate the obligatory nature of the ceremony for ... Section 1516 ... unequivocally requires the exercises to be held every school day in every school in the Commonwealth. The exercises are held in the school buildings and perforce are conducted by and under the authority of the local school authorities and during school sessions. Since the statute requires the reading of the 'Holy Bible,' a Christian document, the practice ... prefers the Christian religion. The record demonstrates that it was the intention of ... the Commonwealth ... to introduce a religious ceremony into the public schools of the Commonwealth." 201 F. Supp., at 819.

No. 119. In 1905 the Board of School Commissioners of Baltimore City adopted a rule pursuant to Art. 77, § 202 of the Annotated Code of Maryland. The rule provided for the holding of opening exercises in the schools of the city consisting primarily of the "reading, without comment, of a chapter in the Holy Bible and/or the use of the Lord's Prayer." The petitioners, Mrs. Madalyn Murray and her son, William J. Murray, III, are both professed atheists. Following unsuccessful attempts to have the respondent school board rescind the rule this suit was filed for mandamus to compel its rescission and cancellation. It was alleged that William was a student in a public school of the city and Mrs. Murray, his mother, was a taxpayer therein; that it was the practice under the rule to have a reading on each school morning from the King James version of the Bible; that at petitioners' insistence the rule was amended[4] to permit children to be excused from the exercise on request of the parent and that William had been excused pursuant thereto; that nevertheless the rule as amended was in violation of the petitioners' rights "to freedom of religion under the First and Fourteenth Amendments" and in violation of "the

principle of separation between church and state, contained therein. . . ." The petition particularized the petitioners' atheistic beliefs
and stated that the rule, as practiced, violated their rights

> "in that it threatens their religious liberty by placing a
> premium on belief as against non-belief and subjects their
> freedom of conscience to the rule of the majority; it pro-
> nounces belief in God as the source of all moral and spiritual
> values, equating these values with religious values, and there-
> by renders sinister, alien and suspect the beliefs and ideals
> of. . . . Petitioners, promoting doubt and question of their
> morality, good citizenship and good faith."

The respondents demurred and the trial court, recognizing
that the demurrer admitted all facts well pleaded, sustained it
without leave to amend. The Maryland Court of Appeals affirmed,
the majority of four justices holding the exercise not in violation
of the First and Fourteenth Amendments, with three justices dissenting. 228 Md. 239, 179 A. 2d 698. We granted certiorari. 371
U. S. 809.

II.

It is true that religion has been closely identified with our
history and government. As we said in *Engel* v. *Vitale*, 370 U. S.
421, 434 (1962), "The history of man is inseparable from the
history of religion. And . . . since the beginning of that history
many people have devoutly believed that 'More things are wrought
by prayer than this world dreams of.' " In *Zorach* v. *Clauson*, 343
U. S. 306, 313 (1952), we gave specific recognition to the proposition that "[w]e are a religious people whose institutions presuppose
a Supreme Being." The fact that the Founding Fathers believed
devotedly that there was a God and that the unalienable rights of
man were rooted in Him is clearly evidenced in their writings,
from the Mayflower Compact to the Constitution itself. This background is evidenced today in our public life through the con-
tinuance in our oaths of office from the Presidency to the Alderman
of the final supplication, "So help me God." Likewise each House
of the Congress provides through its Chaplain an opening prayer,
and the sessions of this Court are declared open by the crier in a

short ceremony, the final phrase of which invokes the grace of God. Again, there are such manifestations in our military forces, where those of our citizens who are under the restrictions of military service wish to engage in voluntary worship. Indeed, only last year an official survey of the country indicated that 64% of our people have church membership, Bureau of Census, U. S. Department of Commerce, Statistical Abstract of the United States, 48 (83d ed. 1962), while less than 3% profess no religion whatever. *Id.,* at p. 46. It can be truly said, therefore, that today, as in the beginning, our national life reflects a religious people who, in the words of Madison, are "earnestly praying, as . . . in duty bound, that the Supreme Lawgiver of the Universe . . . guide them into every measure which may be worthy of his . . . blessing. . . ." Memorial and Remonstrance Against Religious Assessments, quoted in *Everson* v. *Board of Education,* 330 U. S. 1, 71-72 (1947) (Appendix to dissenting opinion of Rutledge, J.).

This is not to say, however, that religion has been so identified with our history and government that religious freedom is not likewise as strongly imbedded in our public and private life. Nothing but the most telling of personal experiences in religious persecution suffered by our forebears, see *Everson* v. *Board of Education, supra,* at 8-11, could have planted our belief in liberty of religious opinion any more deeply in our heritage. It is true that this liberty frequently was not realized by the colonists, but this is readily accountable to their close ties to the Mother Country.[5] However, the views of Madison and Jefferson, preceded by Roger Williams,[6] came to be incorporated not only in the Federal Constitution but likewise in those of most of our States. This freedom to worship was indispensable in a country whose people came from the four quarters of the earth and brought with them a diversity of religious opinion. Today authorities list 83 separate religious bodies, each with memberships exceeding 50,000, existing among our people, as well as innumerable smaller groups. Bureau of Census, *op. cit., supra,* at 46-47.

III.

Almost a hundred years ago in *Minor* v. *Board of Education of Cincinnati,*[7] Judge Alphonzo Taft, father of the revered Chief Justice, in an unpublished opinion stated the ideal of our people as to religious freedom as one of "absolute equality before the law of all religious opinions and sects . . . ."

.   .   .   .   .

"The government is neutral, and, while protecting all, it prefers none, and it disparages none."

Before examining this "neutral" position in which the Establishment and Free Exercise Clauses of the First Amendment place our government it is well that we discuss the reach of the Amendment under the cases of this Court.

First, this Court has decisively settled that the First Amendment's mandate that "Congress shall make no law respecting an establishment of religion, or prohibiting the free exercise thereof" has been made wholly applicable to the states by the Fourteenth Amendment. Twenty-three years ago in *Cantwell* v. *Connecticut,* 310 U. S. 296, 303 (1940), this Court, through Mr. Justice Roberts, said:

"The fundamental concept of liberty embodied in that [Fourteenth] Amendment embraces the liberties guaranteed by the First Amendment. The First Amendment declares that Congress shall make no law respecting an establishment of religion or prohibiting the free exercise thereof. The Fourteenth Amendment has rendered the legislatures of the states as incompetent as Congress to enact such laws. . . ."[8]

In a series of cases since *Cantwell* the Court has repeatedly reaffirmed that doctrine, and we do so now. *Murdock* v. *Pennsylvania,* 319 U. S. 105, 108 (1943); *Everson* v. *Board of Education, supra; Illinois ex rel. McCollum* v. *Board of Education,* 333 U. S. 203, 210-211 (1948); *Zorach* v. *Clauson, supra; McGowan* v. *Maryland,* 366 U. S. 420 (1961); *Torcaso* v. *Watkins,* 367 U. S. 488 (1961); and *Engel* v. *Vitale, supra.*

Second, this Court has rejected unequivocally the contention that the establishment clause forbids only governmental preference of one religion over another. Almost 20 years ago in *Everson, supra,* at 15, the Court said that "[n]either a state nor the Federal government can set up a church. Neither can pass laws which aid one religion, aid all religions, or prefer one religion over another." And Mr. Justice Jackson, dissenting, agreed:

"There is no answer to the proposition ... that the effect of the religious freedom Amendment to our Constitution was to take every form of propagation of religion out of the realm of things which could directly or indirectly be made public business and thereby be supported in whole or in part at taxpayers' expense.... This freedom was first in the Bill of Rights because it was first in the forefathers' minds; it was set forth in absolute terms, and its strength is its rigidity." *Id.,* at 26.

Further, Mr. Justice Rutledge, joined by Justices Frankfurter, Jackson and Burton, declared:

"The [First] Amendment's purpose was not to strike merely at the official establishment of a single sect, creed or religion, outlawing only a formal relation such as had prevailed in England and some of the Colonies. Necessarily it was to uproot all such relationships. But the object was broader than separating church and state in this narrow sense. It was to create a complete and permanent separation of the spheres of religious activity and civil authority by comprehensively forbidding every form of public aid or support for religion." *Id.,* at 31-32.

The same conclusion has been firmly maintained ever since that time, see *Illinois ex rel. McCollum, supra,* at pp. 210-211; *McGowan* v. *Maryland, supra,* at 442-443; *Torcaso* v. *Watkins, supra,* at 492-493, 495, and we reaffirm it now.

While none of the parties to either of these cases has questioned these basic conclusions of the Court, both of which have been long established, recognized and consistently reaffirmed, others continue to question their history, logic and efficacy. Such contentions, in the light of the consistent interpretation in cases of this Court, seem entirely untenable and of value only as academic exercises.

IV.

The interrelationship of the Establishment and the Free Exercise Clauses was first touched upon by Mr. Justice Roberts for the Court in *Cantwell* v. *Connecticut, supra,* at 303, where it was said that their "inhibition of legislation" had

> "a double aspect. On the one hand, it forestalls compulsion by law of the acceptance of any creed or the practice of any form of worship. Freedom of conscience and freedom to adhere to such religious organization or form of worship as the individual may choose cannot be restricted by law. On the other hand, it safeguards the free exercise of the chosen form of religion. Thus the Amendment embraces two concepts—freedom to believe and freedom to act. The first is absolute but, in the nature of things, the second cannot be."

A half dozen years later in *Everson* v. *Board of Education, supra,* at 14-15, this Court, through MR. JUSTICE BLACK, stated that the "scope of the First Amendment . . . was designed forever to suppress" the establishment of religion or the prohibition of the free exercise thereof. In short, the Court held that the Amendment

> "requires the state to be a neutral in its relations with groups of religious believers and non-believers; it does not require the state to be their adversary. State power is no more to be used so as to handicap religions than it is to favor them." *Id.,* at 18.

And Mr. Justice Jackson, in dissent, declared that public schools are organized

> "on the premise that secular education can be isolated from all religious teaching so that the school can inculcate all needed temporal knowledge and also maintain a strict and lofty neutrality as to religion. The assumption is that after the individual has been instructed in worldly wisdom he will be better fitted to choose his religion." *Id.,* at 23-24.

Moreover, all of the four dissenters, speaking through Mr. Justice Rutledge, agreed that

> "Our constitutional policy. . . . [D]oes not deny the value or necessity for religious training, teaching or observance. Rather it secures their free exercise. But to that end it does deny that the state can undertake or sustain them in

any form or degree. For this reason the sphere of religious activity, as distinguished from the secular intellectual liberties, has been given the two-fold protection and, as the state cannot forbid, neither can it perform or aid in performing the religious function. The dual prohibition makes that function altogether private." *Id.,* at 52.

Only one year later the Court was asked to reconsider and repudiate the doctrine of these cases in *McCollum* v. *Board of Education.* It was argued that "historically the First Amendment was intended to forbid only government preference of one religion over another. . . . In addition they ask that we distinguish or overrule our holding in the *Everson* case that the Fourteenth Amendment made the 'establishment of religion' clause of the First Amendment applicable as a prohibition against the States." 333 U. S., at 211. The Court, with Mr. Justice Reed alone dissenting, was unable to "accept either of these contentions." *Ibid.* Mr. Justice Frankfurter, joined by Justices Jackson, Rutledge and Burton, wrote a very comprehensive and scholarly concurrence in which he said that "[s]eparation is a requirement to abstain from fusing functions of government and of religious sects, not merely to treat them all equally." *Id.,* at 227. Continuing, he stated that:

"the Constitution . . . prohibited the government common to all from becoming embroiled, however innocently, in the destructive religious conflicts of which the history of even this country records some dark pages." *Id.,* at 228.

In 1952 in *Zorach* v. *Clauson, supra,* MR. JUSTICE DOUGLAS for the Court reiterated:

"There cannot be the slightest doubt that the First Amendment reflects the philosophy that Church and State should be separated. And so far as interference with the 'free exercise' of religion and an 'establishment' of religion are concerned, the separation must be complete and unequivocal. The First Amendment within the scope of its coverage permits no exception; the prohibition is absolute. The First Amendment, however, does not say that in every and all respects there shall be a separation of Church and State. Rather, it studiously defines the manner, the specific ways, in which there shall be no concert or union or dependency one on the other. That is the common sense of the matter." 343 U. S. at 312.

And then in 1961 in *McGowan* v. *Maryland* and in *Torcaso* v. *Watkins* each of these cases was discussed and approved. CHIEF JUSTICE WARREN in *McGowan*, for a unanimous Court on this point, said:

> "But, the First Amendment, in its final form, did not simply bar a congressional enactment *establishing a church*; it forbade all laws *respecting an establishment of religion.* Thus this Court has given the Amendment a 'broad interpretation ... in the light of its history and the evils it was designed forever to suppress. . . .' " 366 U. S. at 441-442.

And MR. JUSTICE BLACK for the Court in *Torcaso,* without dissent but with Justices Frankfurter and HARLAN concurring in the result, used this language:

> "We repeat and again reaffirm that neither a State nor the Federal Government can constitutionally force a person 'to profess a belief or disbelief in any religion.' Neither can constitutionally pass laws or impose requirements which aid all religions as against non-believers, and neither can aid those religions based on a belief in the existence of God as against those religions founded on different beliefs." 367 U. S. at 495.

Finally, in *Engel* v. *Vitale,* only last year, these principles were so universally recognized that the Court without the citation of a single case and over the sole dissent of MR. JUSTICE STEWART reaffirmed them. The Court found the 22-word prayer used in "New York's program of daily classroom invocation of God's blessings as prescribed in the Regents' prayer ... [to be] a religious activity." 370 U. S., at 424. It held that "it is no part of the business of government to compose official prayers for any group of the American people to recite as a part of a religious program carried on by the government." *Id.,* at 425. In discussing the reach of the Establishment and Free Exercise Clauses of the First Amendment the Court said:

"Although these two clauses may in certain instances overlap, they forbid two quite different kinds of governmental encroachment upon religious freedom. The Establishment Clause, unlike the Free Exercise Clause, does not depend upon any showing of direct governmental compulsion and is violated by the enactment of laws which establish an official religion whether those laws operate directly to coerce non-observing individuals or not. This is not to say, of course, that laws officially prescribing a particular form of religious worship do not involve coercion of such individuals. When the power, prestige and financial support of government is placed behind a particular religious belief, the indirect coercive pressure upon religious minorities to conform to the prevailing officially approved religion is plain." *Id.*, at 430-431.

And in further elaboration the Court found that the "first and most immediate purpose [of the Establishment Clause] rested on a belief that a union of government and religion tends to destroy government and to degrade religion." *Id.*, at 431. When government, the Court said, allies itself with one particular form of religion, the inevitable result is that it incurs "the hatred, disrespect and even contempt of those who held contrary beliefs." *Ibid.*

V.

The wholesome "neutrality" of which this Court's cases speak thus stems from a recognition of the teachings of history that powerful sects or groups might bring about a fusion of governmental and religious functions or a concert or dependency of one upon the other to the end that official support of the State or Federal Government would be placed behind the tenets of one or of all orthodoxies. This the Establishment Clause prohibits. And a further reason for neutrality is found in the Free Exercise Clause, which recognizes the value of religious training, teaching and observance and, more particularly, the right of every person to freely choose his own course with reference thereto, free of any compulsion from the state. This the Free Exercise Clause guarantees. Thus, as we have seen, the two clauses may overlap. As we have indicated, the Establishment Clause has been directly considered by this Court eight times in the past score of years and, with only one Justice dissenting on the point, it has consistently held that the clause withdrew all legislative power respecting religious belief or the expression thereof. The test may be stated as follows: what are the purpose and the primary effect of the enactment? If either is the advancement or inhibition of religion then the enactment exceeds the scope of legislative power as circumscribed by the Constitution. That is to say that to withstand the strictures of the Establishment Clause there must be a secular legislative purpose and a primary effect that neither advances nor inhibits religion. *Everson* v. *Board of Education, supra; McGowan* v. *Maryland, supra*, at 442. The Free Exercise Clause, likewise considered many times here, withdraws from legislative power, state and federal, the exertion of any restraint on the free exercise of religion. Its purpose is to secure religious liberty in the individual by prohibiting any invasions thereof by civil authority. Hence it is necessary in a free exercise case for one to show the coercive effect of the enactment as it operates against him in the practice of his religion. The distinction between the two clauses is apparent—a violation of the Free Exercise Clause is predicated on coercion while the Establishment Clause violation need not be so attended.

Applying the Establishment Clause principles to the cases at bar we find that the States are requiring the selection and reading at the opening of the school day of verses from the Holy Bible and the recitation of the Lord's Prayer by the students in unison. These exercises are prescribed as part of the curricular activities of students who are required by law to attend school. They are held in the school buildings under the supervision and with the participation of teachers employed in those schools. None of these factors, other than compulsory school attendance, was present in the program upheld in *Zorach* v. *Clauson*. The trial court in No. 142 has found that such an opening exercise is a religious ceremony and was intended by the State to be so. We agree with the trial court's finding is to the religious character of the exercises. Given that finding the exercises and the law requiring them are in violation of the Establishment Clause.

There is no such specific finding as to the religious character of the exercises in No. 119, and the State contends (as does the State in No. 142) that the program is an effort to extend its benefits to all public school children without regard to their religious belief. Included within its secular purposes, it says, are the promotion of moral values, the contradiction to the materialistic trends of our

times, the perpetuation of our institutions and the teaching of literature. The case came up on demurrer, of course, to a petition which
alleged that the uniform practice under the rule had been to read
from the King James version of the Bible and that the exercise was
sectarian. The short answer, therefore, is that the religious character of the exercise was admitted by the State. But even if its purpose
is not strictly religious, it is sought to be accomplished through
readings, without comment, from the Bible. Surely the place of the
Bible as an instrument of religion cannot be gainsaid, and the
State's recognition of the pervading religious character of the ceremony is evident from the rule's specific permission of the alternative use of the Catholic Douay version as well as the recent amendment permitting nonattendance at the exercises. None of these
factors is consistent with the contention that the Bible is here used
either as an instrument for nonreligious moral inspiration or as a
reference for the teaching of secular subjects.

The conclusion follows that in both cases the laws require
religious exercises and such exercises are being conducted in direct
violation of the rights of the appellees and petitioners.[9] Nor are
these required exercises mitigated by the fact that individual students may absent themselves upon parental request, for that fact
furnishes no defense to a claim of unconstitutionality under the
Establishment Clause. See *Engel* v. *Vitale, supra,* at 430. Further,
it is no defense to urge that the religious practices here may be relatively minor encroachments on the First Amendment. The breach
of neutrality that is today a trickling stream may all too soon become a raging torrent and, in the words of Madison, "it is proper
to take alarm at the first experiment on our liberties." Memorial
and Remonstrance Against Religious Assessments, quoted in *Everson, supra,* at 65.

It is insisted that unless these religious exercises are permitted
a "religion of secularism" is established in the schools. We agree of
course that the State may not establish a "religion of secularism"
in the sense of affirmatively opposing or showing hostility to religion, thus "preferring those who believe in no religion over those
who do believe." *Zorach* v. *Clauson, supra,* at 314. We do not agree,
however, that this decision in any sense has that effect. In addition,
it might well be said that one's education is not complete without
a study of comparative religion or the history of religion and its
relationship to the advancement of civilization. It certainly may
be said that the Bible is worthy of study for its literary and historic

qualities. Nothing we have said here indicates that such study of the Bible or of religion, when presented objectively as part of a secular program of education, may not be effected consistent with the First Amendment. But the exercises here do not fall into those categories. They are religious exercises, required by the States in violation of the command of the First Amendment that the Government maintain strict neutrality, neither aiding nor opposing religion.

Finally, we cannot accept that the concept of neutrality, which does not permit a State to require a religious exercise even with the consent of the majority of those affected, collides with the majority's right to free exercise of religion.[10] While the Free Exercise Clause clearly prohibits the use of state action to deny the rights of free exercise to *anyone,* it has never meant that a majority could use the machinery of the State to practice its beliefs. Such a contention was effectively answered by Mr. Justice Jackson for the Court in *West Virginia Board of Education* v. *Barnette,* 319 U. S. 624, 638 (1943):

> "The very purpose of a Bill of Rights was to withdraw certain subjects from the vicissitudes of political controversy, to place them beyond the reach of majorities and officials and to establish them as legal principles to be applied by the courts. One's right to ... freedom of worship ... and other fundamental rights may not be submitted to vote; they depend on the outcome of no elections."

The place of religion in our society is an exalted one, achieved through a long tradition of reliance on the home, the church and the inviolable citadel of the individual heart and mind. We have come to recognize through bitter experience that it is not within the power of government to invade that citadel, whether its purpose or effect be to aid or oppose, to advance or retard. In the relationship between man and religion, the State is firmly committed to a position of neutrality. Though the application of that rule requires interpretation of a delicate sort, the rule itself is clearly and consisely stated in the words of the First Amendment. Applying that rule to the facts of these cases, we affirm the judgment in No. 142. In No. 119, the judgment is reversed and the cause remanded to the Maryland Court of Appeals for further proceedings consistent with this opinion.

It is so ordered.

(Chief Justice Warren and Associate Justices Black, Brennan, Douglas, Goldberg, Harlan and White joined with Justice Clark in the foregoing judgment of the Court. Justice Brennan wrote a 76-page concurring opinion; Justice Douglas contributed a 3-page separate concurrence; and Justice Goldberg wrote a 4-page concurring opinion in which he was joined by Justice Harlan. For space reasons we are compelled to omit the separate concurring opinions. The Brennan opinion is especially commended for legal students.)

MR. JUSTICE STEWART, dissenting.

I think the records in the two cases before us are so fundamentally deficient as to make impossible an informed or responsible determination of the constitutional issues presented. Specifically, I cannot agree that on these records we can say that the Establishment Clause has necessarily been violated.[11] But I think there exist serious questions under both that provision and the Free Exercise Clause—insofar as each is imbedded in the Fourteenth Amendment—which require the remand of these cases for the taking of additional evidence.

I.

The First Amendment declares that "Congress shall make no law respecting an establishment of religion, or prohibiting the free exercise thereof. . . ." It is, I think, a fallacious oversimplification to regard these two provisions as establishing a single constitutional standard of "separation of church and state," which can be mechanically applied in every case to delineate the required boundaries between government and religion. We err in the first place if we do not recognize, as a matter of history and as a matter of the imperatives of our free society, that religion and government must necessarily interact in countless ways. Secondly, the fact is that while in many contexts the Establishment Clause and the Free Exercise Clause fully complement each other, there are areas in which a doctrinaire reading of the Establishment Clause leads to irreconcilable conflict with the Free Exercise Clause.

A single obvious example should suffice to make the point. Spending federal funds to employ chaplains for the armed forces might be said to violate the Establishment Clause. Yet a lonely soldier stationed at some faraway outpost could surely complain that a government which did *not* provide him the opportunity for pastoral guidance was affirmatively prohibiting the free exercise of his religion. And such examples could readily be multiplied. The short of the matter is simply that the two relevant clauses of the First Amendment cannot accurately be reflected in a sterile metaphor which by its very nature may distort rather than illumine the problems involved in a particular case. Cf. *Sherbert* v. *Verner, post,* p. ——.

II.

As a matter of history, the First Amendment was adopted solely as a limitation upon the newly created National Government. The events leading to its adoption strongly suggest that the Establishment Clause was primarily an attempt to insure that Congress not only would be powerless to establish a national church, but would also be unable to interfere with existing state establishments. See *McGowan* v. *Maryland,* 366 U. S. 420, 440-441. Each State was left free to go its own way and pursue its own policy with respect to religion. Thus Virginia from the beginning pursued a policy of disestablishmentarianism. Massachusetts, by contrast, had an established church until well into the nineteenth century.

So matters stood until the adoption of the Fourteenth Amendment, or more accurately, until this Court's decision in *Cantwell* v. *Connecticut,* in 1940. 310 U. S. 296. In that case the Court said: "The First Amendment declares that Congress shall make no law respecting an establishment of religion or prohibiting the free exercise thereof. The Fourteenth Amendment has rendered the legislatures of the states as incompetent as Congress to enact such laws."[12]

I accept without question that the liberty guaranteed by the Fourteenth Amendment against impairment by the States embraces in full the right of free exercise of religion protected by the First Amendment, and I yield to no one in my conception of the breadth of that freedom. See *Braunfeld* v. *Brown,* 366 U. S. 599, 616 (dissenting opinion). I accept too the proposition that the Fourteenth Amendment has somehow absorbed the Establishment

Clause, although it is not without irony that a constitutional provision evidently designed to leave the States free to go their own way should now have become a restriction upon their autonomy. But I cannot agree with what seems to me the insensitive definition of the Establishment Clause contained in the Court's opinion, nor with the different but, I think, equally mechanistic definitions contained in the separate opinions which have been filed.

III.

Since the *Cantwell* pronouncement in 1940, this Court has only twice held invalid state laws on the ground that they were laws "respecting an establishment of religion" in violation of the Fourteenth Amendment. *McCollum* v. *Board of Education*, 333 U. S. 203; *Engel* v. *Vitale*, 370 U. S. 421. On the other hand, the Court has upheld against such a challenge laws establishing Sunday as a compulsory day of rest, *McGowan* v. *Maryland*, 366 U. S. 420, and a law authorizing reimbursement from public funds for the transportation of parochial school pupils. *Everson* v. *Board of Education*, 330 U. S. 1.

Unlike other First Amendment guarantees, there is an inherent limitation upon the applicability of the Establishment Clause's ban on state support to religion. That limitation was succinctly put in *Everson* v. *Board of Education*, 330 U. S. 1, 18: "State power is no more to be used so as to handicap religions than it is to favor them."[13] And in a later case, this Court recognized that the limitation was one which was itself compelled by the free exercise guarantee. "To hold that a state cannot consistently with the First and Fourteenth Amendments utilize its public school system to aid any or all religious faiths or sects in the dissemination of their doctrines and ideals does not . . . manifest a governmental hostility to religion or religious teaching. A manifestation of such hostility would be at war with our national tradition as embodied in the First Amendment's guaranty of the free exercise of religion." *McCollum* v. *Board of Education*, 333 U. S. 203, 211-212.

That the central value embodied in the First Amendment— and, more particularly, in the guarantee of "liberty" contained in the Fourteenth—is the safeguarding of an individual's right to free exercise of his religion has been consistently recognized. Thus, in the case of *Hamilton* v. *Regents,* 293 U. S. 245, 265, Mr. Justice Cardozo, concurring, assumed that it was ". . . *the religious liberty* protected by the First Amendment against invasion by the nation [which] is protected by the Fourteenth Amendment against invasion by the states." (Emphasis added.) And in *Cantwell* v. *Connecticut, supra,* the purpose of those guarantees was described in the following terms: "On the one hand, it forestalls compulsion by law of the acceptance of any creed or the practice of any form of worship. Freedom of conscience and freedom to adhere to such religious organization or form of worship as the individual may choose cannot be restricted by law. On the other hand, it safeguards the free exercise of the chosen form of religion." 310 U. S., at 303.

It is this concept of constitutional protection embodied in our decisions which makes the cases before us such difficult ones for me. For there is involved in these cases a substantial free exercise claim on the part of those who affirmatively desire to have their children's school day open with the reading of passages from the Bible.

It has become accepted that the decision in *Pierce* v. *Society of Sisters,* 268 U. S. 510, upholding the right of parents to send their children to nonpublic schools, was ultimately based upon the recognition of the validity of the free exercise claim involved in that situation. It might be argued here that parents who wanted their children to be exposed to religious influences in school could, under *Pierce,* send their children to private or parochial schools. But the consideration which renders this contention too facile to be determinative has already been recognized by the Court: "Freedom of speech, freedom of the press, freedom of religion are available to all, not merely to those who can pay their own way." *Murdock* v. *Pennsylvania,* 319 U. S. 105, 111.

It might also be argued that parents who want their children exposed to religious influences can adequately fulfill that wish off school property and outside school time. With all its surface persuasiveness, however, this argument seriously misconceives the basic constitutional justification for permitting the exercises at issue in these cases. For a compulsory state educational system so structures a child's life that if religious exercises are held to be an impermissible activity in schools, religion is placed at an artificial and state-created disadvantage. Viewed in this light, permission of such exercises for those who want them is necessary if the schools are truly to be neutral in the matter of religion. And a refusal to permit religious exercises thus is seen, not as the realization of state neutrality, but rather as the establishment of a religion of secularism, or at the least, as government support of the beliefs of those who think that religious exercises should be conducted only in private.

What seems to me to be of paramount importance, then, is recognition of the fact that the claim advanced here in favor of Bible reading is sufficiently substantial to make simple reference to the constitutional phrase "establishment of religion" as inadequate an analysis of the cases before us as the ritualistic invocation of the nonconstitutional phrase "separation of church and state." What these cases compel, rather, is an analysis of just what the "neutrality" is which is required by the interplay of the Establishment and Free Exercise Clauses of the First Amendment, as imbedded in the Fourteenth.

IV.

Our decisions make clear that there is no constitutional bar to the use of government property for religious purposes. On the contrary, this Court has consistently held that the discriminatory barring of religious groups from public property is itself a violation of First and Fourteenth Amendment guarantees. *Fowler* v. *Rhode Island,* 345 U. S. 67; *Niemotko* v. *Maryland,* 340 U. S. 268. A different standard has been applied to public school property, because of the coercive effect which the use by religious sects of a compulsory school system would necessarily have upon the children involved. *McCollum* v. *Board of Education,* 333 U. S. 203. But insofar as the *McCollum* decision rests on the Establishment rather than the Free Exercise Clause, it is clear that its effect is limited to religious instruction—to government support of proselytizing activities of religious sects by throwing the weight of secular authority behind the dissemination of religious tenets.[14]

The dangers both to government and to religion inherent in official support of instruction in the tenets of various religious sects are absent in the present cases, which involve only a reading from the Bible unaccompanied by comments which might otherwise constitute instruction. Indeed, since, from all that appears in either record, any teacher who does not wish to do so is free not to participate,[15] it cannot even be contended that some infinitesimal part of the salaries paid by the State are made contingent upon the performance of a religious function.

In the absence of evidence that the legislature or school board intended to prohibit local schools from substituting a different set of readings where parents requested such a change, we should not assume that the provisions before us—as actually administered—may not be construed simply as authorizing religious exercises, nor that the designations may not be treated simply as indications of the promulgating body's view as to the community's preference. We are under a duty to interpret these provisions so as to render them constitutional if reasonably possible. Compare *Two Guys* v. *McGinley*, 366 U. S. 582, 592-595; *Everson* v. *Board of Education*, 330 U. S. 1, 4, and n. 2. In the *Schempp* case there is evidence which indicates that variations were in fact permitted by the very school there involved, and that further variations were not introduced only because of the absence of requests from parents. And in the *Murray* case the Baltimore rule itself contains a provision permitting another version of the Bible to be substituted for the King James version.

If the provisions are not so construed, I think that their validity under the Establishment Clause would be extremely doubtful, because of the designation of a particular religious book and a denominational prayer. But since, even if the provisions are construed as I believe they must be, I think that the cases before us must be remanded for further evidence on other issues—thus affording the plaintiffs an opportunity to prove that local variations are not in fact permitted—I shall for the balance of this dissenting opinion treat the provisions before us as making the variety and content of the exercises, as well as a choice as to their implementation, matters which ultimately reflect the concensus of each local school community. In the absence of coercion upon those who do not wish to participate—because they hold less strong beliefs, other beliefs, or no beliefs at all—such provisions cannot, in my view, be held to represent the type of support of religion barred by the Establishment Clause. For the only support which such rules provide for religion is the withholding of state hostility—a simple acknowledgment on the part of secular authorities that the Constitution does not require extirpation of all expression of religious belief.

V.

I have said that these provisions authorizing religious exercises are properly to be regarded as measures making possible the free exercise of religion. But it is important to stress that, strictly speaking, what is at issue here is a privilege rather than a right. In other words, the question presented is not whether exercises such as those at issue here are constitutionally compelled, but rather whether they are constitutionally invalid. And that issue, in my view, turns on the question of coercion.

It is clear that the dangers of coercion involved in the holding of religious exercises in a schoolroom differ qualitatively from those presented by the use of similar exercises or affirmations in ceremonies attended by adults. Even as to children, however, the duty laid upon government in connection with religious exercises in the public schools is that of refraining from so structuring the school environment as to put any kind of pressure on a child to participate in those exercises; it is not that of providing an atmosphere in which children are kept scrupulously insulated from any awareness that some of their fellows may want to open the school day with prayer, or of the fact that there exist in our pluralistic society differences of religious belief.

These are not, it must be stressed, cases like *Brown* v. *Board of Education,* 347 U. S. 483, in which this Court held that, in the sphere of public education, the Fourteenth Amendment's guarantee of equal protection of the laws required that race not be treated as a relevant factor. A segregated school system is not invalid because its operation is coercive; it is invalid simply because our Constitution presupposes that men are created equal, and that therefore racial differences cannot provide a valid basis for governmental action. Accommodation of religious differences on the part of the State, however, is not only permitted but required by that same Constitution.

The governmental neutrality which the First and Fourteenth Amendments require in the cases before us, in other words, is the extension of even-handed treatment to all who believe, doubt, or disbelieve—a refusal on the part of the State to weight the scales of private choice. In these cases, therefore, what is involved is not state action based on impermissible categories, but rather an attempt by the State to accommodate those differences which the existence in our society of a variety of religious beliefs make inevitable. The Constitution requires that such efforts be struck down only if they are proven to entail the use of the secular authority of government to coerce a preference among such beliefs.

It may well be, as has been argued to us, that even the supposed benefits to be derived from noncoercive religious exercises in public schools are incommensurate with the administrative problems which they would create. The choice involved, however, is one for each local community and its school board, and not for this Court. For, as I have said, religious exercises are not constitutionally invalid if they simply reflect differences which exist in the society from which the school draws its pupils. They become constitutionally invalid only if their administration places the sanction of secular authority behind one or more particular religious or irreligious beliefs.

To be specific, it seems to me clear that certain types of exercises would present situations in which no possibility of coercion on the part of secular officials could be claimed to exist. Thus, if such exercises were held either before or after the official school day, or if the school schedule were such that participation were merely one among a number of desirable alternatives,[16] it could hardly be contended that the exercises did anything more than to provide an opportunity for the voluntary expression of religious belief. On the other hand, a law which provided for religious exercises during the school day and which contained no excusal provision would obviously be unconstitutionally coercive upon those who did not wish to participate. And even under a law containing an excusal provision, if the exercises were held during the school day, and no equally desirable alternative were provided by the school authorities, the likelihood that children might be under at least some psychological compulsion to participate would be great. In a case such as the latter, however, I think we would err if we *assumed* such coercion in the absence of any evidence."[17]

VI.

Viewed in this light, it seems to me clear that the records in both of the cases before us are wholly inadequate to support an informed or responsible decision. Both cases involve provisions which explicitly permit any student who wishes, to be excused from participation in the exercises. There is no evidence in either case as to whether there would exist any coercion of any kind upon a student who did not want to participate. No evidence at all was adduced in the *Murray* case, because it was decided upon a demurrer. All that we have in that case, therefore, is the conclusory language of a pleading. While such conclusory allegations are acceptable for procedural purposes, I think that the nature of the constitutional problem involved here clearly demands that no decision be made except upon evidence. In the *Schempp* case the record shows no more than a subjective prophecy by a parent of what he thought would happen if a request were made to be excused from participation in the exercises under the amended statute. No such request was ever made, and there is no evidence whatever as to what might or would actually happen, nor of what administrative arrangements the school actually might or could make to free from pressure of any kind those who do not want to participate in the exercises. There were no District Court findings on this issue, since the case under the amended statute was decided exclusively on Establishment Clause grounds. 201 F. Supp. 815.

What our Constitution indispensably protects is the freedom of each of us, be he Jew or Agnostic, Christian or Atheist, Buddhist or Freethinker, to believe or disbelieve, to worship or not worship, to pray or keep silent, according to his own conscience, uncoerced and unrestrained by government. It is conceivable that these school boards, or even all school boards, might eventually find it impossible to administer a system of religious exercises during school hours in such a way as to meet this constitutional standard—in such a way as completely to free from any kind of official coercion those who do not affirmatively want to participate.[18] But I think we must not assume that school boards so lack the qualities of inventiveness and good will as to make impossible the achievement of that goal.

I would remand both cases for further hearings.

NOTES

[1] The action was brought in 1958, prior to the 1959 amendment of § 15-1516 authorizing a child's nonattendance at the exercises upon parental request. The three-judge court held the statute and the practices complained of unconstitutional under both the Establishment Clause and the Free Exercise Clause. 177 F. Supp. 398. Pending appeal to this Court by the school district, the statute was so amended, and we vacated the judgment and remanded for further pro-

(Footnote 1—continued.)

ceedings. 364 U. S. 298. The same three-judge court granted appellees' motion to amend the pleadings, 195 F. Supp. 518, held a hearing on the amended pleadings and rendered the judgment, 201 F. Supp. 815, from which appeal is now taken.

[2] The statute as amended imposes no penalty upon a teacher refusing to obey its mandate. However, it remains to be seen whether one refusing could have his contract of employment terminated for "wilful violation of the school laws." 24 Pa. Stat. (Supp. 1960) §11-1122.

[3] The trial court summarized his testimony as follows:

"Edward Schempp, the children's father, testified that after careful consideration he had decided that he should not have Roger or Donna excused from attendance at these morning ceremonies. Among his reasons were the following. He said that he thought his children would be 'labeled as "odd balls" ' before their teachers and classmates every school day; that children, like Roger's and Donna's classmates, were liable 'to lump all particular religious difference[s] or religious objections [together] as "atheism" ' and that today the word 'atheism' is often connected with 'atheistic communism,' and has 'very bad' connotations, such as 'un-American' or 'anti-Red,' with overtones of possible immorality. Mr. Schempp pointed out that due to the events of the morning exercises following in rapid succession, the Bible reading, the Lord's Prayer, the Flag Salute, and the announcements, excusing his children from the Bible reading would mean that probably they would miss hearing the announcements so important to children. He testified also that if Roger and Donna were excused from Bible reading they would have to stand in the hall outside their 'homeroom' and that this carried with it the imputation of punishment for bad conduct." 201 F. Supp., at 818.

[4] The rule as amended provides as follows:

"Opening Exercise. Each school, either collectively or in classes, shall be opened by the reading, without comment, of a chapter in the Holy Bible and/or the use of the Lord's Prayer. The Douay version may be used by those pupils who prefer it. Appropriate patriotic exercises should be held as a part of the general opening exercise of the school or class. Any child shall be excused from participating in the opening exercises or from attending the opening exercises upon written request of his parent or guardian."

[5] There were established churches in at least eight of the original colonies, and various degrees of religious support in others as late as the Revolutionary War. See *Engel* v. *Vitale, supra*, at 428, n. 10.

[6] "There goes many a ship to sea, with many hundred souls in one ship, whose weal and woe is common, and is a true picture of a commonwealth, or human combination, or society. It hath fallen out sometimes, that both Papists and Protestants, Jews and Turks, may be embarked in one ship; upon which supposal, I affirm that all the liberty of conscience I ever pleaded for, turns upon these two hinges, that none of the Papists, Protestants, Jews, or Turks be forced to come to the ship's prayers or worship, nor compelled from their own particular prayers or worship, if they practice any."

[7] Superior Court of Cincinnati, February 1870. The opinion is not reported but is published under the title, The Bible in the Common Schools (Cincinnati: Robert Clarke & Co. 1870). Judge Taft's views, expressed in dissent,

(Footnote 7—continued.)

prevailed on appeal. See *Board of Education of Cincinnati* v. *Minor,* 23 Ohio St. 211, 253 (1872), in which the Ohio Supreme Court held that:

"The great bulk of human affairs and human interests is left by any free government to individual enterprise and individual action. Religion is eminently one of these interests, lying outside the true and legitimate province of government."

[8] Application to the States of other clauses of the First Amendment obtained even before *Cantwell.* Almost 40 years ago in the opinion of the Court in *Gitlow* v. *New York,* 268 U. S. 652, 666 (1925), Mr. Justice Sanford said: "For present purposes we may and do assume that freedom of speech and of the press —which are protected by the First Amendment from abridgement by Congress— are among the fundamental personal rights and 'liberties' protected by the Due Process Clause of the Fourteenth Amendment from impairment by the States."

[9] It goes without saying that the laws and practices involved here can be challenged only by persons having standing to complain. But the requirements for standing to challenge state action under the Establishment Clause, unlike those relating to the Free Exercise Clause, do not include proof that particular religious freedoms are infringed. *McGowan* v. *Maryland, supra,* at 429-430. The parties here are school children and their parents, who are directly affected by the laws and practices against which their complaints are directed. These interests surely suffice to give the parties standing to complain. See *Engel* v. *Vitale, supra.* Cf. *McCollum* v. *Board of Education, supra; Everson* v. *Board of Education, supra.* Compare *Doremus* v. *Board of Education,* 342 U. S. 429 (1952), which involved the same substantive issues presented here. The appeal was there dismissed upon the graduation of the school child involved and because of the appellants' failure to establish standing as taxpayers.

[10] We are not of course presented with and therefore do not pass upon a situations such as military service, where the Government regulates the temporal and geographic environment of individuals to a point that, unless it permits voluntary religious services to be conducted with the use of government facilities, military personnel would be unable to engage in the practice of their faiths.

[11] It is instructive, in this connection, to examine the complaints in the two cases before us. Neither complaint attacks the challenged practices as "establishments." What both allege as the basis for their causes of actions are, rather, violations of religious liberty.

[12] 310 U. S., at 303. The Court's statement as to the Establishment Clause in *Cantwell* was dictum. The case was decided on free exercise grounds.

[13] See also, in this connection, *Zorach* v. *Clauson,* 343 U. S. 306, 314: "Government may not finance religious groups nor undertake religious instruction nor blend secular and sectarian education nor use secular institutions to force one or some religion on any person. But we find no constitutional requirement which makes it necessary for government to be hostile to religion and to throw its weight against efforts to widen the effective scope of religious influence."

[14] "This is beyond all question a utilization of the tax-established and tax-supported public school system to aid religious groups *to spread their faith.*" *McCollum* v. *Board of Education,* 333 U. S. 203, 210. (Emphasis added.)

[15] The Pennsylvania statute was specifically amended to remove the compulsion upon teachers. Act of December 17, 1959, P. L. 1928, 24 Purdon's Pa.

(Footnote 15—continued.)

Stat. Ann. § 15-1516. Since the Maryland case is here on a demurrer, the issue of whether or not a teacher could be dismissed for refusal to participate seems, among many others, never to have been raised.

[16] See, *e. g.*, the description of a plan permitting religious instruction off school property contained in *McCollum* v. *Board of Education*, 333 U. S. 203, 224 (separate opinion of Mr. Justice Frankfurter).

[17] Cf. "The task of separating the secular from the religious in education is one of magnitude, intricacy and delicacy. To lay down a sweeping constitutional doctrine as demanded by complainant and apparently approved by the Court, applicable alike to all school boards of the nation,... is to decree a uniform, rigid and, if we are consistent, an unchanging standard for countless school boards representing and serving highly localized groups which not only differ from each other but which themselves from time to time change attitudes. It seems to me that to do so is to allow zeal for our own ideas of what is good in public instruction to induce us to accept the role of a super board of education for every school district in the nation." *McCollum* v. *Board of Education*, 333 U. S. 203, 237 (concurring opinion of Mr. Justice Jackson).

[18] For example, if the record in the *Schempp* case contained proof (rather than mere prophecy) that the timing of morning announcements by the school was such as to handicap children who did not want to listen to the Bible reading, or that the excusal provision was so administered as to carry any overtones of social inferiority, then impermissible coercion would clearly exist.

Appendix III

Important Church-State Legal Cases

Abington v. *Schempp*, see Appendix II (1963).

Berghorn v. *Reorganized School District*, 364 Mo. 121 (1953).

Billard v. *Board of Education*, 69 Kan. 53 (1904).

Board of Education v. *Minor*, 23 Ohio St. 211 (1872).

Cantwell v. *Connecticut*, 310 U.S. 296 (1940).

Carden v. *Bland*, 199 Tenn. 665 (1956).

Chamberlin v. *Dade County*, 143 So. 2d 21 (1962).

Church v. *Bullock*, 104 Tex. 1 (1908).

Cochran v. *Louisiana*, 281 U.S. 370 (1930).

Commonwealth v. *Herr*, 229 Pa. 132 (1910).

Conway, State ex rel., v. *District Board*, 162 Wis. 482 (1916).

Dearle, State ex rel., v. *Frazier*, 102 Wash. 369 (1918).

Dickman v. *School District*, 366 Pac. 2d. 533 (1962).

Donahoe v. *Richards*, 38 Me. 379 (1854).

Doremus v. *Board of Education*, 342 U.S. 429 (1952).

Engel v. *Vitale*, 370 U.S. 421 (1962).

Everson v. *Board of Education*, 330 U.S. 1 (1947).

Finger, State ex rel., v. *Weedman*, 55 S.D. 343 (1929).

Freeman, State ex rel., v *Weedman*, 55 Neb. 853 (1902).

Gerhard v. *Heid*, 66 N.D. 444 (1936).

Gurney v. *Ferguson*, 190 Okla. 254 (1941).

Hackett v. *Brooksville Graded District*, 120 Ky. 608 (1905).

Harfst v. *Hoegen*, 349 Mo. 808 (1941).

Herold v. *Parish Board*, 136 La. 1034 (1915).

Hysong v. *School District*, 164 Pa. 629 (1894).

Johnson v. *Boyd*, 217 Ind. 348 (1940).

Judd v. *Board of Education*, 278 N.Y. 200 (1938).

Kaplan v. *School District*, 171 Minn. (1927).

Knowlton v. *Baumhover*, 182 Ia. 691 (1918).

Lewis v. *Board of Education*, 157 Misc. (N.Y.) 520 (1935).

McCollum v. *Board of Education*, 333 U.S. 203 (1948).

McGowan v. *Maryland*, 366 U.S. 420 (1961).

Massachusetts v. *Mellon*, 262 U.S. 447 (1923).

Matthews v. *Quinton*, 362 P. 2d. 932 (1961).

Meyer v. *Nebraska*, 262 U.S. 390 (1923).

Miller v. *Cooper*, 56 N.M. 355 (1952).

Moore v. *Monroe* 64 Ia. 367 (1884).

Murray v. *Curlett*, see Appendix II (1963).

North v. *Trustees U. of Illinois*, 137 Ill. 296 (1891).

O'Connor v. *Hendrick*, 184 N.Y. 421 (1906).

People v. *Stanley*, 81 Col. 276 (1927).

Permoli v. *New Orleans*, 3 How (U.S.) 589 (1845).

Pierce v. *Society of Sisters*, 268 U.S. 510 (1925).

Quick Bear v. *Leupp*, 210 U.S. 50 (1908).

Resnick v. *Dade County*, Fla. Supreme Court, No. 31, 546 (1962).

Reynolds v. *United States*, 98 U.S. 145 (1878).

Reynolds, State ex rel., v. *Nussbaum*, 171 Wis. 2d. 148 (1952).

Public School No 6, State ex rel., v. *Taylor*, 122 Neb. 454 (1932).

Ring v. *Board of Education*, 245 Ill. 334 (1910).

Torcaso v. *Watkins*, 367 U.S. 488 (1961).

Tudor v. *Board of Education*, 14 N.J. 31 (1953), Certiorari denied.

Schempp v. *School District* (1963).

Snyder v. *Town of Newton*, 147 Conn. 374 (1961). Appeal dismissed.

Spiller v. *Inhabitants of Woburn*, 12 Allen (Mass.) 127 (1866).

Swart v. *South Burlington*, 122 Vt. 177 (1961). Certiorari denied.

Visser v. *Nooksack*, 33 Wash. 2d. 699 (1949).

Vollmer v. *Stanley*, 81 Col. 276 (1927).

Washington Ethical Society v. *District of Columbia*, 249 F. 2d. 127 (1957).

Watson v. *Jones*, 13 Wall (U.S.) 679 (1872).

Weiss, State ex rel., v. *District Board*, 76 Wis. 177 (1890).

Williams v. *Stanton School District*, 173 Ky. 708 (1917).

Zellers v. *Huff*, 55 N.M. 501 (1951).

Zorach v. *Clauson*, 343 U.S. 306 (1952).

Bibliography

American Civil Liberties Union, Annual Reports.

Annals of the American Academy, "Organized Religion in the United States" (March, 1948).

Beale, Howard K. *A History of Freedom of Teaching in American Schools.* Charles Scribner's Sons, 1941.

Bennett, John C. *Christians and the State.* Charles Scribner's Sons, 1958.

Blanshard, Paul. *American Freedom and Catholic Power.* Beacon Press, 1958.

———. *God and Man in Washington.* Beacon Press, 1960.

Blau, Joseph L. *Cornerstones of Religious Freedom in America.* Beacon Press, 1949.

Blum, Virgil. *Freedom of Choice in Education.* The Macmillan Company, 1958.

Boles, Donald E. *The Bible, Religion and the Public Schools.* Iowa State University Press, 1963.

Bouscaren, T. Lincoln, and Adam C. Ellis. *Canon Law: Text and Commentary.* Bruce Publishing Co., 1948.

Brant, Irving. *James Madison.* The Bobbs-Merrill Company, Inc., 1941-1961.

Brown, Samuel W. *The Secularization of American Education.* Columbia University Press, 1912.

Butts, R. Freeman. *The American Tradition in Religion and Education.* Beacon Press, 1950.

Cahn, Edmond. "Government and Prayer," *New York University Law Review* (December, 1962).

Cobb, Sanford H. *The Rise of Religious Liberty in America.* The Macmillan Company, 1902.

Conant, James B. *Education in a Divided World.* Harvard University Press, 1948.

Connell, Francis J. *Morals in Politics and Professions.* The Newman Press, 1946.

Cousins, Norman. *In God We Trust.* Harper and Row, Publishers, 1958.

Cubberley, Elwood P. *Public Education in the United States.* Houghton Mifflin Company, 1919.

Dierenfield, Richard B. *Religion in American Public Schools.* Public Affairs Press, 1962.

Drinan, Robert F. *Religion, the Courts and Public Policy,* McGraw-Hill Book Co., Inc., 1963.

Dumbauld, Edward. *The Bill of Rights.* University of Oklahoma Press, 1957.

Fellman, David. *The Supreme Court and Education.* Teachers College, Columbia Univ., Bureau of Publications, 1962.

Five Great Encyclicals, Paulist Press, 1962.

Foote, Henry Wilder. *Thomas Jefferson.* Beacon Press, 1947.

Fund for the Republic (pamphlets), *Religion and the Free Society,* by William Lee Miller and others, 1958.

———. *Religion and the Schools,* by Robert Gordis and others, 1959.

Hachten, William A. "Journalism and the Prayer Decision," *Columbia Journalism Review* (Fall, 1962).

Healey, Robert M. *Jefferson and Religion in Public Education."* Yale University Press, 1962.

Honeywell, Roy J. *The Educational Work of Thomas Jefferson.* Harvard University Press, 1931.

Jacobson, Philip. *Religion in Public Education.* American Jewish Committee (165 East 56th St., New York 22) , 1963.

Johnson, Alvin W. and Frank H. Yost. *Separation of Church and State in the United States.* University of Minnesota Press, 1948.

Konvitz, Milton R. *Bill of Rights Reader.* Cornell University Press, 1954.

Kurland, Philip B. *Religion and the Law.* Aldine Publishing Co., 1962.

————, ed. *The Supreme Court Review, 1962,* University of Chicago Press, 1962.

LaNoue, George. "Religious Schools and 'Secular' Subjects,"*Harvard Educational Review* (Summer, 1962) .

Law and Contemporary Problems, "Religion and the State" (Winter, 1949) .

Levy, Leonard. "School Prayers and the Founding Fathers," *Commentary* (September, 1962) .

Lowell, C. Stanley. *Federal Aid to Parochial Schools.* Protestants and Other Americans United, 1961.

McCluskey, Neil G. *Public Schools and Moral Education.* Columbia University Press, 1958.

————. *Catholic Viewpoint on Education.* Doubleday & Company, Inc., 1962.

McCollum, Vashti. *One Woman's Fight.* Beacon Press, 1961.

McGrath, John J. *Church and State in American Law.* Bruce Publishing Co., 1962.

MacGregor, Geddes. *The Bible in the Making.* Lippincott, 1959.

Moehlman, Conrad H. *School and Church: The American Way.* Harper and Row, Publishers, 1944.

————. *The Church as Educator.* Hinds, Hayden and Eldridge, 1947.

————. *The Wall of Separation Between Church and State.* Beacon Press, 1951.

Moral and Spiritual Values in the Public Schools. National Education Association, 1951.

Murray, John Courtney. *We Hold These Truths.* Sheed and Ward, 1960.

National Catholic Almanac, 1963. Doubleday & Company, Inc.

O'Neill, James M. *Religion and Education Under the Constitution.* Harper and Row, Publishers, 1949.

Padover, Saul. *Jefferson.* Harcourt, Brace & World, Inc., 1942.

Parsons, Wilfred. *The First Freedom.* Declan X. McMullen, 1948.

Pfeffer, Leo. *Church, State and Freedom.* Beacon Press, 1953.

Rosenfield, Harry N. "Separation of Church and State and the Public Schools," *University of Pittsburgh Law Review* (March, 1961) .

Smylie, James H. "The First Amendment and Bishop Pike," *The Christian Century* (October 31, 1962) .

The State and Nonpublic Schools (legal compilation) . U.S. Office of Education, 1958.

Stokes, Anson Phelps. *Church and State in the United States.* 3 vols., Harper and Row, Publishers, 1950.

Sweet, William Warren. *Religion in Colonial America.* Charles Scribner's Sons, 1942.

Torpey, William G. *Judicial Doctrines of Religious Rights in America.* University of North Carolina Press, 1948.

Thayer, Vivian T. *The Attack Upon the American Secular School.* Beacon Press, 1951.

U.S. Senate Hearings Before the Committee on the Judiciary on "Prayers in Public Schools and Other Matters" (July 26 and August 2, 1962). U.S. Government Printing Office.

Van Dusen, Henry P. *God in Education.* Charles Scribner's Sons, 1951.

Walter, Erich A. *Religion and the State University.* University of Michigan Press, 1958.

Waterhouse, Howard A. "Is Released Time Worth While?" *The Christian Century* (October 2, 1957).

Notes

Books listed in the Bibliography are referred to by the author's surname. The following abbreviations of titles are used: *CR* for *Congressional Record; NYT* for *New York Times.*

CHAPTER 1

1. *Engel* v. *Vitale*, 370 U.S. 421 (1962), reprinted in Appendix I.

2. Nearly all American religious statistics are questionable because of differing methods in calculating membership and the custom of carrying "dead wood" members on the rolls of some churches. The 1963 *Yearbook of American Churches* estimated that, in 1961, 63.4 per cent of Americans were members of churches and synagogues, a slight percentage decline from the previous year. The 1963 *Official Catholic Directory* estimated the Catholic population of the United States at 43,859,000, but this included all baptized infants. *The Yearbook* indicated a Protestant membership of 63,669,000, but some Protestant sects do not submit figures, and the usual Protestant practice is not to count infants as members. For background material *see Religious Perspectives in American Culture,* edited by James W. Smith and A. Leland Jamison, Princeton University Press, 1961. A 1962 Gallup poll indicated church attendance in a typical week at 46 per cent of the population (*Washington Post,* January 5, 1963).

3. Cobb, p. 496.

4. For colonial and early national religious history, *see* Cobb; Brown; Cousins; Moehlman, *School and Church: The American Way;* Butts, Chapters 2 and 3; Blau; Stokes I; Torpey; Beale, Chapters 1 and 2; and Dorchester.

5. Cobb, p. 507.

6. The *Remonstrance* is published in full in Blau; and in *Everson* v. *Board of Education,* 330 U.S. 1 (1947). *See* Brant for Madison facts.

7. Cousins, p. 323.

8. Winfred E. Garrison, in *Annals of the American Academy,* March, 1948, p. 20, says: "In 1800, less than 10 per cent of the people of the United States were members of any church." *See* Pfeffer, p. 85 and Stokes I, p. 229 for other estimates.

9. Padover, pp. 76-77; for attack on Calvinism, p. 371. Charles and Mary Beard, *The Rise of American Civilization* I, p. 449, include Washington with Jefferson, Paine, John Adams, Franklin and Madison "to be reckoned among either the Unitarians or Deists." Stokes I, pp. 292 ff. is a little optimistic in classifying these leaders among believers, although they all had some deep religious convictions. *See* Foote for extended discussion of Jefferson and religion, and Brant for discussion of Madison. Cousins' short sketches are excellent. A 1963 work by Robert M. Healey, *Jefferson and Religion in Public Education,* stresses Jefferson's faith but says (p. 257): "But let us not forget that to Jefferson the fundamentals of Christian theism were limited to the principles of morality, the utilitarian arguments for moral behavior, and the rational and philosophic proofs for God's existence." Thomas Cuming Hall, in *The Religious Background of American Culture,* classes Washington, Madison and Jefferson as "more or less Deists and skeptics," and says (p. 163) that Washington's church membership "implied no sort of living interest in the issues upon which organized religion lays stress." *See* also *New Repub-*

lic, July 3, 1962 for Brant article, "Madison and the Prayer Case."

10. Foote, p. 3; Padover, p. 274.

11. Ellwood P. Cubberly, *Public Education in the United States*, p. 33.

12. P. 1.

13. *See* Blau, pp. 157-201; and a friendly treatment of Mann by Father Neil G. McCluskey, S.J., *Public Schools and Moral Education.*

14. Beale, p. 100; Stokes I, p. 830.

15. *NYT*, September 24, 1961. Beale, Chapter 4, discusses the whole period.

16. Quoted in dissent in *McCollum* v. *Board of Education.* 333 U.S. 203; also in Pfeffer, p. 289.

17. *Cantwell* v. *Connecticut*, 310 U.S. 296 (1940). The principle had been sustained earlier by three justices in *Hamilton* v. *Regents*, 293 U.S. 245 (1934).

18. *Cochran* v. *Louisiana*, 281 U.S. 370 (1930).

19. *Doremus* v. *Board of Education*, 342 U.S. 429 (1952). This is discussed at length by Boles, pp. 86 ff.

20. *Elliott* v. *White*, 23 F. 2d, 997 (1928). The old standard case against the right to sue is *Massachusetts* v. *Mellon*, 262 U.S. 447 (1923).

21. *Cantwell* v. *Connecticut, supra.*

22. The five cases cited in this paragraph are: *Everson* v. *Board of Education*, 330 U.S. 1 (1947); *McCollum* v. *Board of Education*, 333 U.S. 203; *Zorach* v. *Clauson*, 343 U.S. 306 (1952); *Torcaso* v. *Watkins*, 367 U.S. 488 (1961); and *Engel* v. *Vitale*, 370 U.S. 421 (1962).

23. Text of the Spellman-Roosevelt correspondence in Appendix II of my *Communism, Democracy and Catholic Power.*

24. Canon 1374, as published in *Canon Law; a Text and Commentary*, by T. Lincoln Bouscaren and Adam C. Ellis, p. 704, reads:

Catholic children may not attend non-Catholic. neutral. or mixed schools, that is, those which are open also to non-Catholics, and it pertains exclusively to the Ordinary [bishop] of the place to decide, in accordance with instruction of the Holy See, under what circumstances and with what precautions against the danger of perversion, attendance at such schools may be tolerated.

25. *NYT*, September 14, 1960.

26. The official American bishops' statement of 1948, "The Christian in Action," covering the bishops' interpretation of the separation of church and state, was published in full in *NYT*, November 21, 1948. It was probably the strongest attack ever made by an ecclesiastical body upon the United States Supreme Court. The bishops criticized the McCollum decision severely, ridiculed the alleged misuse of Jefferson's wall metaphor as a "shibboleth of doctrinaire secularism," and committed themselves to a multiple establishment view of the First Amendment which would allow nonpreferential tax support for their schools. They pledged themselves to work "peacefully, patiently and perseveringly" for this interpretation of the Constitution. This view was supported in many subsequent publications.

The 1948 statement used by the Democratic National Committee as a "Statement of the Catholic Bishops," published in part in *NYT*, September 9, 1960, was actually an individual comment by Archbishop John T. McNicholas, chairman of the administrative board of the National Catholic Welfare Conference, in reply to a Manifesto by POAU. When Kennedy and the Committee referred to it, only three sentences were plucked out: "We deny absolutely and without qualification that the Catholic Bishops of the United States are seeking a union of church and state by any endeavors whatsoever, either proximately or remotely. If tomorrow Catholics constituted a majority in our country, they would not seek a union of church and state. They would, then as now, uphold the Constitution and all its Amendments, recognizing the moral obligation imposed upon all Catholics to observe and defend the Constitution and its Amendments."

When the latter portion of the Mc-Nicholas statement is analyzed and compared with the official bishops' statement of November, 1948, it is apparent that the quoted sentences of the Archbishop did not commit the bishops in any way to support the wall of separation as defined by the Supreme Court. Actually, the McNicholas statement supported the legality of federal aid to parochial schools, the gravamen of the "religious issue" as it was raised at Houston, and declared: "The First Amendment is being distorted today, especially by those who advocate secularism in education." The full text of the McNicholas statement is in Stokes II, p. 715.

CHAPTER 2

1. The opinions in *Engel* v. *Vitale*, together with many background facts, were published in *NYT*, June 26, 1962, and the issue of July 1, 1962 contained a summary of editorial opinion. *See also Time*, July 6, 1962 and *The Tablet*, *passim*.

2. *See* Vashti McCollum, *One Woman's Fight*, Beacon Press, 1952 (rev. ed. 1961).

3. Column of February 24, 1959.

4. *Journal of Church and State*, November, 1960.

5. From files of the American Civil Liberties Union.

6. June 22, 1957. The old Ten Commandments battle is summarized in a letter in *The Progressive*, August, 1962, by a 15-year resident of New Hyde Park who declared that as early

as 1957 the district was "the most turbulent battleground in New York State, if not in the whole country, on the issue of religion in the public schools." The B'nai B'rith statement was in *NYT*, December 2, 1956.

7. *NYT*, February 12, 1962.

8. *America*, December 15, 1951.

9. 10 N.Y. 2d 174; reprinted *CR*, July 2, 1962, p. 1152.

10. *Catholic Criterion*, September 9, 1962; and *The Tablet*, September 8, 1962.

11. The opposing brief of the intervenors in support of the prayer was published in *CR*, July 2, 1962, p. 11525.

CHAPTER 3

1. *NYT*, June 28, 1962; and *National Catholic Almanac*, 1963, p. 69.

2. *CR*, January 15, 1963, pp. 341 ff.

3. *CR*, August 25, 1962, p. 16520.

4. *CR*, August 2, 1962, p. A5957.

5. *CR*, September 21, 1962, p. 19139.

6. *Hearings Before the Committee on the Judiciary*, U.S. Senate, Eighty-seventh Congress, on "Prayers in Public Schools and Other Matters," July 26 and August 2, 1962, p. 140 ff.—hereinafter called *Hearings*. Text of governor's resolution at p. 210.

7. *NYT*, July 4, 1962.

8. *America*, July 14, 1962.

9. *Christianity and Crisis*, July 23, 1962; *see also* his article in *New Leader*, July 9, 1962.

10. The Niebuhr attack was in a statement signed by 25 Protestant leaders in *Christianity and Crisis*, July 5, 1948; the Spellman attack was in the Catholic bishops' statement, *NYT*, November 21, 1948.

11. *NYT*, June 26, 1962.

12. Summarized with other editorials, *NYT*, June 29, 1962.

13. *NYT*, August 3, 1962.

14. July 29, 1962.

15. *America*, July 7, 1962.

16. April 22, 1962.

17. *CR*, July 11, 1962, p. A5239.

18. *National Catholic Almanac,* 1963, pp. 115 ff.

19. *Commonweal,* July 13, 1962.

20. *Ibid.,* July 27, 1962. Mr. Ball's legal arguments which were in *The Catholic Lawyer,* Summer and Autumn, 1962, included the claim that the public schools under the decision would not be neutral but "promoters of Secular Humanist Sectarianism."

21. *NYT,* July 11, 1962.

22. Pamphlet, "Prayer in the Public Schools," Community Relations Service, 165 East 56th St., N.Y. 22, for this and other religious reactions.

23. *NYT,* June 26, 1962. More complete statement by Unitarian Fellowship of Social Justice, *Hearings,* p. 163.

24. POAU press release; more complete statements in *Hearings,* p. 163 and p. 230.

25. *Hearings,* p. 107; subsequent statement by Dr. Hobbs, p. 146.

26. *NYT,* July 1, 1962.

27. *NYT,* June 26, 1962; and Mr. Kelley's letter in *America,* August 11, 1962. An official review of National Council policy up to the summer of 1962 was in *Hearings,* pp. 150 ff. The National Council statement of June 7, 1963 is available from 475 Riverside Drive, N.Y. 27.

28. *Christianity and Crisis,* October 15, 1962. *See also* issue of August 6, 1962 for editorial opposing Court.

29. July 20, 1962. This represented some departure from previous attitudes, e.g. *Christianity Today,* September 2, 1957.

30. Text in Community Relations pamphlet, *supra; Christian Century* editorial, July 4, 1962.

31. *NYT,* May 22, 1963.

32. *The Humanist,* No. 2, 1962, p. 43.

33. Text in *Hearings,* p. 166; story in *NYT,* November 11, 1962. Important statements by Jewish organizations in support of the Court are in *Hearings,* pp. 94, 97, 104, 135 and 136.

An excellent summary of opinion in the press, for and against the Court's ruling, was prepared by Theodore Leskes, American Jewish Committee, 165 East 56th St., N.Y. 22.

34. *America,* September 2, 1962.

35. *Hearings,* p. 64.

36. *Harvard Law Review,* November, 1962.

37. *See Columbia Journalism Review,* Fall, 1962, for article "Journalism and the School-Prayer Decision"; also summary by Theodore Leskes, *supra.*

38. *NYT,* June 27, 1962.

39. *Washington Post,* June 29, 1962.

CHAPTER 4

1. *Law and Contemporary Problems* (Duke University), Winter, 1949, p. 52.

2. *Brown* v. *Board of Education,* 347 U.S. 483 (1954).

3. *Bradfield* v. *Roberts,* 175 U.S. 291 (1899).

4. *Cochran* v. *Board of Education,* 281 U.S. 370 (1930); and the companion case, *Borden* v. *Louisiana,* 168 La. 1006 (1929).

5. *New York University Law Review,* December, 1962.

6. Everson, *supra.* The decision in Torcaso, *supra,* disposes of the claim that this paragraph was mere dictum.

7. McCollum, *supra.*

8. *National Catholic Almanac,* 1963, p. 681.

9. Zorach, *supra.*

10. *McGowan* v. *Maryland,* 366 U.S. 420 (1961).

11. Torcaso, *supra.*

12. *Washington Ethical Society* v. *District of Columbia,* 249 F. 2d. 127 (1957).

13. Its article in issue of September, 1962, "Freedom of Religion or Freedom From Religion" by Geral Kirvin, quoted more extensively from the rejected opinion of Justice Desmond of

New York than from the Supreme Court itself.

14. *CR*, March 19, 1963; 1949 statement in Pfeffer, p. 290 from *Social Action*, February 15, 1949.

15. *The Supreme Court Review*, 1962, University of Chicago, p. 33. Professor Kurland's summation is notable, with many bibliographical references.

16. A Gallup poll released about seven weeks after the prayer decision showed 79 to 80 per cent approval of religious observances in public schools. The White House mail on the subject in the first two weeks was ten to one against the decision.

17. Cardinal Spellman said of the prayer decision: "This is the establishment of a new religion of secularism." *Tablet*, August 4, 1962.

18. Professor Arthur E. Sutherland Jr., *Harvard Law Review*, November, 1962. Prof. Sutherland's earlier discussion of the right to sue was in Vol. 62, pp. 1343-1344. Pfeffer, pp. 165 ff. has a thorough discussion of the right to sue. *See also Harvard Law Review*, May, 1961, "Standing to Secure Judicial Review" by Louis L. Jaffe.

19. The two basic authorities are *Annals of Congress*, ed. Joseph Gales, Washington, 1834; and Jonathan Elliott, *The Debates on the Adoption of the Federal Constitution*, 5 vols., Washington, 1827; 2d. edition, Philadelphia, 1881. Butts, Ch. 4, discusses Madison's comments and the variations and wordings listed in this paragraph. Dumbauld has complete texts of Madison amendments of June 8, 1789, amendments reported by a select committee on July 28, 1789, amendments reported by the House of Representatives on August 24, 1789, and amendments reported by the Senate on September 9, 1789, with documented discussion. *See* historical treatment in *Columbia Law Review*, January, 1963. *See also* Pfeffer, "Church and State; Something Less than Separation," *University of Chicago Law Review*, Autumn, 1951; and, for earlier views opposing the Supreme Court, O'Neill; and articles by Father John Courtney Murray, S.J. and Edward S. Corwin, *Law and Contemporary Problems*, Winter, 1949.

20. *Commentary*, September, 1962, available in reprint form from American Jewish Committee, 165 East 56th St., N.Y. 22. Professor Levy has done extensive research in the whole field of multiple establishments in colonial and early national history. Among the books available to sustain his thesis as applied to various sections of the country are M. Louise Green, *The Development of Religious Liberty in Connecticut;* Jacob C. Meyer, *Church and State in Massachusetts from 1740 to 1833*; Reba Strickland, *Religion and the State in Georgia in the 18th Century*; George A. Stewart, *A History of Religious Education in Connecticut to the Middle of the Nineteenth Century*; and, for massive documentation in 7 volumes, Francis N. Thorpe, *The Federal and State Constitutions, Colonial Charters and Other Organic Laws*.

21. In his *The American Tradition in Religion and Education*, Chapters 2, 3 and 4.

22. *Home Building* v. *Blaisdell*, 290 U.S. 398 (1934).

23. *Washington Post*, February 15, 1963. Philip B. Kurland in his *Religion and the Law*, p. 17, expresses a similar thought about the two concepts in the First Amendment, religious liberty and the separation of church and state: "Nor were these two concepts closed systems at the time of the adoption of the first amendment. The objectives of the provisions were clear, but the means of their attainment were still to be developed and, indeed, are still in the course of development. Thus, like the other great clauses of the Constitution, the religion clauses cannot now be confined

to the application they might have received in 1789."

CHAPTER 5

1. *School District of Abington* v. *Schempp*, No. 142, October term, 1962; and *William J. Murray III* v. *Curlett*, No. 119, hereinafter called the Schempp-Murray decision. Majority and dissenting texts in Appendix II.

2. *Ring* v. *Board of Education*, 245 Ill. 334 (1910); *Tudor* v. *Board of Education*, 14 N.J. 31 (1953).

3. *School Life*, July, 1962, available as leaflet from U.S. Office of Education, contains also legal citations. For somewhat different categories *see International Journal of Education*, March 19, 1956.

4. Dierenfield, pp. 49-58.

5. Transcript of Record, *Schempp* v. *Abington*, 177 F. Supp. 398 (1959); vacated and remanded, 364 U.S. 298 (1960).

6. *Progressive World*, January, 1961.

7. *Chamberlin* v. *Dade County*, 143 S. 2d. 21 (1962); *Resnick* v. *Dade County*, Fla. Supreme Court, No. 31, 546 (1962); facts and quotes from *Jurisdictional Statement* by Appellants, U.S. Supreme Court, October term, 1962, No. 520.

8. Dierenfield, p. 50.

9. Unpublished thesis, "Religious Practices in Texas Public Schools" by Earl L. Humble, Southwestern Baptist Theological Seminary, Fort Worth, Texas.

10. *See* Appendix II for ruling and dissent.

11. For Congressional quotations in this summary *see* CR, June 19, 1963, pp. 10461-10514.

12. *NYT*, June 18, 1963.

13. *Ibid.*, June 19, 1963.

14. Final statement, "The Churches and the Public Schools," June 7, 1963. Stories in *NYT*, June 7 and 14, 1963; *Tablet*, June 13, 1963. Presbyterian statement *NYT*, May 22, 1963.

15. *NYT*, June 19, 1963.

CHAPTER 6

1. The Bible of Catholic educational doctrine is the 1929 encyclical of Pope Pius XI, "Christian Education of Youth," in *Five Encyclicals*, pp. 37-68, which reinforces the educational provisions in Canons 1372-1383, *Bouscaren and Ellis*, pp. 703-709. Pius referred only briefly to the "distributive justice" evidenced by the "financial aid granted by the State." He flatly rejected both neutral schools and all schools "in which the students are provided with separate religious instruction, but receive other lessons in common with non-Catholic pupils from non-Catholic teachers." He declared: "And first of all education belongs pre-eminently to the Church, by reason of a double title in the supernatural order, conferred exclusively upon her by God Himself, absolutely superior therefore to any other title in the natural order." Among the many later papal statements about church financial rights in education is that of Pius XII in an address on September 15, 1951 to teaching nuns in Rome in which he expressed the demand that church schools should not be "placed in a worse condition than state schools"—full text in Brooklyn *Tablet*, November 3, 1951. The National Catholic Welfare Conference submitted to a hearing of the House Committee on Education and Labor in 1947 (pp. 310-311) a statement saying: "Since government itself has nothing to teach, and because government receives a full return from its educational investment when a school produces well-trained citizens, therefore, every school to which parents may send their children in compliance with the compulsory educational laws of the State is entitled to a fair share of tax funds."

2. Some phases of European school systems are discussed in my *Commu-*

nism, Democracy and Catholic Power, pp. 153-58; and in *The Irish and Catholic Power,* Chapter 6. *See* "Religious Education in Sweden" by John Sjorgren, *Religious Education,* May-June, 1963; and, for chief terms in the Vatican-Hitler Concordat, "Germany," *Catholic Encyclopedia Supplement.*

3. *Look,* May, 1961.

4. McCluskey, *Catholic Viewpoint,* p. 81.

5. *NYT,* June 20, 1949, and August 6, 1949. The Spellman attack on Mrs. Roosevelt was in *NYT,* July 23, 1949 and Mrs. Roosevelt's reply July 28. Other comments were published in *The Churchman,* July and September, 1949; and *The Christian Century,* July 6, 1949. *See also* McCluskey, *Catholic Viewpoint,* p. 167.

6. Spellman statement January 17, 1961; Kennedy inaugural address January 20; first Kennedy educational message February 20; good summary of events in *Look,* May 23, 1961, "The Bishops *vs.* Kennedy," by Fletcher Knebel. For comprehensive summary of 1961 facts and opinions, *see* House Hearings on Federal Aid to Schools, Part I, March 13-20, 1961, with National Council of Churches statement at p. 390; Catholic statement at p. 335; and my testimony at p. 375.

7. *Look,* March, 1959; summarized *NYT,* February 17, 1959.

8. *Commonweal,* October 13, 1961.

9. NCWC release March 3, 1961 in *Register,* March 12. A longer version is in *Naitonal Catholic Almanac* (1962), p. 114.

10. Statement of February 22, 1961, National Council of Churches, 475 Riverside Drive, N.Y. 27. *See also* statement of Protestant leaders, *NYT,* March 16, 1961; and also issue of March 17, 1961.

11. *Time,* March 24, 1961.

12. *NYT,* March 30, 1961.

13. *Ibid,* June 23, 1961. Editorial quote, *NYT,* June 17, 1961. Senators Morse and Clark proved that they were acting in good faith by writing in to their legislative proposals a provision for a court test of the church-state issue. *See CR,* April 2, 1962, p. 5236.

14. *Tablet,* July 22, 1961.

15. March 13, 1961.

16. March 17, 1961.

17. March 5, 1961.

18. *The Register,* February 18, 1962; *Tablet,* February 17, 1962.

19. *NYT,* November 8, 1962.

20. Delaney defended his scheme in *CR,* January 22, 1962, p. 505; *see also NYT,* January 24, 1961; lobby summary *NYT,* April 17, 1961.

21. P. 526; Hochwalt statement in *Tablet,* February 14, 1963. *See also* McCluskey, *Catholic Viewpoint,* pp. 21 and 32. The Gannon statement was in *Tablet,* June 13, 1963.

22. P. 155. *See also* article by Fred Hechinger, *NYT,* March 12, 1961.

23. Most constitutional and statutory provisions are in *The State and Nonpublic Schools,* pp. 31-152. A recent state constitutional summary is in *Hearings,* pp. 268-285.

24. *See* next chapter.

25. *Washington Post,* April 8, 1961, for editorial and Hochwalt statement.

26. *Swart* v. *South Burlington,* 122 Vt. 177 (1961). Certiorari denied.

27. *Notre Dame Lawyer,* August, 1962, p. 677. This issue contains valuable summary of recent church-state cases.

28. The Catholic legal reply to the administration's legal memorandum was published in *Georgetown Law Journal* (1961), Vol. 50, and summarized in *NYT,* December 15, 1961.

29. 1963, p. 526.

30. Kurland, *Religion,* p. 27.

31. *Washington Post,* April 30, 1961.

32. *Catholic World,* April, 1955.

33. *See* Blum, Chapters 6-9; and C.E.F. literature, obtainable from 3109 South Grand Blvd., St. Louis 18, Mo.

34. *CR,* May 20, 1963, p. 8500; *NYT,*

May 21, 1963. *See also Harvard Law Review*, December, 1962, for article, "Federal Tax Incentives for Higher Education."

35. *NYT*, May 26, 1963; for McIntyre statement, *ibid*, May 21, 1963.

36. The reader is referred to McCluskey and Blum as illustrations of this type of persuasion.

37. Moehlman, *The Church as Educator*, p. 131.

38. *Five Encyclicals*, p. 60.

39. Bouscaren and Ellis, pp. 458-464.

40. *NYT*, April 23, 1963.

41. Bennett, p. 246.

CHAPTER 7

1. *CR* (House debates on college aid), January 30, 1962, pp. 1012 and 1015; and *CR*, August 8, 1962, p. 14868; also *Higher Education*, October-November, 1962 (U.S. Office of Education), article by Wilbur J. Cohen. For Senate debates *see CR*, February 2, 5 and 6, 1962. For systematic compilation of facts *see* Senate Hearings on Aid for Higher Education, August 17-21, 1961, with Bibliography at p. 144.

2. HR 8900 and S 1241, 87th Congress, first session, both contained the weak church-state formula excluding expenditures for chapels and divinity schools without coming to grips with other forms of religious promotion. See *CR*, September 19, 1962, p. 18840. A compromise agreement for a bill appropriating about $2,350,000,000 was reached after a four-month deadlock —see *CR*, September 19, 1962, p. 18840 and September 21, 1962, p. 19169; and *NYT*, September 21, 1962—but it was defeated in the House by a margin of about 30 votes. From the church-state-separation point of view the House bill was more dangerous because it provided outright matching grants for sectarian colleges.

3. HEW Memorandum to Wayne Morse, *CR*, August 8, 1962, p. 14867.

4. A Yale Divinity School seminar, reviewing practices in 70 public universities, found religious courses for credit in all but 2, with an average of 9 courses per institution in religion (*Religious Education*, May-June, 1959). For general review and discussion of college practices, *see* Walter.

5. *North* v. *Trustees of U. of Ill.*, 137 Ill. 296 (1891). For regulations concerning armed forces chapels, *see* Douglas opinion in *Engel* v. *Vitale*, footnote 2.

6. For example, the Notre Dame *General Bulletin*, 1962-1963, p. 73, says: "Every Catholic student is required to take courses in religion as part of his college education.... While attendance at Mass is required only on days prescribed by the Church, the students are urged to attend Mass and receive Holy Communion every day." The university trustees are all Holy Cross priests.

7. See *College Hearings*, pp. 559 ff. for this quotation and other details about college practices submitted in opposition to sectarian college aid by Dr. Edgar Fuller, Executive Secretary, Council of Chief State School Officers. The demand by 28 Jesuit college presidents for across-the-board grants was in *NYT*, January 5, 1958.

8. Catalogue, 1962-1963. For list of Protestant church-related colleges, *see* Information Service, National Council of Churches, February 3, 1962, which points out that such institutions vary all the way from complete independence with some historical connection to "actual current control."

9. *Everson* v. *Board of Education, supra*.

10. *Visser* v. *Nooksack*, 33 Wash. 2d. 699 (1949).

11. *McVey* v. *Hawkins*, 364 Mo. 44 (1953).

12. *Matthews* v. *Quinton*, 362 P. 2d. 932.

13. *Reynolds, State* ex rel. v. *Nussbaum,* 171 Wis. 2d. 148 (1952).

14. *Dickman* v. *School District,* 366 P. 2d. 533 (1962.).

15. *Gurney* v. *Ferguson,* 190 Okla. 254 (1941).

16. Daily newspapers of March 1, 1957 ff. and May 7, 1957; *Tablet,* May 30, 1959, and *America,* June 13, 1959.

17. *NYT,* May 4-10, 1963; *Register,* May 19, 1963; *Tablet,* May 9, 1963.

18. *Catholic World,* April, 1955.

19. Blum, p. 113.

20. *Register,* January 15, 1956.

21. *Snyder* v. *Town of Newton,* 147 Conn. 374 (1961).

22. *Dickman* v. *School District, supra.*

23. *Cochran* v. *Louisiana,* 281 U.S. 370 (1930).

24. Partially summarized in *NYT,* May 11, 1962.

25. Dierenfield, pp. 96 and 62. *See also* Pfeffer, pp. 418 ff.; and Boles, pp. 146 ff.

26. *Washington Star,* May 23, 1957.

27. *Minneapolis Star,* March 11, 1958.

28. Statement of December, 1957, summarized in *Kennebec Journal,* March 24, 1958.

29. *Chamberlin* v. *Dade County,* 143 So. 2d. 21 (1962). In *Miller* v. *Cooper,* 56 N.M. 355 (1952), the New Mexico Supreme Court permitted baccalaureate services in a Baptist church because there was no suitable auditorium except in a church. *See also Conway, State* ex rel. v. *District Board,* 162 Wis. 482, discussed in Boles, p. 146.

30. Dierenfield's summary, p. 68, indicates that 88 per cent of American public schools observe Christmas with some kind of activities, and about 58 per cent observe Easter.

31. *Christianity and Crisis,* November 12, 1962. *See also* Pfeffer pp. 399-412; Jacobson; Rosenfield; article by John C. Bennett, "When Christmas Becomes Divisive," *Christianity and Crisis,* November 24, 1958; article by Philip Jacobson, "Should the Ayes Always Have It?" *The Christian Century,* October 22, 1958; and the 42nd Annual Report of the American Civil Liberties Union.

32. January 3, 1963; Sharon story in all Boston dailies December 17, 1962 ff.

33. *Wall Street Journal,* December 24, 1962. Ossining citation, *Baer* v. *Kolmorgen,* 14 Misc. 2d. 1015, 181 N.Y.S. 2d. 230.

34. Jacobson, p. 2.

35. There are no completely reliable statistics covering nuns and captive schools, and these figures are only estimates based partially on my personal investigations in Indiana, Kansas, Kentucky and Ohio. *See* Pfeffer, pp. 412 ff.; my *American Freedom and Catholic Power,* 1958 edition, pp. 124 ff.; also *Church and State* (published by POAU), January, May and October, 1959. A 1946 NEA survey indicated that in actual practice only 12 states permitted costumed nuns to teach in public classrooms, and since then two states have discontinued the practice, but the nominal permissiveness extends to several other states.

36. *Religious Education,* May-June 1962, article by William W. Boyer.

37. *See* my article in *Presbyterian Life,* January 15, 1960. The Jasper, Indiana "Catholic public" school (St. Joseph's) is only four blocks away from the genuine public school and it has been carried for many years under two different names in the *National Catholic Directory* and in the Indiana public school directory.

38. *Zellers* v. *Huff,* 55 N.M. 501 (1951).

39. *Berghorn* v. *Reorganized School District,* 364 Mo. 121 (1953). *See also Harfst* v. *Hoegen,* 349 Mo. 808 (1941).

40. Dissenting opinion of Judge Williams in *Hysong* v. *School District,* 164 Pa. 629 (1894). For later Pennsylvania case upholding a statute barring

nun teachers, *see Commonwealth* v. *Herr*, 229 Pa. 132 (1910).

CHAPTER 8

1. *America*, May 25, 1963. The cardinals' statements were in *NYT*, June 19, 1963.

2. *Hearings*, p. 43.

3. *CR*, June 19, 1963, p. 10465; Eastland amendment in *Hearings*, p. 2.

4. *Ibid.*, pp. 51 ff.; *CR*, July 7, 1962, p. A5806.

5. *Thought* (Fordham quarterly) Winter, 1962.

6. *Christianity and Crisis,* July 23, 1962.

7. *See* Dierenfield, Ch. 6; Pfeffer, Ch. 10; and historical review by Justice Frankfurter in McCollum case.

8. Dierenfield, p. 101; and Waterhouse. A scholarly study of released time in the Chicago area, published in *The Humanist*, No. 4, 1948, indicated that less than 10 per cent of students used the released time plan in Chicago, and that in both New York and Chicago only a tiny minority of Protestants and Jews used the plan. The City Club of New York *Bulletin,* October 31, 1962, noted that after 20 years of effort less than one-fifth of New York City's pupils have been enlisted for released time, and "there is little meaningful educational programming for the 80 per cent who do not seek religious instruction."

9. *The Mormons,* by Thomas F. O'Dea, p. 228; and Dierenfield, p. 73.

10. *CR*, February 22, 1963, p. A881.

11. In symposium, "Shared Time," by Harry L. Stearns and others, *Religious Education*, January-February, 1962.

12. February 27, 1963.

13. Dierenfield, p. 45; for general discussion *see* Thayer, Ch. 10; and special issue of *International Journal of Religious Education*, May, 1958.

14. Published by NEA, Washington, D.C., 1951. For New York City struggle, *see Newsweek*, November 14, 1955; and Dierenfield, pp. 40 ff.

15. *National Catholic Almanac,* 1953, p. 102.

16. *The Nation*, November 17, 1951.

17. When the King James version was produced in 1611, there were less than a dozen Greek manuscripts available for translation; today there are some 4,500. Protestant scholars have produced the British Revised Version in the 1880's, with the Apocrypha in 1895; the American Standard Version in 1901; the American Revised Standard Version (RSV) in 1946, 1952, and 1957; followed by the New English Bible which will not be completed until 1967. All accepted Catholic versions in English go back to the translation by St. Jerome into Latin in the 4th century—the Vulgate. This was translated and published in English at Rheims, France (the New Testament) in 1582 and at Douay, France (the Old Testament) in 1609. The total product is now universally called the Douay version although the most popular version for American Catholics is the 1750 Bishop Challoner revision, approved by American Catholic bishops in 1810. *See* MacGregor; "Bible," *Encyclopedia Brittanica*; and Sir Frederick Kenyon, *Our Bible and the Ancient Manuscripts*, Harper and Row, Publishers, 1958.

18. *Bouscaren and Ellis,* p. 726. *See also* "Bible," *Catholic Encyclopedia; The Catholic Church and the Bible* by Hugh Pope O.P., The Macmillan Company, 1928; and for recent rulings of the Pontifical Biblical Commission, *Rome and the Study of Scripture*, St. Meinrod Abbey, Indiana, 1953. For article on possible "common Bible," *see America*, October 22, 1960.

19. *Suggested Bible Readings for Maine Public Schools*, State Department of Education, Augusta, 1958, p. 3. Most states leave the preparation of

suitable Bible lists to local school authorities.

20. *Washington Post,* January 26, 1963.

21. NAE leaflet, "A Framework for Service," 108 North Main St., Wheaton, Ill.

22. *Washington Post,* March 9, 1963. For a popular summary of the criticisms of Rudolf Bultmann and his disciples *see Time,* June 21, 1963.

23. *Washington Post,* February 26, 1963.

24. *This Believing World,* p. 226. *See also* Walter Kaufman, *Critique of Religion and Philosophy* (Doubleday & Company, Inc.)

25. *National Education Association News,* May 16, 1952.

Index